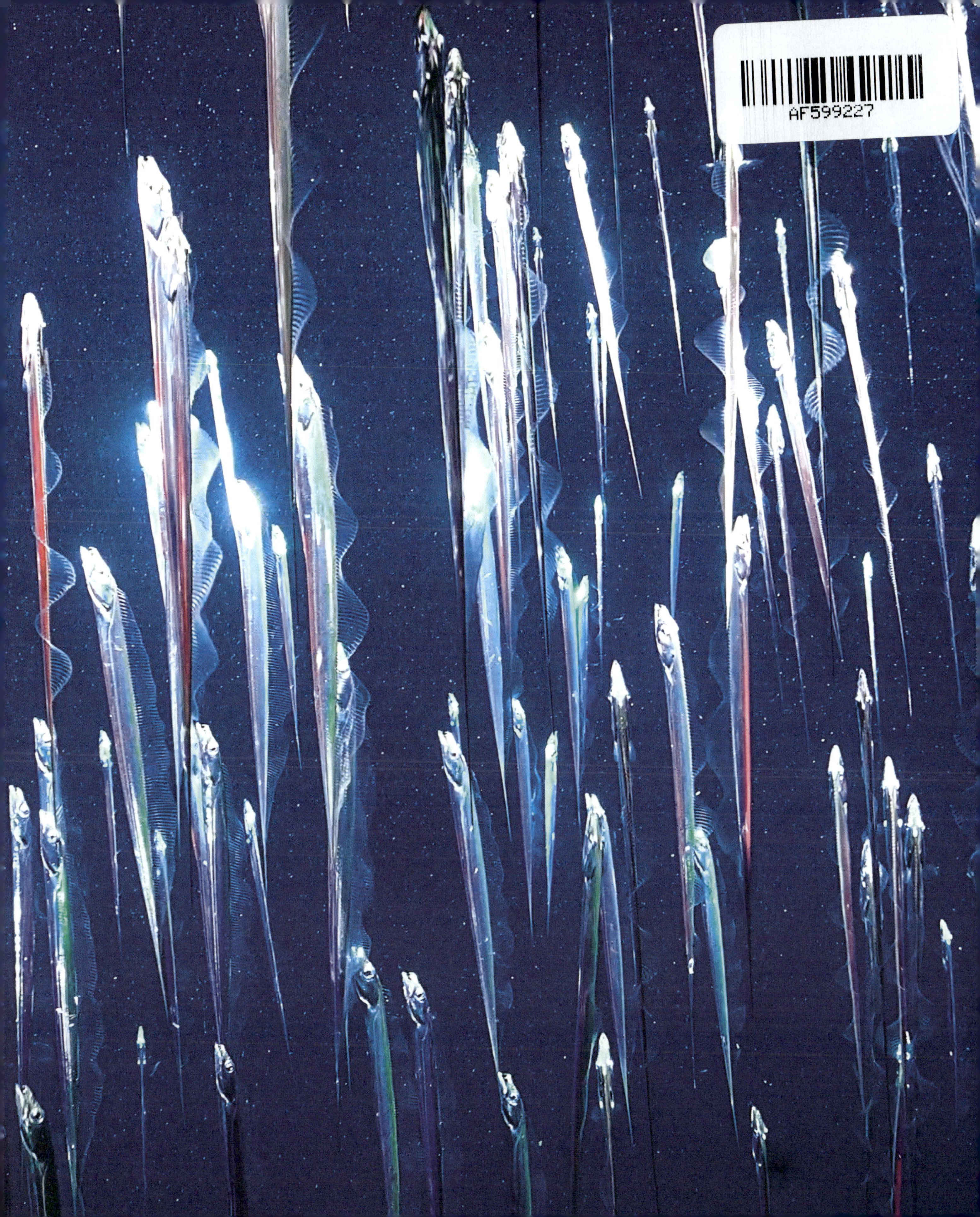

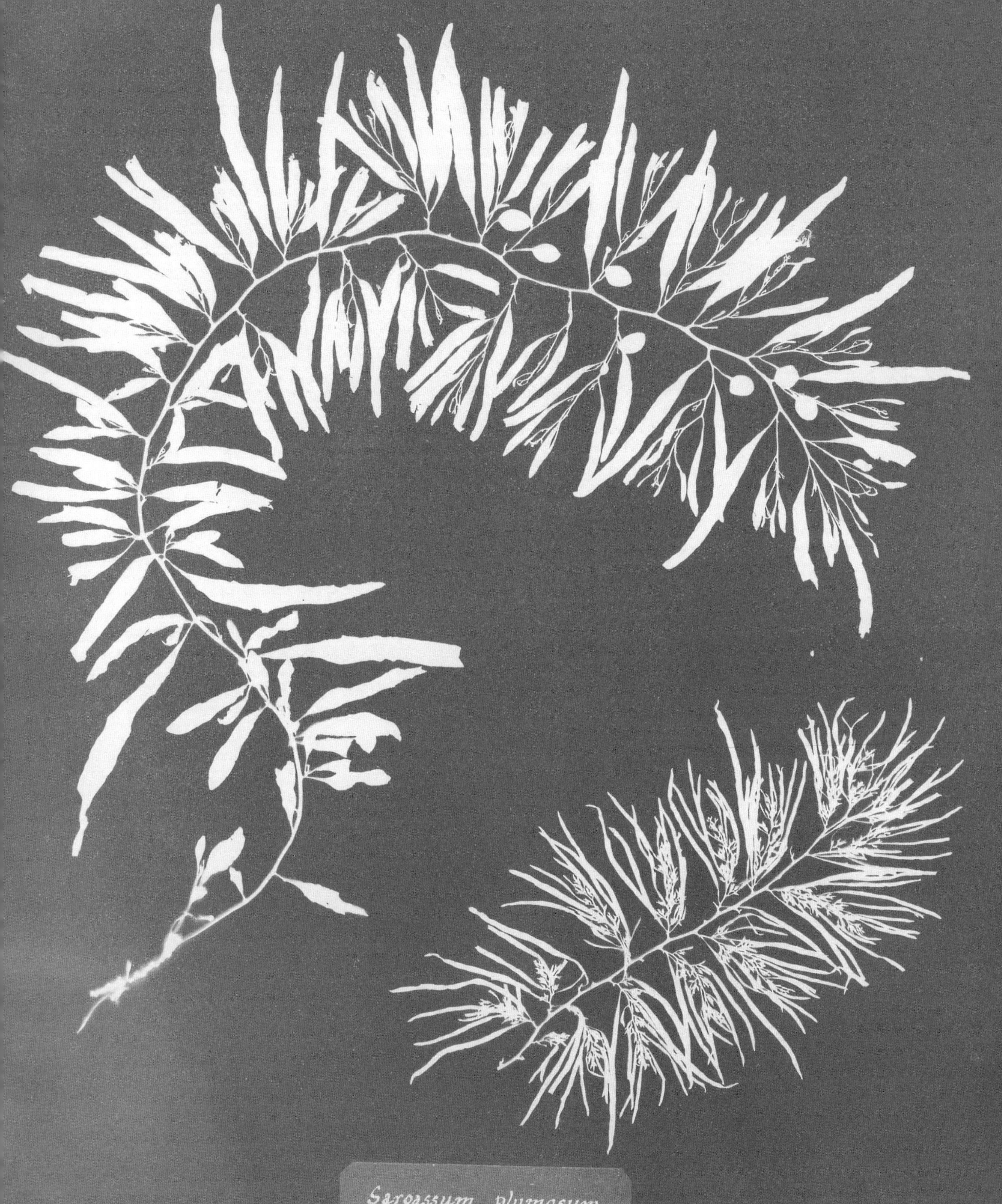

Sargassum plumosum.

OCEAN

Louisiana Museum of Modern Art

Page 2, 4-11, 13 and endpapers
ANNA ATKINS
Pages of the book *Photographs of British Algae: Cyanoptype Impressions,* 1843-1853

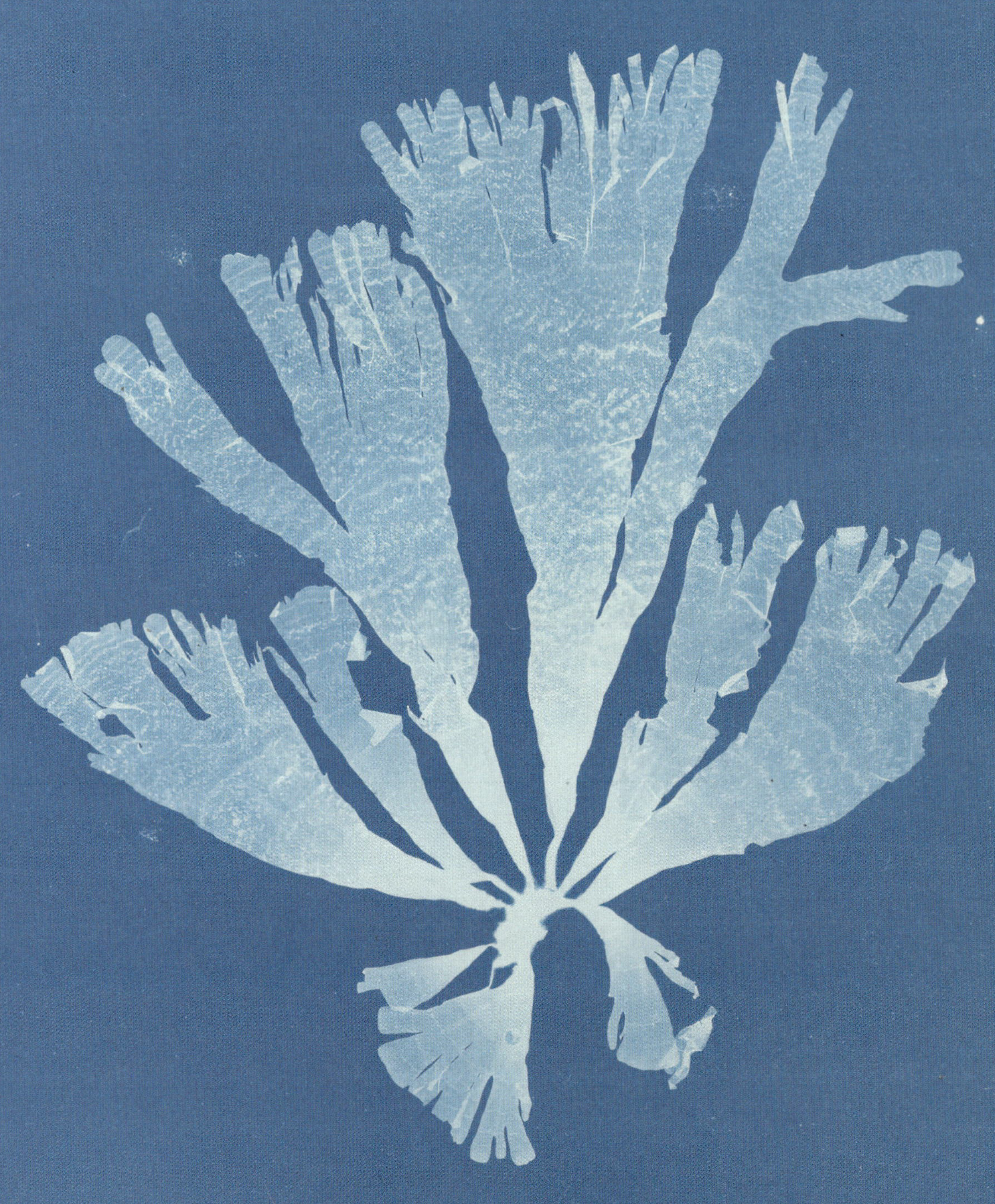

Dictyota atomaria.

Content

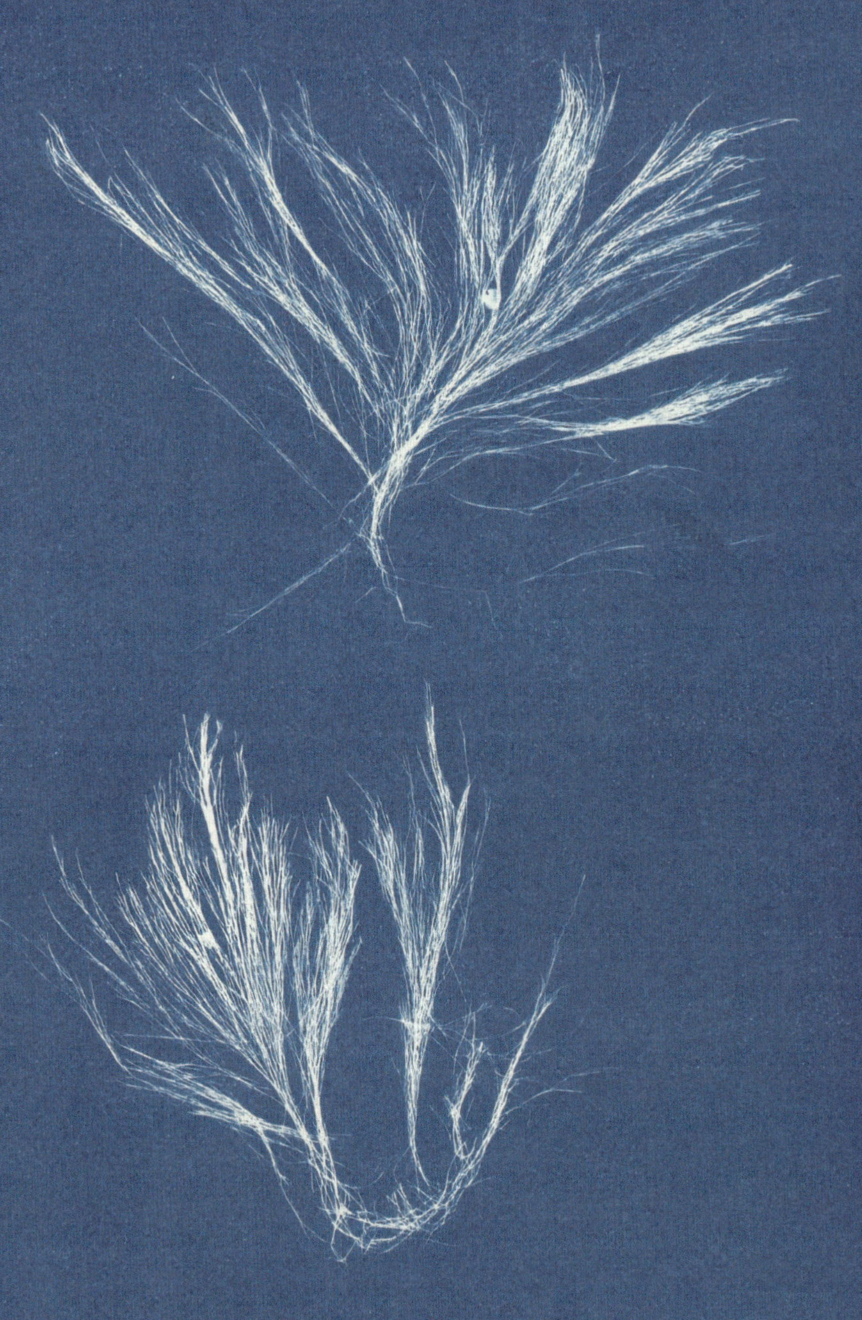

Polysiphonia urceolata.

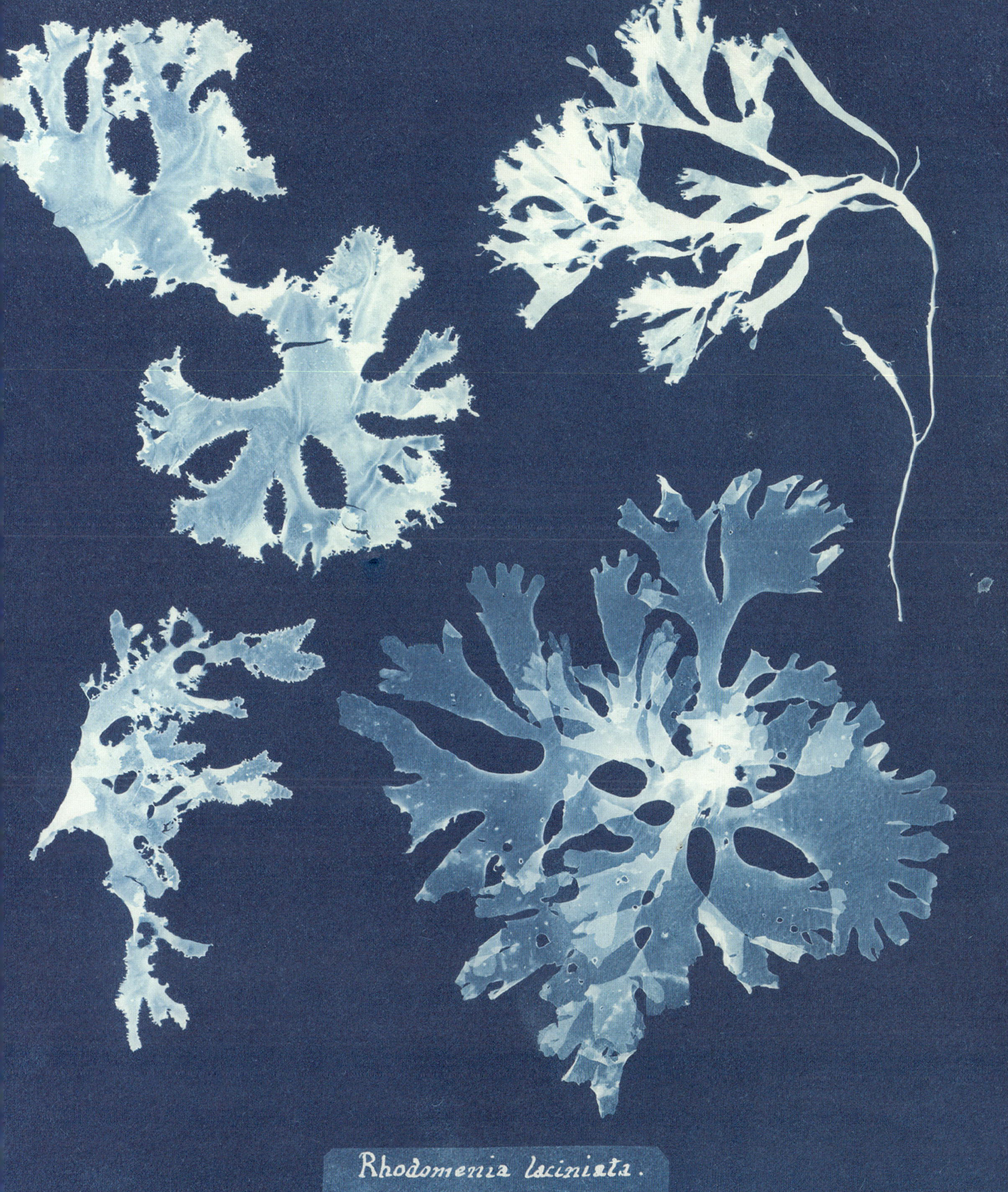

Rhodomenia laciniata.

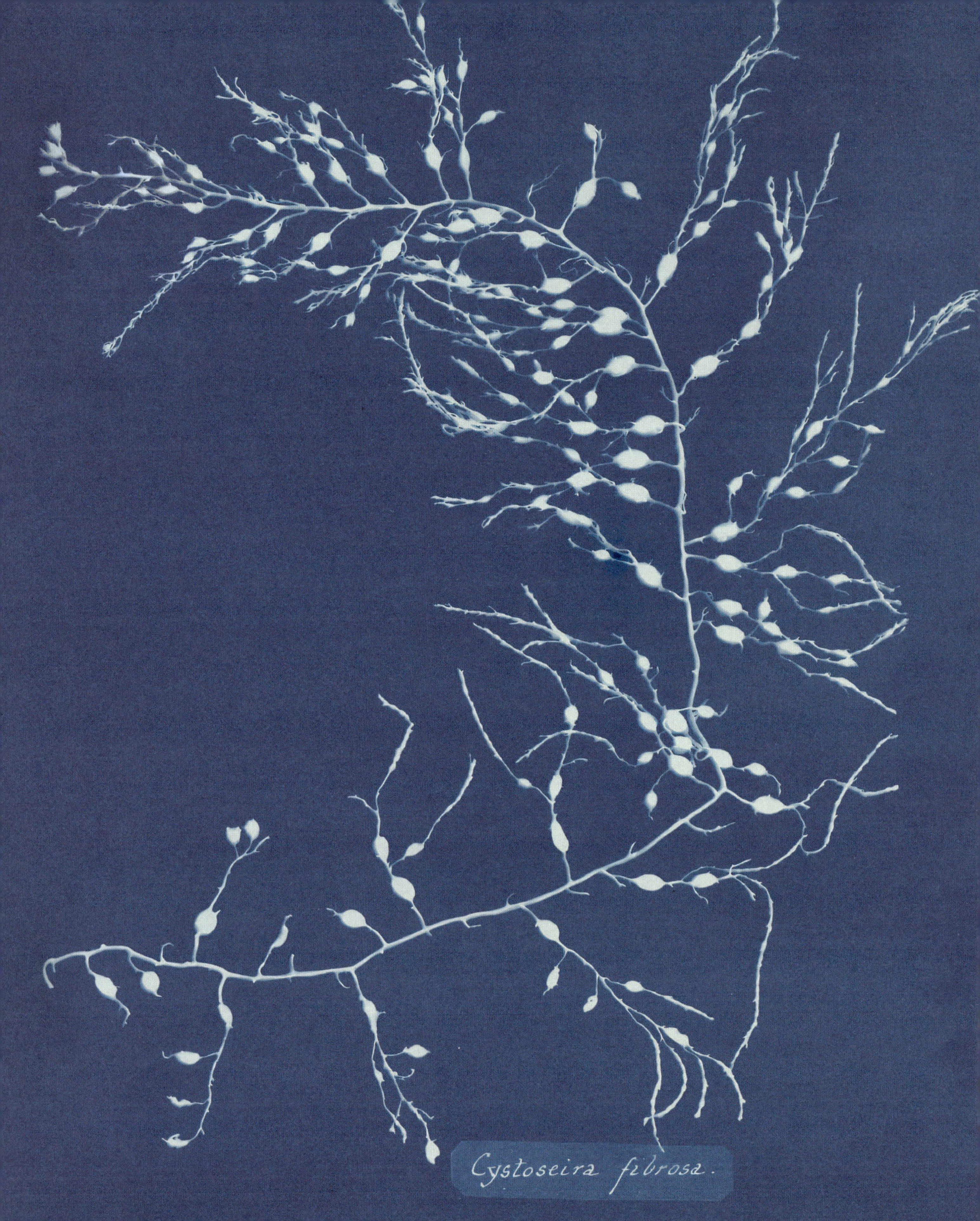
Cystoseira fibrosa.

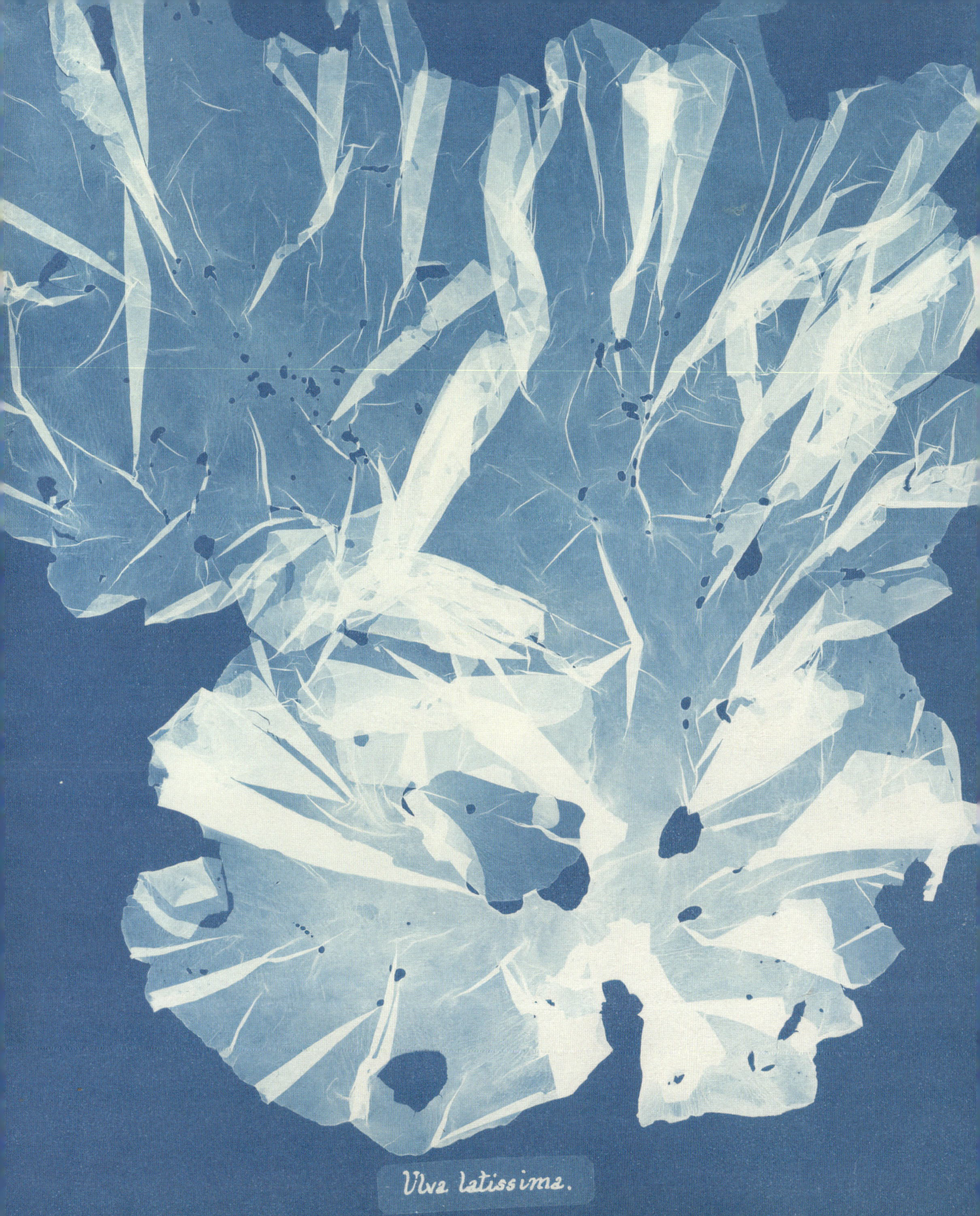

Ulva latissima.

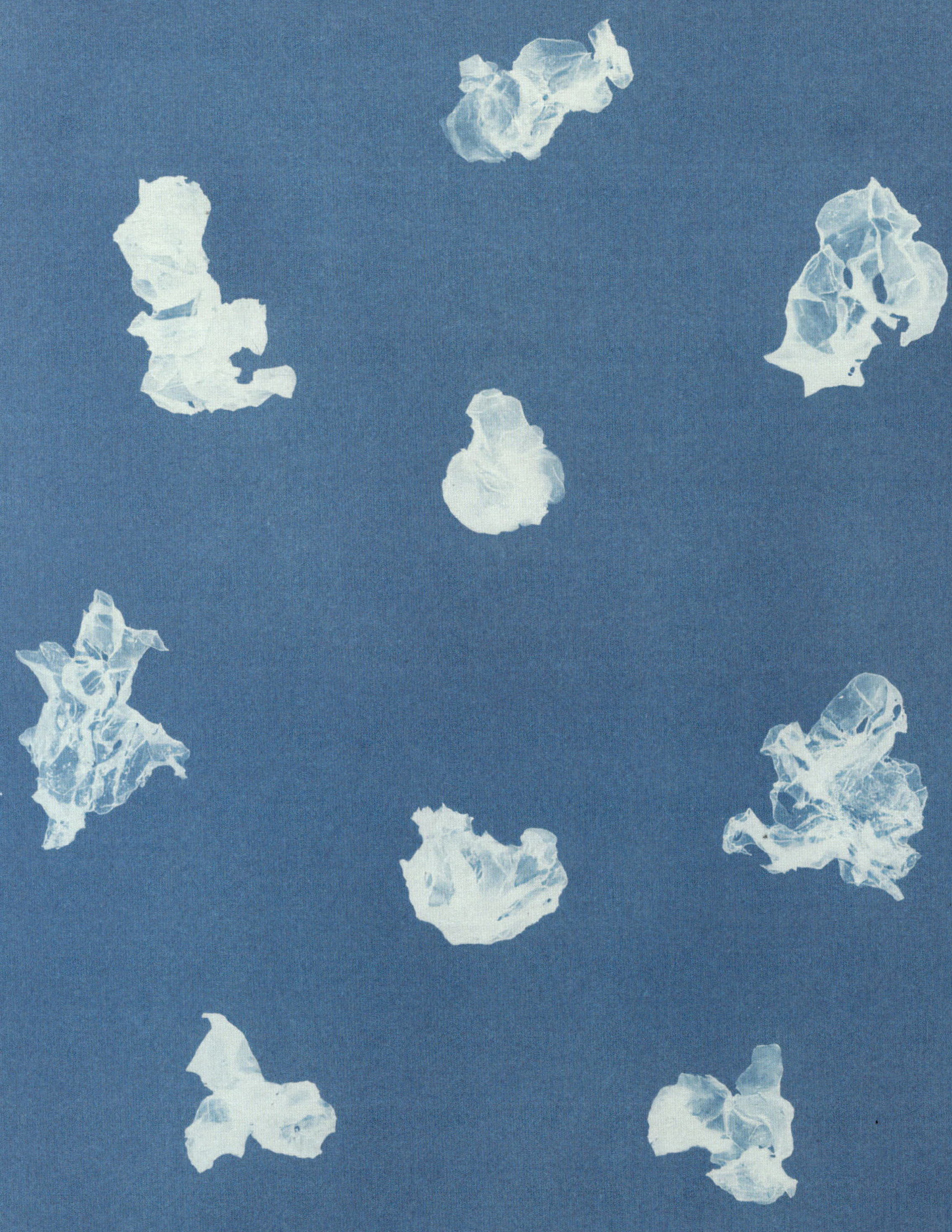

Nostoc commune

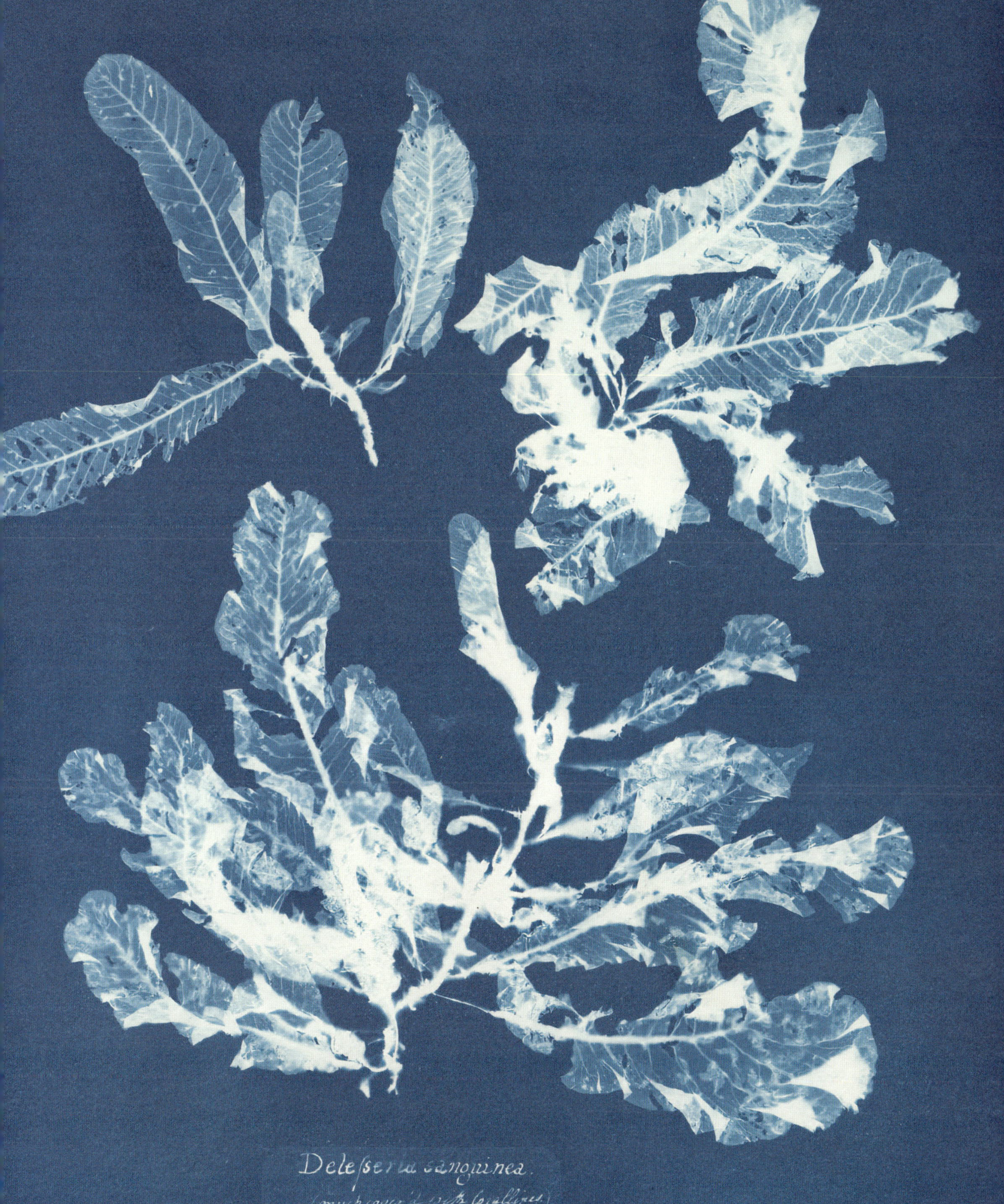

Delesseria sanguinea.
(much cover'd with corallines)

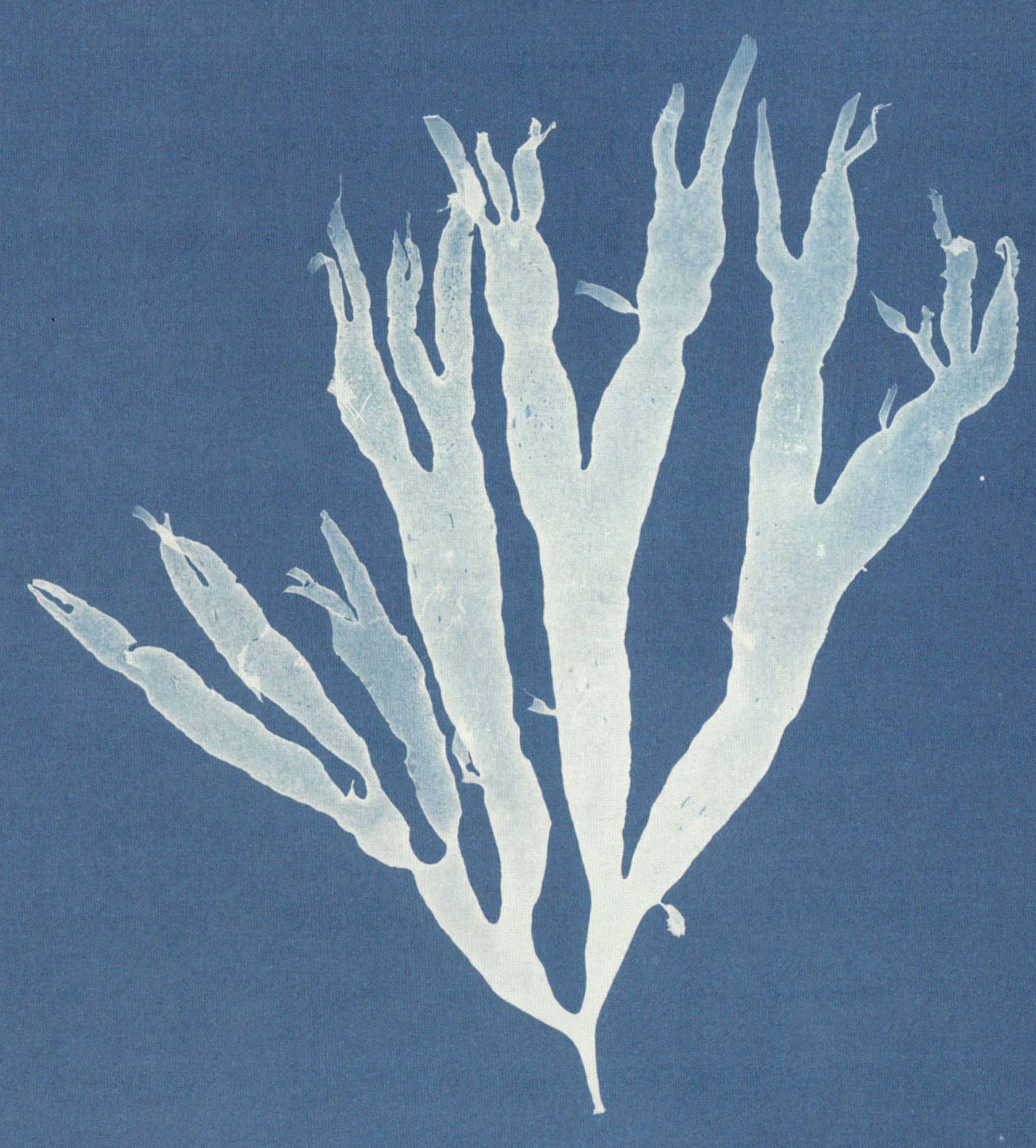

Halymenia ligulata, var. latifolia.

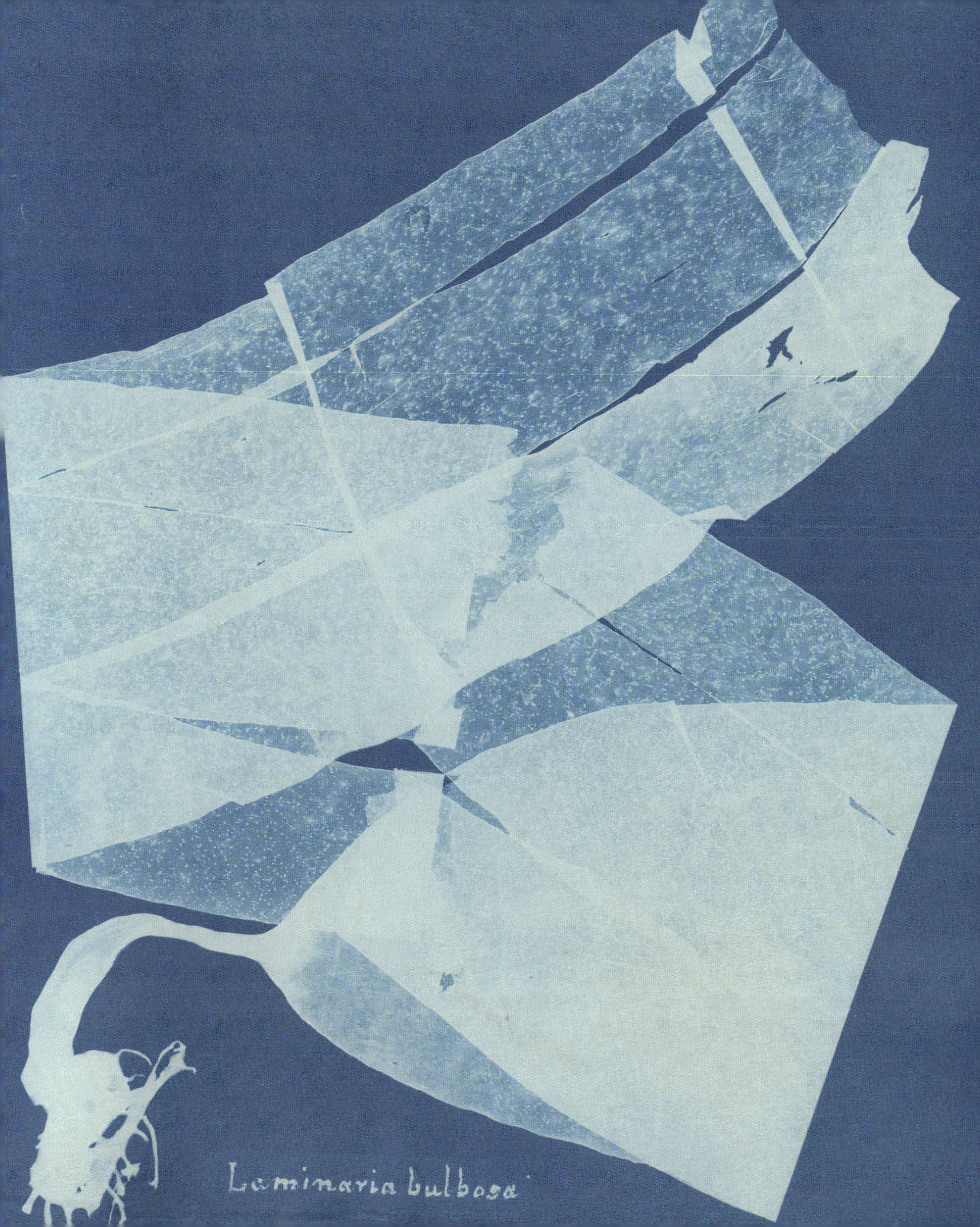
Laminaria bulbosa

Foreword

"No one could write truthfully about the sea and leave out the poetry," said the pioneering American marine biologist Rachel Carson in the middle of last century. She was so knowledgeable about her subject that it was difficult for people – read: men – to believe she was a woman (one researcher long insisted, against his better judgement, on addressing her as a man). With poetry, one can convey the immense importance the ocean has had and continues to have as a motif, theme, figure, condition, element, frontier, myth, terror and fascination.

The ocean can be the object of all desires, and it can be the maelstrom of waywardness and damnation. "The sea! The sea!" shouted ten thousand soldiers once they escaped Persian enemy territory and saw the promised freedom of the Black Sea, according to Greek historian Xenophon. Jonah was whisked away on a journey beneath the waves, but the Lord took mercy and deposited him on the shore. Odysseus, meanwhile, stepped ashore in all the wrong places during his endless journey home across the sea. Melville's Captain Ahab found home in his eternal quest for Moby Dick, and Jules Verne's Nemo found his in the *Nautilus* among the aquatic cosmos.

The ocean connects kingdoms and countries with one another – it separates them, too. Then again, isn't the sea the very negation of this segmented mindset? What is my water today will lap upon your shore tomorrow ... One cannot write truthfully about the ocean while disregarding the fact that it flows together as a single, all-encompassing whole touching everyone and everything.

Over the past ten years, Louisiana Museum of Modern Art has organised a series of exhibitions in which poetry, the arts, has been the driving force behind our curatorial expeditions, first to the *Arctic* and then *The Moon* – two major exhibitions in 2013 and 2018, respectively. Both are remote places that, by virtue of their inaccessibility, have a magnetic draw on us.

Both have required the mobilisation of extraordinary forces, technology hanging at poetry's heel. The sea, on the other hand, is much closer to human reach – in Denmark, it is never more than 51 kilometres away, no matter where you end up and no matter how much the Moon tugs at it. And the fact that in Humlebæk the ocean has had to wait in line behind the Moon is unquestionably an insight in its own right: we currently know more about the Moon than we do about the depths of the ocean.

Just as with the exhibitions on the Arctic and the Moon, our exhibition on the ocean is organised so as to cut across the histories of culture and art. And, once again, visitors will learn that objects from cultural history are also aesthetic objects, that scientific discoveries are also impelled by the same wonder from which poetry can emerge, and, finally, that art – which we so often refer to as something 'in its own right' – has infinite potential to tell us about the world of which it is also a part.

There is not, as far as we know, anything so distinct as ocean art or ocean artists – but we do know that there is much in our art and culture about the ocean. That attentiveness is a good thing because, whether it rises or not, without the ocean, we're finished. This is another reason why the exhibition at the Louisiana is a tribute to the ocean, not just the poetry. The bond between art and the world has always been important to the museum – and has nothing to do with what most people call the art world.

Welcome to *Ocean*.

Poul Erik Tøjner
Director, Louisiana

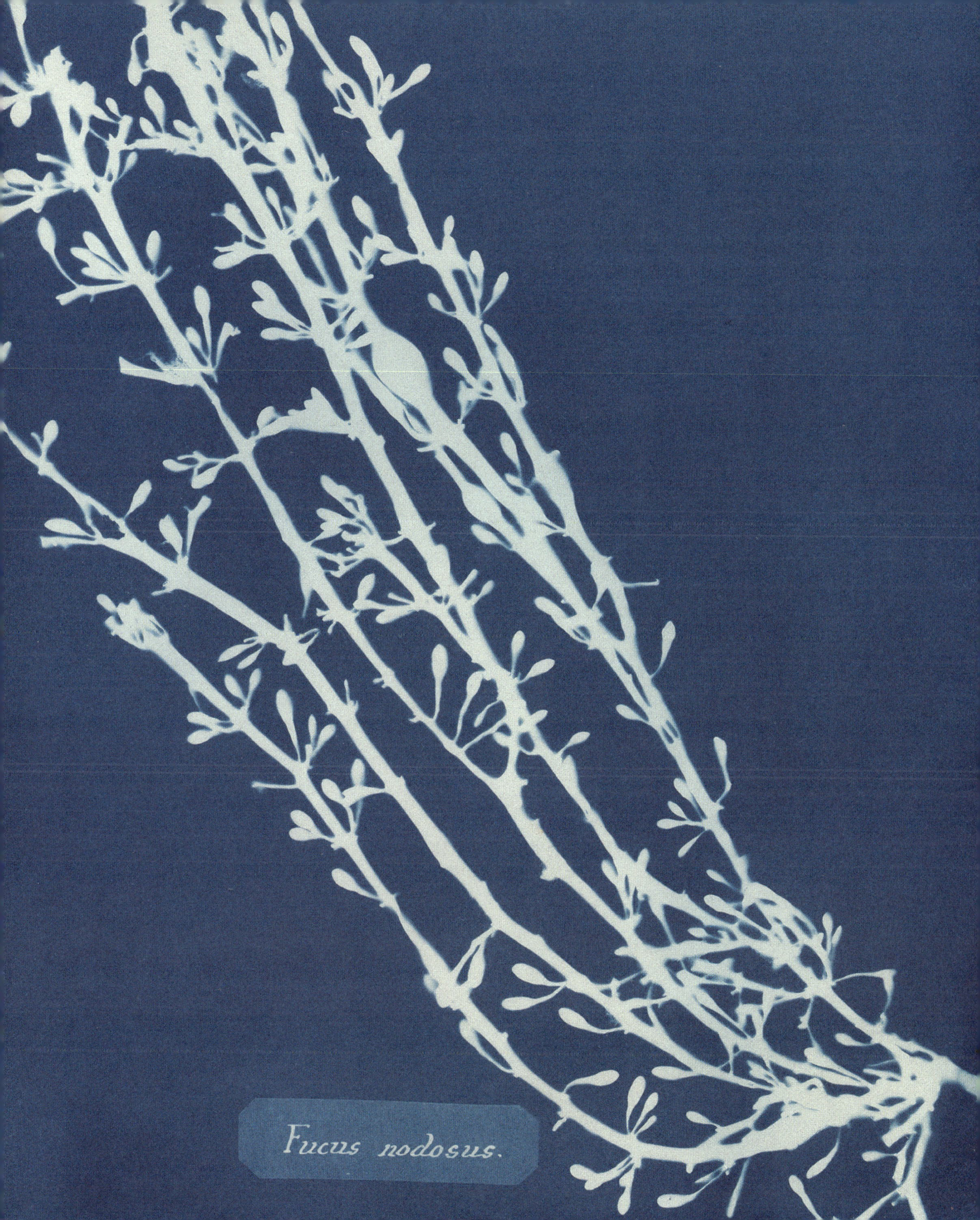
Fucus nodosus.

THANK YOU

We are grateful for the generous support of the Aage and Johanne Louis-Hansen Foundation and The Obel Family Foundation for the three thematic exhibitions *Mother* (2021), *The Irreplaceable Human* (2023) and *Ocean* (2024).

Many thanks to Dorthe Jørgensen and Katherine Richardson, who have written new articles for this publication providing us with new insights on the sea from the perspectives of philosophy, theology and marine science.

We have been in contact with many professional authorities during our preparations for the exhibition, and have been met with kindness, interest and dedication by all. We appreciate and are thankful for the fruitful contributions and conversations.

Last but not least, a big thank you to all the participating artists and to the private individuals and institutions that have supported the exhibition by lending crucial works.

LENDERS

Amgueddfa Cymru – Museum Wales
Archives Jean Painlevé / Les Documents Cinématographiques
Collection of Marcus Rediker
Dallas Museum of Art
Emilija Škarnulytė
Galleri Tom Christoffersen; Kirsten Justesen
Garth Greenan Gallery, New York; Howardena Pindell
THE GEORGE ECONOMU COLLECTION
The Gundersen Collection
GEUS
Hauser & Wirth
Hellenic Ministry of Culture, National Archaeological Museum
Jeannette Ehlers Studio
Julia M. Otte, MPI/AWI, Germany
Kunsten Museum of Modern Art Aalborg
Kunstmuseum Brandts
Lena Maria Thüring
Lillehammer Art Museum
Lisson Gallery; Smoking Dogs Films, Estate of Susan Hiller
MAK – Museum of Applied Arts, Vienna
Museum Boijmans Van Beuningen
Niceaunties
October Gallery; El Anatsui
P. & N. de Boer Foundation, Amsterdam
Pace Gallery; Trevor Paglen
Peter Freeman, Inc., New York; Elisabetta Benassi
Rijksmuseum, Amsterdam
SMK, National Gallery of Denmark
Natural History Museum Denmark
SUPERFLEX, Courtesy of Nils Stærk
TBA21 Thyssen-Bornemisza Art Contemporary Collection
Victoria and Albert Museum, London
Wang Yuyan
Gagosian Gallery, Inc.; Woodman Family Foundation
Zephirin/Giannetta Gallery
Zoological Collection of the University of Rostock

And lenders who wish to remain anonymous.

The exhibition is endorsed as an activity under United Nations Decade of Ocean Science for Sustainable Development.

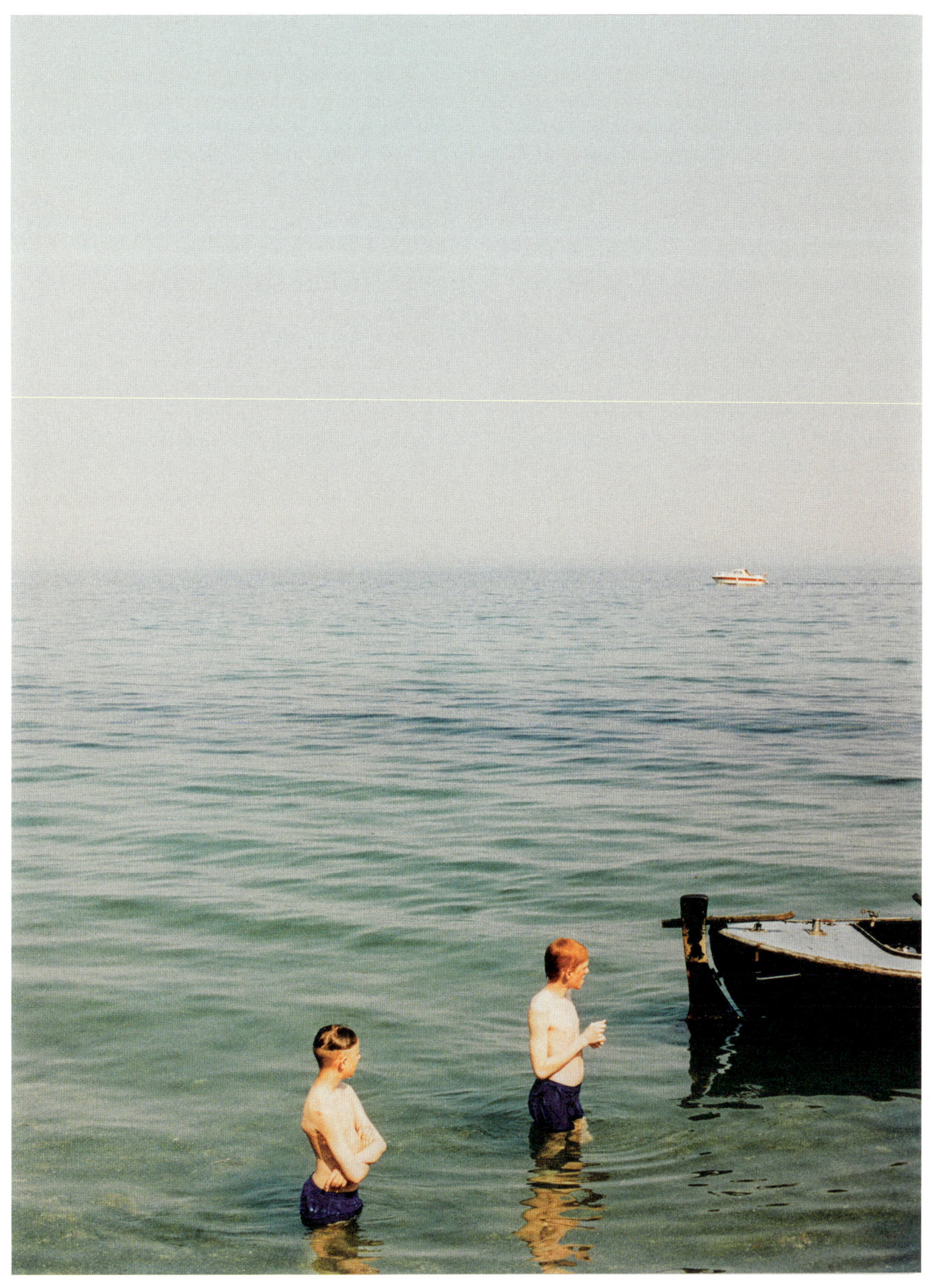

WOLFGANG TILLMANS
Louisiana, 1996

Ocean.
A Brief Introduction to the Exhibition

Tine Colstrup

We can start with the dizzying fact that all life comes from the sea. Unlike sea creatures, we landlubbers left the watery element and now cling to the mere 29 percent of the planet's surface that is *not* covered in water. The ocean wraps around the globe, stretching beyond the horizon where the eye cannot follow. What we see and think when contemplating the ocean may vary. But this much is sure: the seas are rising, not only as a watery, physical mass but also in human consciousness as a significant and complex phenomenon.

For humans, the ocean has always been both abstract and concrete. The ocean is a reservoir of myths, dreams and longings. It's the planet's subconscious and a mirror of existential questions. A highway for trading goods and people. Escape route, destiny, larder, natural-resource storehouse, garbage dump – and lung. Today, we know that the ocean makes up 99 percent of the planet's biosphere, that it generates half of the oxygen we breathe and absorbs nearly a third of the carbon dioxide we emit.

This exhibition introduces the vast diversity of the sea. Presenting art, new and old, alongside objects of cultural history and science, the exhibition takes us by turns below and above water – between past and future, beauty and horror, myth and politics, capitalism and climate realities. What follows is a brief introduction to the exhibition and some of the objects and artworks featured in it.

The ocean, between art and science

The exhibition begins under the sea, a world teeming with marvellous life that has existed for hundreds of millions of years before the arrival of humans. Advances in technology have enabled us to descend ever deeper into the abyss, where scientists encounter new life-forms as well as dispiriting traces of the modern human lifestyle. Emilija Škarnulytė's (b. 1987) visually sumptuous video work *Aphotic Zone* (2022, on the following spread) brings together underwater beauty, deep time and dystopian science fiction. The title refers to the part of the ocean not reached by sunlight. Škarnulytė combines documentary footage from a research project studying climate change at the bottom of the Gulf of Mexico with her own digitally

SIGURDUR GUDMUNDSSON
Horizontal Thoughts (study), 1970-1971

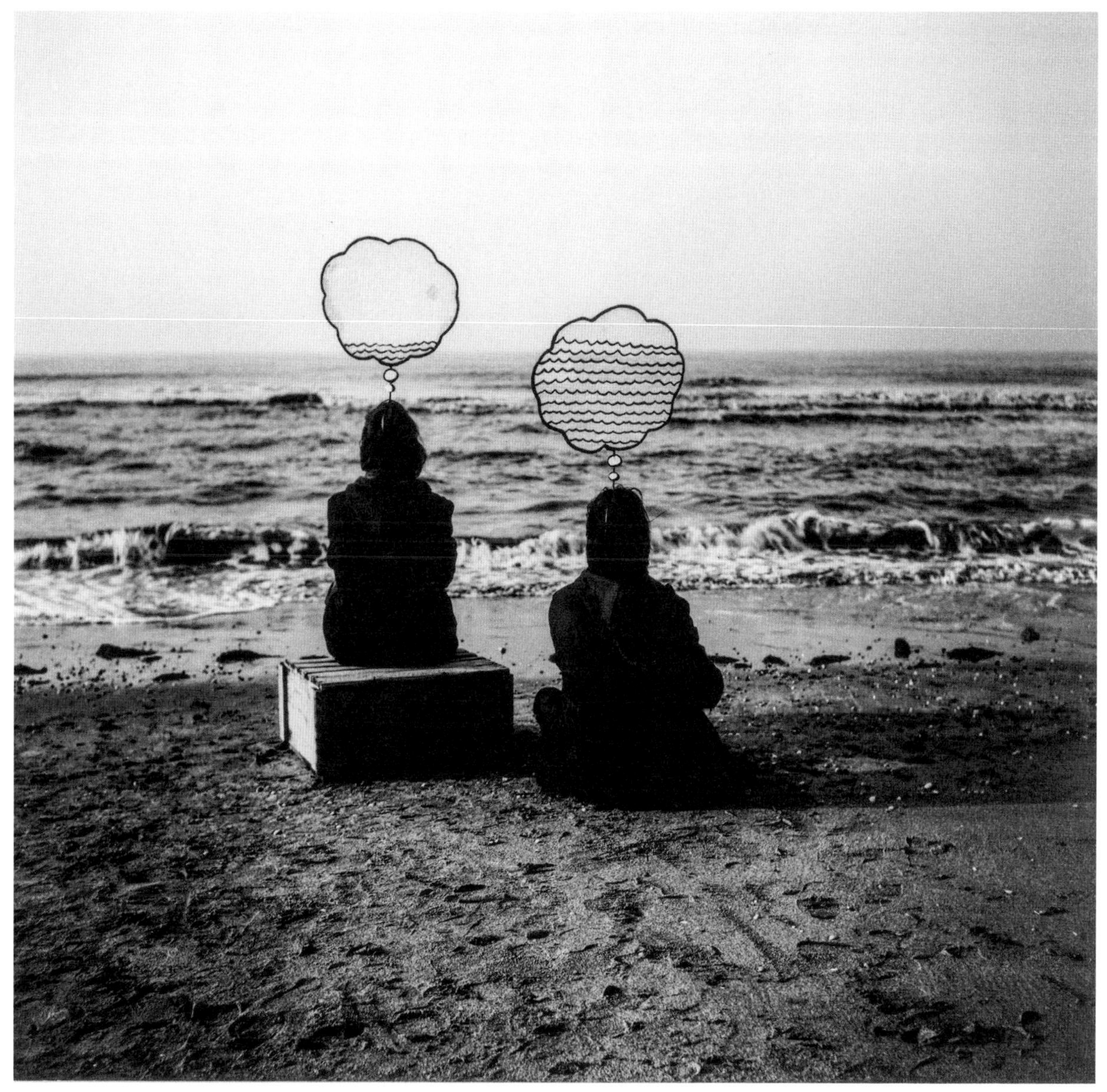

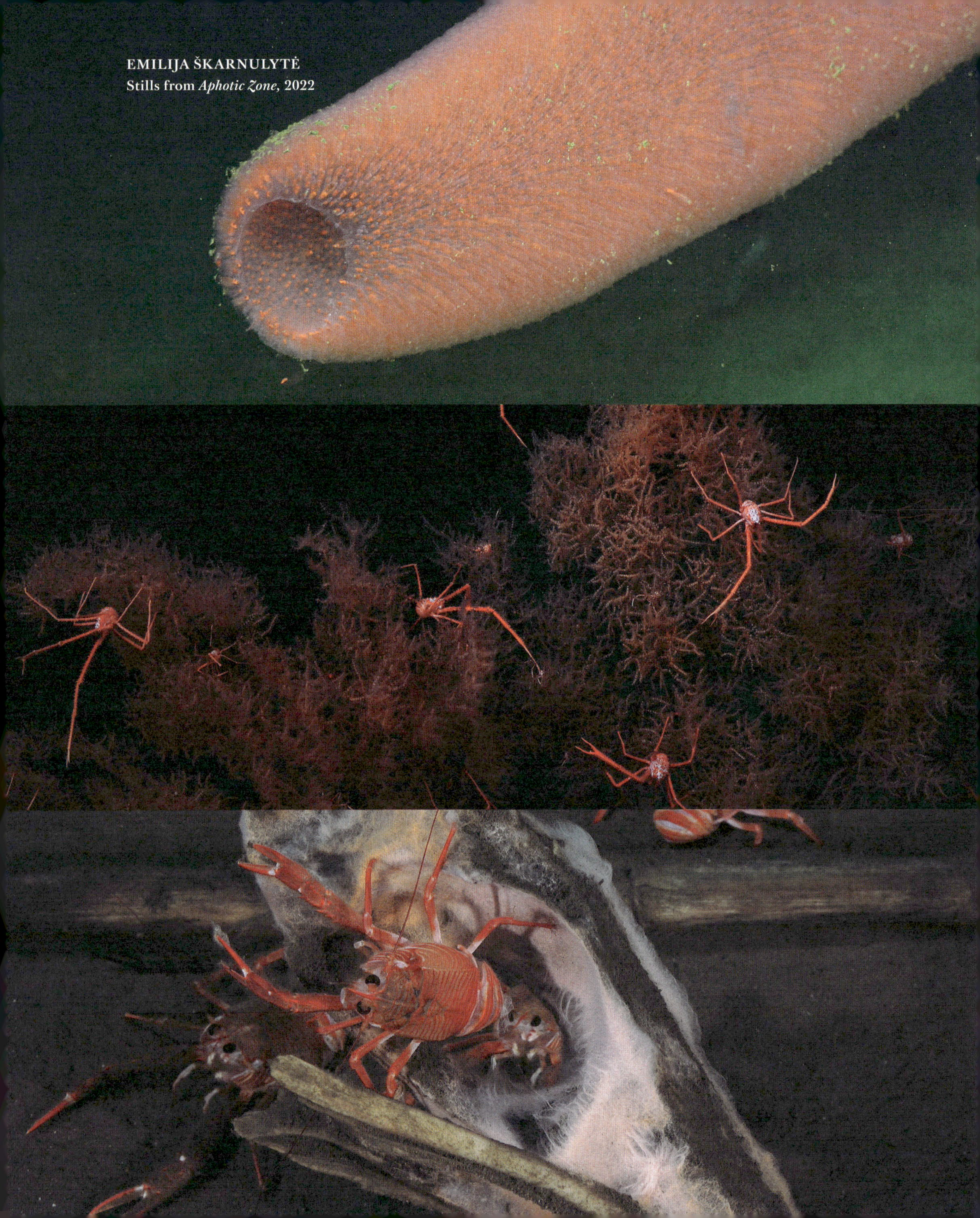

EMILIJA ŠKARNULYTĖ
Stills from *Aphotic Zone*, 2022

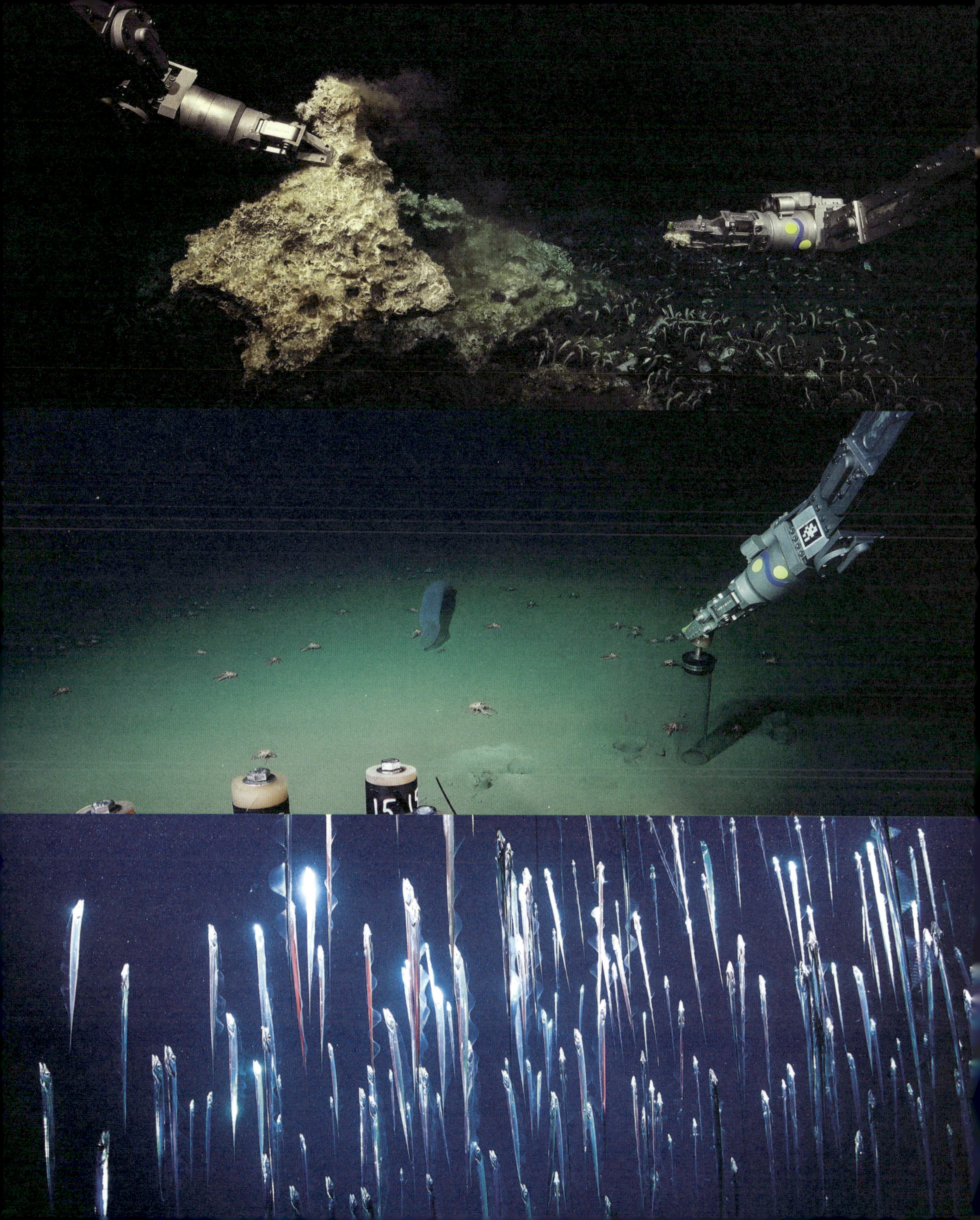

generated images of a future where the Earth is flooded and relics of industrious, warlike humanity stand like strange growths on the ocean floor.

A throughline in the exhibition is the human fascination and exploration of deep-sea life and beauty. The French filmmaker and photographer Jean Painlevé (1902-1989, p. 41-43), a pioneer of underwater photography and film, was part of the Surrealist movement on the experimental Paris art scene in the 1920s and 1930s. With a gaze that was both scientific and coloured by the contemporary fascination with the subconscious, Painlevé documented the captivating creatures of the sea, conveying the ocean as a sphere of cultural counter-narratives. His 1934 film *The Sea Horse* shows that, in this species, the male gives birth, squirting the young from a small hole in his swollen belly. In several films, Painlevé demonstrated that the so-called natural relationship between the sexes is a complex and nuanced affair across the animal kingdom, and not least in the sea.

Before advances in diving and camera technologies enabled a clear view of the underwater world, other (artistic) techniques were used to capture the ocean's flora and fauna. The exhibition presents a selection of the many books of artfully drawn and coloured illustrations cataloguing and communicating marine life. A key work is *Photographs of British Algae: Cyanotype Impressions* (1843-1853, p. 2, 4-11, 13, 127) by the English botanist and photographer Anna Atkins (1799-1871), which has been called the world's first photo book. Using the newly invented cyanotype technique, Atkins placed seaweed on a light-sensitive emulsion that turns blue when exposed to light, at once leaving white shadows of the specimen as a precise impression and poetic abstraction.

The interplay between science, art and craftsmanship is also evident in the exhibition's 29 glass models of invertebrates, made in the late 19th century when interest in the ocean was on the rise. It was difficult to preserve marine invertebrates for scientific collections, since species like jellyfish, octopuses and sea cucumbers lose their structure and colour in alcohol. In response, talented father-and-son glassmakers Leopold and Rudolf Blaschka (1822-1895/1857-1939) began producing accurate, lifelike models of invertebrates (p. 44-45), which were purchased by universities and others for research and educational purposes.

Starting in the 17th century, another beautiful object from the sea, the seashell, sparked scientific interest and an outright collecting craze. The exhibition's chapter on seashells includes a shell cabinet constructed by master cabinetmaker and seashell expert Lorenz Spengler in 1762 for Frederiksdal Castle, where the extensive seashell collection would aid the education of the family's son (p. 53). Objects of beauty and collector's items, seashells were traded for vast sums of money. The exotic shells also testify to colonialism and the growing global transport of goods on merchant ships. Works by Georgia O'Keeffe (1887-1986, p. 57) and Francesca Woodman (1958-1981, p. 56) show how the interest in seashells continued into 20th-century Surrealism and modern art, as women artists, in particular, underscored the poetry of seashells and their allusions to female genitalia.

The sublime and mythical sea

The fascination with marine life goes hand in hand with a fascination for the violent and deadly power of the sea. Humanity's smallness in the face of nature has been a fundamental existential theme in myths, religions and art for millennia. The great, violent and sublime ocean became a popular motif in 19th-century Romanticism, not least due to the work of Caspar David Friedrich (1774-1840). His dramatic, symbolic painting *After the Storm* (1817, p. 72) shows a ship dashed against the rocks. Similar grand drama is condensed into small formats in the work of J.C. Dahl (1788-1857, p. 73) and Peder Balke (1804-1887, p. 68). Sea and sky clash in a cosmic conspiracy in August Strindberg's (1849-1912) expressive painting *Storm in the Skerries. "The Flying Dutchman", Dalarö* (1892, p. 66), and in his painting of a massive, black wave rising like a wall before us (p. 67). Romanticism's sublime motifs of oceanic power soon became an exceedingly popular theme in popular culture, as seen in Susan Hiller's (1940-2019) *On the Edge* (2015,

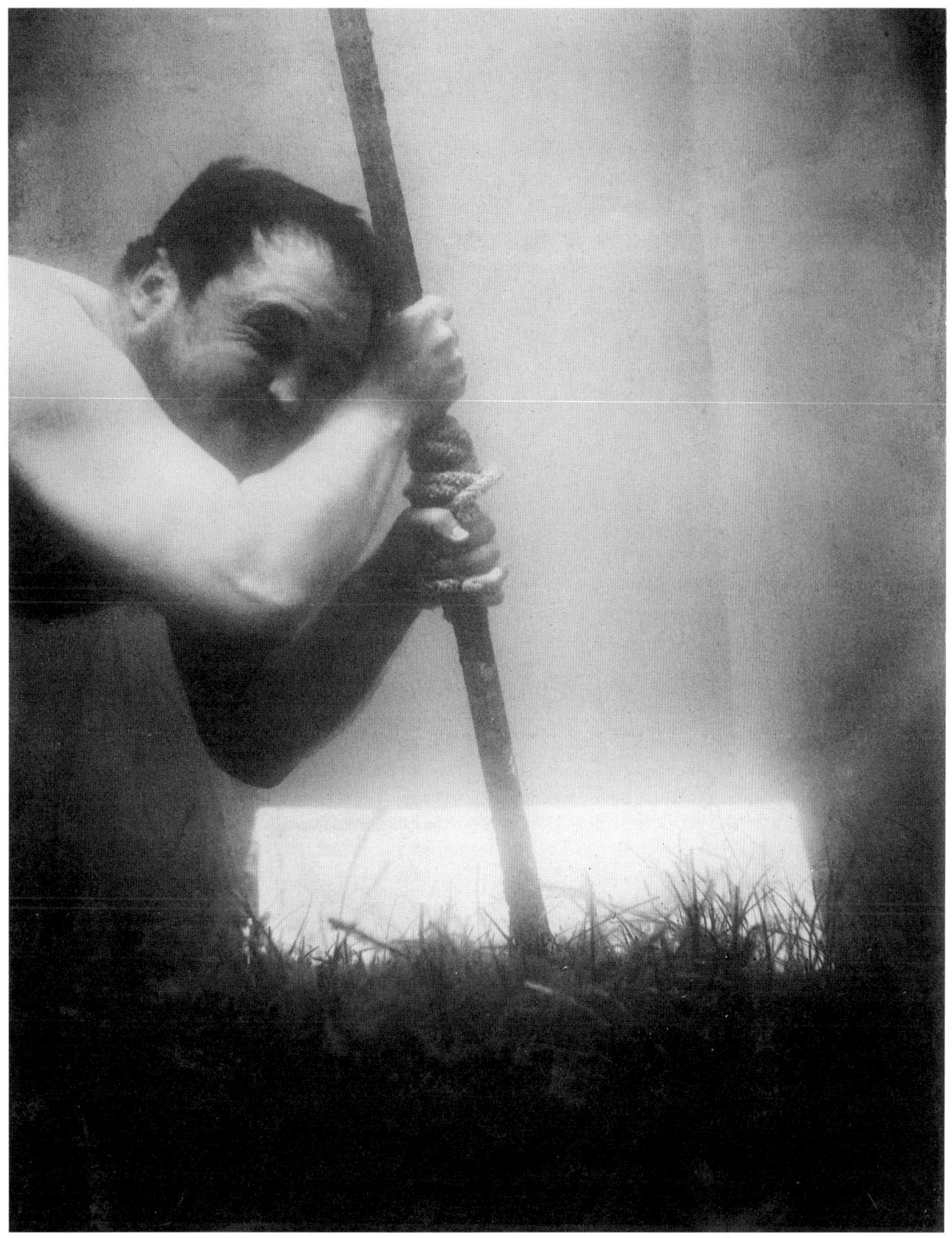

LOUIS BOUTAN

Plongeur avec bâton (Diver with stick), 1898

The French marine biologist and photographer Louis Boutan (1859-1934) developed the first method for taking clear and accurate photographs underwater. Captured by an assistant, this picture of Boutan holding a pole proved that it was possible to take snapshots underwater.

p. 70-71). Up and down the British coast, the artist collected 482 postcards from the 1910s of "rough seas" – violent waves crashing on man-made piers and harbours in seaside towns.

Unlike those dramatic pictures of turbulent seas, Hiroshi Sugimoto's (b. 1948) minimalist images of the infinite ocean open up a different kind of sublime perspective. According to Sugimoto, the view of the sea is one we share across time with the first humans. On-land views have been changed by vegetation and human intervention. Sugimoto reminds us that the ocean has looked the same since the dawn of time, whether we are looking out over the Sea of Marmara from Istanbul, the English Channel or the Tyrrhenian Sea in the Mediterranean (p. 64-65).

Around the world, the ocean is also a mythical space inhabited by gods and fantastical creatures, and new myths continue to emerge. Western culture brims with human-fish hybrids like mermaids and tritons, and sea gods with ideal human bodies. Andrea Mantegna (1431-1506, p. 78) depicts gods locked in savage combat. The sea god Neptune is casually cruising on a pair of dolphins in an engraving by Willem van Swanenburgh (1580-1612, p. 79), while Albrecht Dürer's (1471-1527) *The Sea Monster* (p. 80) shows a woman abducted by a fish-tailed merman on what appears to be an otherwise ordinary day at the beach.

The cruel sea

Sea creatures abound in the paintings of the contemporary artist Frantz Zéphirin (b. 1968). Depicting sea gods of Caribbean mythology and voodoo (p. 84), Zéphirin maintains magic and fantasy as a still active element of oceanic tales while, simultaniously, Western colonialism casts a dark shadow across that universe. The transatlantic slave trade is a central theme in contemporary art about the sea. The large-scale paintings of Ellen Gallagher (b. 1965, p. 86-87) feature fragments of Black bodies in colourful underwater landscapes. The titles are taken from a chapter of Herman Melville's *Moby Dick* (1851), while the artist also elaborates on a more recent myth, Drexciya. Since its creation in the 1990s by the Detroit electronic music duo of the same name, the myth has resonated with a number of artists. Central to Drexciya is the story of pregnant enslaved West African women thrown overboard on the voyage across the Atlantic and giving birth underwater, creating a new civilization of aquatic people. The new Black oceanic mythology stands as an ever clearer counter-image to white, Western mythology and its physically fit sea gods.

Two works in the exhibition directly address Denmark's cruel involvement in the transatlantic slave trade from the 1670s into the 19th century. In Jeanette Ehlers's (b. 1973) photographic work *Atlantic (Endless Row)* (2009, p. 85), a line of reflected Black bodies stretches across a beach and into the sea in Ghana, on Africa's so-called Gold Coast, where Denmark had a number of slave forts. El Anatsui's (b. 1944) large sculptural work *Akua's Surviving Children* (1996, p. 36-37) represents a clan of survivors from the Danish slave trade. The "akua" of the title is a reference to traditional Ghanaian wooden fertility figures. The work is made from driftwood collected by the artist on the beach at Hellebæk, 20 km north of the Louisiana. Anatsui assembled the pieces at Hammermøllen, a local former arms factory, where "Dane guns" were made in the 18th and 19th centuries, providing a key asset in the Danish trade of enslaved people in Ghana.

Who takes out the trash in the human sea?

From bananas to automobiles and flip-flops – many of the things we buy are shipped across the ocean before arriving at the supermarket or parcel shop. In the "Middle Passage" chapter from the text and photo work *Fish Story* (1989-1995, p. 102), Allan Sekula (1951-2013) focusses on the workers and their conditions aboard container ships of the kind that have played a central role in global capitalism since the 1950s. In her video *Hanjin Palermo* (2015, p. 99), Lena Maria Thüring (b. 1981) continues the focus on exploitation and the working conditions at sea, following sailors who, for little pay, move consumer goods around the world. "I can't stop loooving you," crew members sing on the karaoke machine during their breaks, as the enormous ship sails from America to Europe.

An armada of found cruise ship models is suspended from the ceiling in the installation *Fleet* (2024, p. 100-101) by Nina Beier (b. 1975). Millions of people cruise the oceans every year, and the increasingly gigantic ships are international micro-societies promoted with a host of entertainment options. On each model ship, Beier has added a mixture of sugar and sand that, beyond alluding to common holiday treats, recalls the transoceanic trade in sugar and other colonial goods.

That the seas are rising, notably as a consequence of global capitalism, is a recurring theme in the work of the artist group Superflex. The group's 2009 video work *Flooded McDonald's* (p. 106) shows a replica of a McDonald's restaurant slowly filling up with water, as shipwrecked french fries and soggy Happy Meals swirl in a murky whirlpool alongside the figurehead of Ronald McDonald. Superflex's new sculptures are perfectly suited for this occasion, created to be ideal habitats for fish and other sea organisms on the day when even the temples of art are underwater (p. 107).

Connotations of climate change, overconsumption and pollution also appear in the work of Kirsten Justesen (b. 1943), whose photo-documented performance *HAV FRUE / MER MAID* (1990, p. 104) shows a nude mature woman vacuuming the ocean. A barbed comment on art history's countless depictions of passive nude female figures, the scene, spanning classical myths and contemporary climate realities, can be seen as an image of Venus, goddess of love, resolutely and empathically taking action with an industrial vacuum cleaner to save humankind from self-inflicted ocean pollution and rising sea levels. Mature women also take the lead in *Auntlantis* (2024, p. 105), a trilogy by the AI filmmaker known as Niceaunties, showing ageing aunties move through an absurd plastic world, assisting in cleaning the sea.

Pushing aside the plastic waste and descending to the bottom of the deep sea, we find millions of square kilometres of naturally occurring mineral deposits that mining companies are currently lining up to extract in the name of the green transition. Rocks such as manganese nodules (p. 110), specimens of which are on display, contain minerals needed to make batteries for, among other things, electric cars. But the deep-sea ocean floor is also home to organisms and microbial communities that have evolved over millions of years. Scientists warn that commercial mining will cause the collapse of these life-forms, along with important biochemical cycles.

A manganese nodule grows around one millimetre every million years. In comparison, our species, Homo sapiens, is assumed to be about 160,000 years old. The small manganese nodules are not only concentrated materials, they also represent a staggeringly long time. The deep time of the ocean is likewise condensed in *Zoodram 2* (2010/2021, p. 108-109), a saltwater aquarium by Pierre Huyghe (b. 1962) offering an opportunity to reflect on our generally myopic, anthropocentric behaviour, especially considering that humans are an exceedingly young species compared to the creatures of the sea. By contrast, the small yellow cowfish in the aquarium dates back at least 50 million years.

The ocean depths are also home to the physical infrastructure that carries practically all internet traffic, digitally connecting the world. Photographic works by Trevor Paglen (b. 1974) and Taryn Simon (b. 1975), depicting undersea cables (p. 112-113), are a reminder that the internet exists deep down in the sea, not up in the "cloud." Indeed, people used to "surf" the internet. Since those days, the internet has grown into a chaotic deep sea of information and entertainment. In her video work *One Thousand and One Attempts to Be an Ocean* (2021, p. 114-115), Yuyan Wang (b. 1989) goes beachcombing for debris washed ashore from the great internet ocean. A wave-like cut of found "oddly satisfying" footage, the film bears witness to the powerful and sublimely unfathomable digital ocean, but also to the longing for an oceanic feeling of connection that is more than digital.

Vertigo sea

Looking at the sea, we look through eyes whose vitreous humour is 99 percent water. The human body overall is made up of roughly 70 percent water, just as our planet's surface is roughly 70 percent water. A close-up of an eye is among the motifs in Pipilotti Rist's (b. 1962) video installation *Sip My Ocean* (1996, opposite page) where our watery bodies are connected with the ocean in a Rorschach-like corner projection. We are taken into the ocean by a swimming body that bobs up and down on the symbolic and psychologically loaded boundary between the visible above and the more unknown below. The video is set in relatively shallow water, but emotionally it takes us into the deep end.

The exhibition concludes with John Akomfrah's (b. 1957) monumental *Vertigo Sea* (2015, p. 26-27). For many of those who experienced the video installation at the 2015 Venice Biennale, the ocean will have lost its innocence, if it hadn't already. Whales sing, waves roar, seaweed sways, sunlight sparkles on water – it's wonderful. Whales are harpooned, migrants sink, enslaved people drown, an oil rig burns, seagulls shriek – it's horrific. Shown on three large screens, the work is a montage of historical film and TV footage intercut with new scenes using actors. From this union of disparate materials, cutting evocatively between whaling and transatlantic slave transport, a great and complex story emerges. The work embodies the fluid diversity of beauty and horror that is the ocean.

Tine Colstrup is a curator at the Louisiana. In addition to *Ocean*, she has curated exhibitions with among others Marina Abramović, Pipilotti Rist, Tetsumi Kudo, Sonia Delaunay, Ragnar Kjartansson and Pussy Riot.

PIPILOTTI RIST
Still from *Sip My Ocean*, 1996

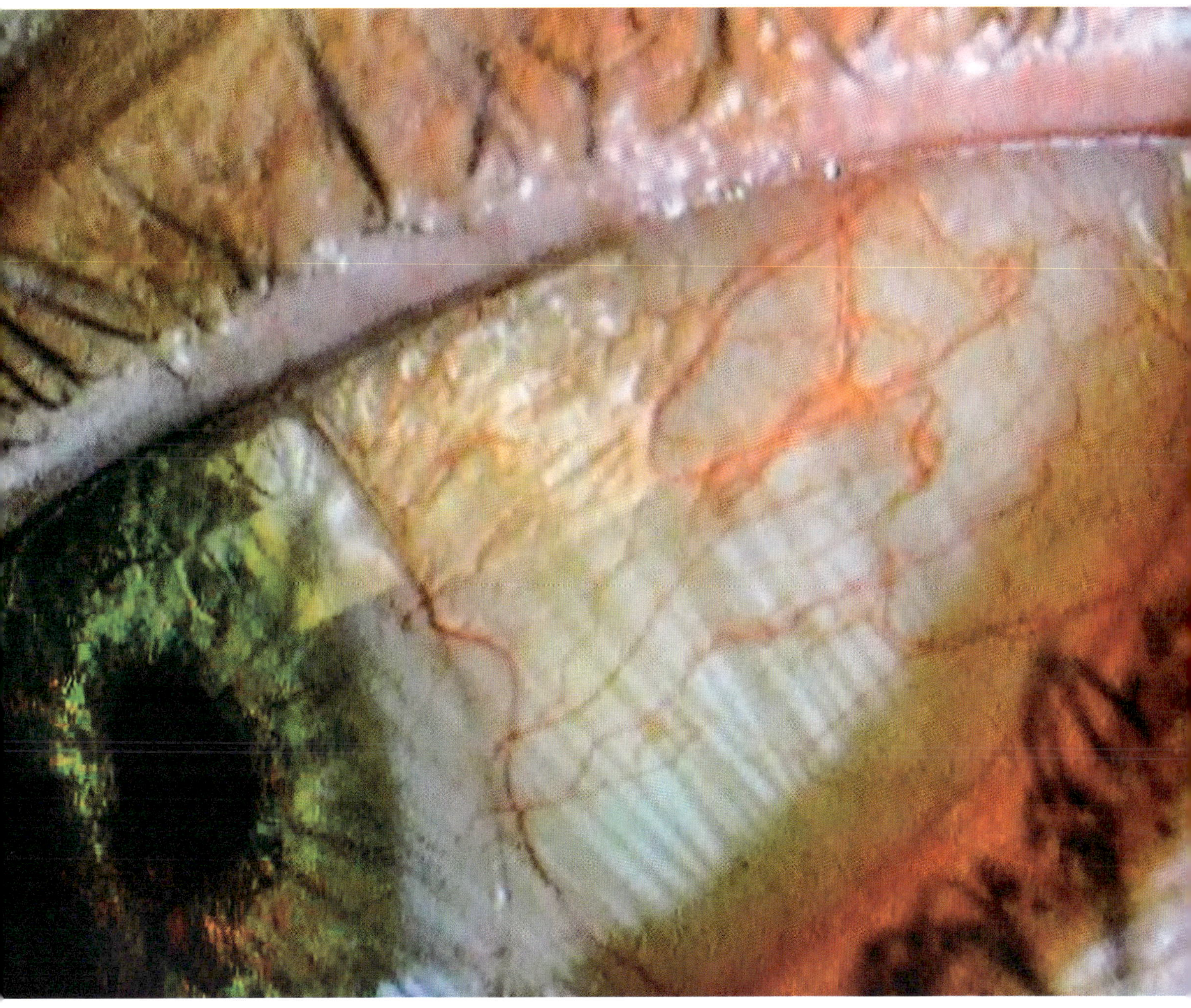

JOHN AKOMFRAH
Vertigo Sea, 2015

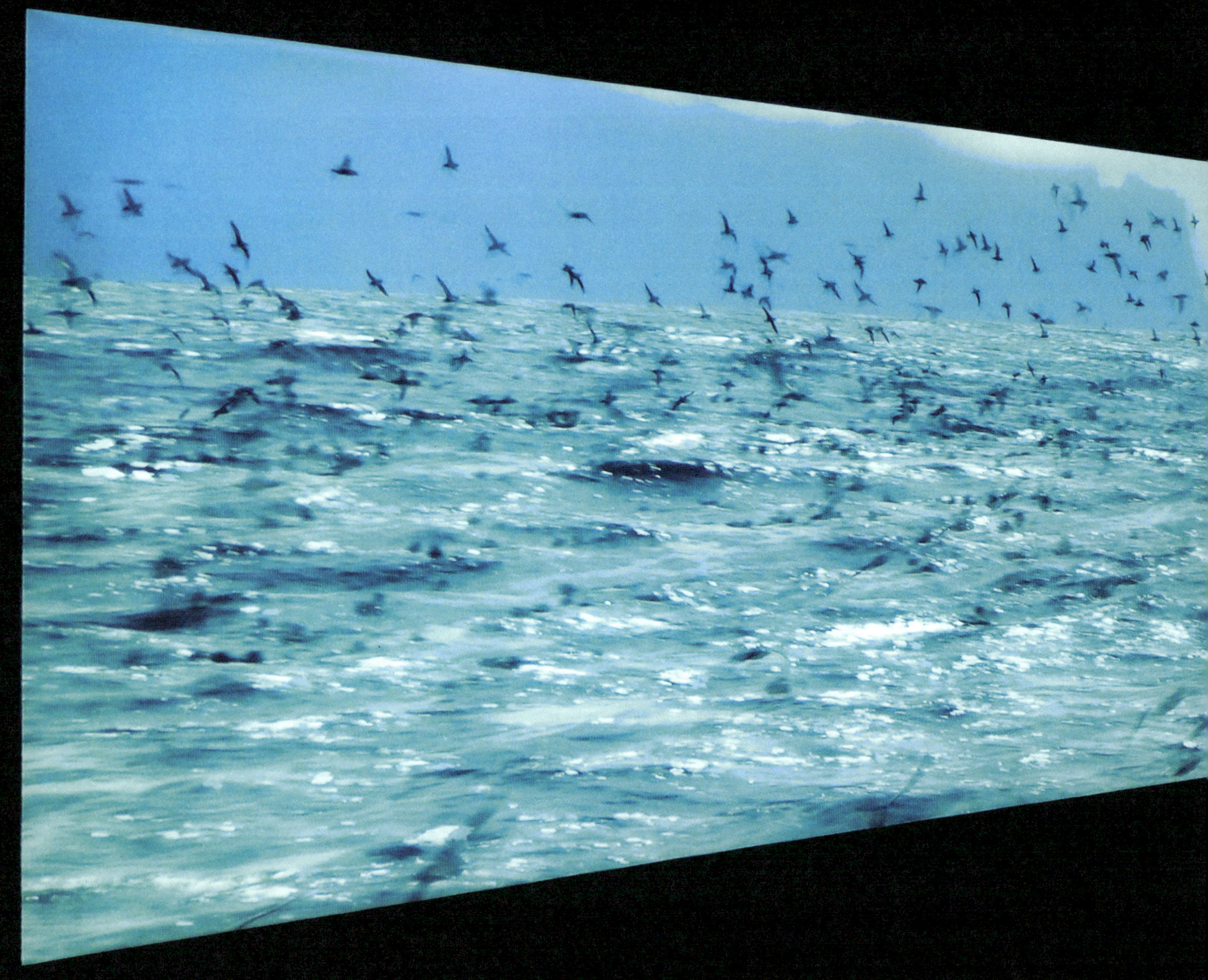

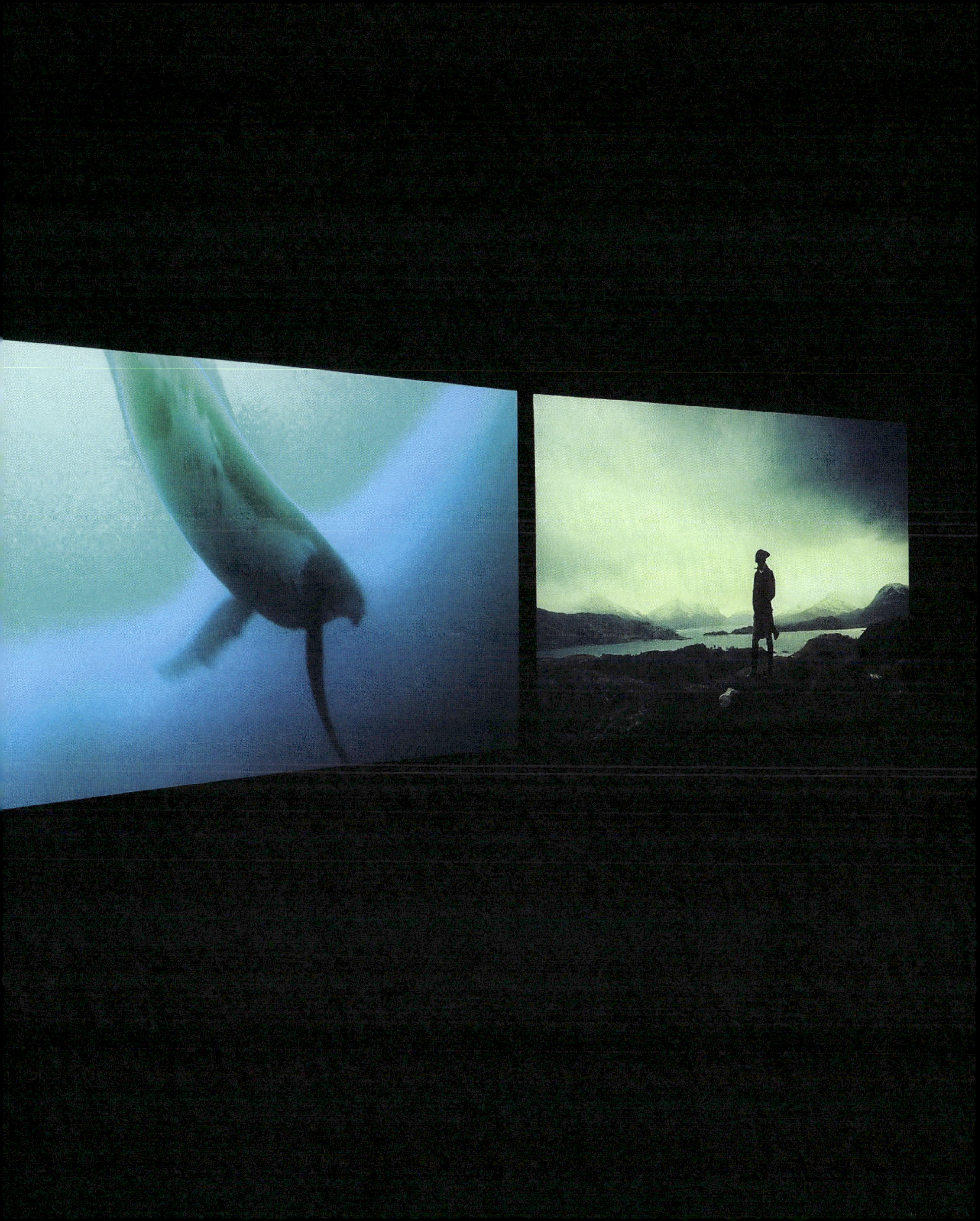

Rebirth in the Sea

Kaspar Thormod

Around Easter 1900, a storm forced a party of sponge divers to seek shelter on the island of Antikythera in the Aegean Sea. Waiting to resume their journey home to Symi, they spent the time diving. Wearing a copper helmet and canvas suit, with an air line to the surface – modern technology that had revolutionised the ancient profession of sponge diving in the 19th century – Ilias Stadiatis descended into the depths. As he neared the bottom, he saw a scattering of decomposed human bodies in the blue twilight. He quickly signalled to be pulled up. But when he told the others what he had seen, they didn't believe him. The captain decided to make a dive himself, and he too witnessed the eerie sight of human bodies rotting on the ocean floor.[1]

As it turned out, the sponge divers had discovered a shipwreck from the 1st century BCE. Partially buried at 45-60 metres were bronze and marble sculptures, among other objects. The marble statues, some of which are on display in the Louisiana's exhibition, uncannily resembled decomposing bodies. Stone-eating microbes had attacked the marble that was exposed to water, while the parts of the statues that were buried in the sand had been perfectly preserved. What Ilias Stadiatis saw were classical gods, heroes and athletes – perfect Greek bodies, but partially disfigured, abstracted. Beyond the sensational circumstances of the shipwreck and its ancient treasures, there is symbolic potential in the image of human bodies on the ocean floor.

All life comes from the sea. Unlike the whales, however, that for inscrutable reasons returned to living underwater some 50 million years ago, humans still live near the sea like "like ants or frogs around a pond," as Plato put it in *Phaedo*.[2] The Antikythera statues remind us that the ocean is an element that can kill us. The threat seems increasingly urgent today as rising sea levels due to climate change bring the ocean ever closer.

Moreover, there is something compelling about the image of human bodies on the ocean floor. As the biologist and author Rachel Carson writes, humans are connected with and attracted to the sea because "as life itself began in the sea, so each of us begins his individual life in a miniature ocean within his mother's womb, and in the stages of his embryonic development

Top: Right hand of a marble male statue, early 1st century BC.
Bottom: Part of the torso of a marble male statue, early 1st century BC.

repeats the steps by which his race evolved, from gill-breathing inhabitants of a water world to creatures able to live on land."[3] In a similar vein, the literary historian Steve Mentz argues for the existence of "an 'oceanic feeling' that many of us recognize, even if we don't know where it comes from."[4] Karen Blixen (Isak Dinesen) put it this way, "There is nothing for which you feel such a great longing as for the sea."[5]

This essay will explore and compare two remarkable visions of a human return to the perilous, beckoning sea. First, there is the French oceanographer Jacques-Yves Cousteau's notion of *Homo aquaticus*, aquatic man. In a speech to the first World Congress on Underwater Activities in London, 1962, Cousteau argued that science could change human anatomy to propel the evolution of a new race of water people.[6] Second, we will look at the so-called myth of Drexciya. Originating in the 1990s, it draws its power from the historical transatlantic slave trade, where enslaved people were thrown overboard on the voyage from Africa to the New World. According to this oceanic myth, pregnant Black women in the depths of the sea gave birth to a new generation of children who had never breathed air above water.

The ocean is not just a natural phenomenon. It is also a metaphorical place onto which humans have always projected their dreams and imaginations. Both *Homo aquaticus* and the Drexciya myth are about rebirth underwater. Comparing these two visions here for the first time will show that the white and the Black aquatic bodies are infused with concepts of politics, gender and race.

White bodies under the sea

Jacques Cousteau is widely known for his popular-science films and series of documentaries on undersea life and mysteries that were broadcast around the world in the 1960s and 1970s. His invention, with Émile Gagnan, of the Aqua-Lung in 1943 had made scuba diving possible. Now, divers could explore the ocean free of air lines to the surface. The late-career Cousteau, the one most of us know, focused on nature conservation and adventure – in 1976, for instance, he helped Greek archaeologists salvage objects from the Antikythera shipwreck.[7] But from the 1940s to the mid-1960s, he was also interested in colonising and exploiting the ocean's resources.[8] It was during this early phase that he articulated his ideas about *Homo aquaticus*.

In his speech to leading oceanographers at the World Congress on Underwater Activities in 1962, Cousteau declared that a new race of humans was evolving, and that we would soon be able to breathe and live underwater – indeed, return to the element our ancestors had once left. "I think there will be a conscious and deliberate evolution of *Homo aquaticus*, spurred by human intelligence rather than the slow blind natural adaptation of species," he said.[9] These new aquatic people would be able to work in the deep sea, farming and producing food as well as discovering oil and minerals. Science would make it possible to surgically implant gills, Cousteau contended. This augmentation of the human anatomy would in turn accelerate evolution, facilitating the emergence of a new race within a few generations rather than over hundreds of thousands of years:

> After living in compressed air habitats for a generation, Water People will be born at the bottom of the sea. They will breathe by extracting oxygen directly from water after operations to surgically implant gills in their throats, bringing humanity full circle back into the sea.[10]

Cousteau was sincere about living in the sea. From 1962 to 1965, he created the underwater habitats Conshelf I, II and III that allowed divers to live on the ocean floor for weeks at a time at depths down to 100 metres.[11] Conshelf II, in the Red Sea off the coast of Sudan, was documented in the film *World Without Sun* (1964), and even today images of the yellow, science-fiction-like steel structures at the bottom of the sea hold tremendous fascination. Throughout the film, pains are taken to normalise life underwater. During a break before leaving the underwater habitat to work, Cousteau and his men are shown seated around a table, nonchalantly smoking pipes and Gauloises while drinking red wine. It is a stretch from hybrid people with surgically

JACQUES-YVES COUSTEAU
Poster for *The Silent World*, 1956

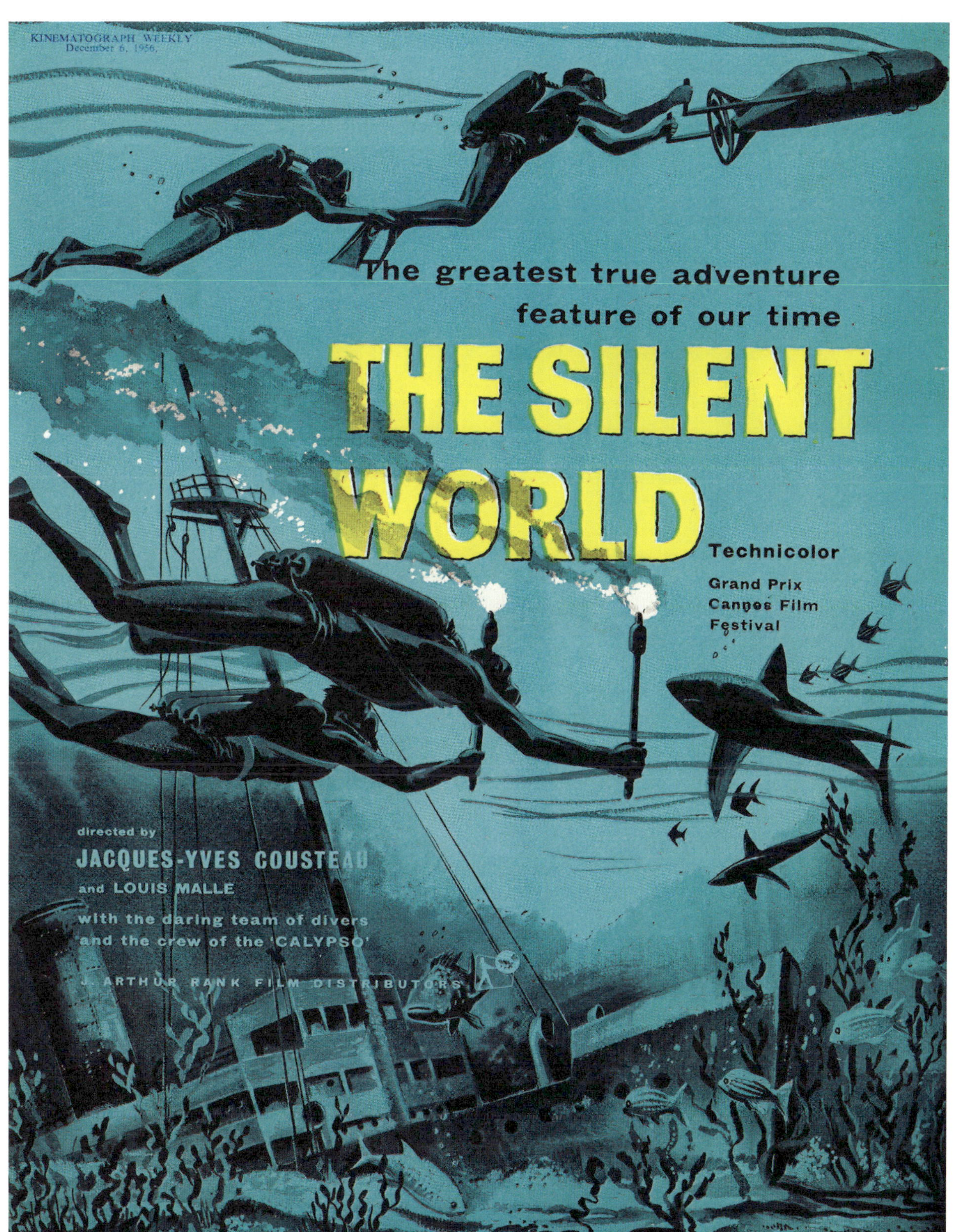

implanted gills to Frenchmen enjoying themselves, but that is how *Homo aquaticus* in Cousteau's world begins his life in the sea.

The fantasy of returning to a life underwater has a long history. Many classical myths feature physical transformation and rebirth in the ocean, and mermaids and tritons have been considered a missing link between us and the wet element.[12] Later, technology played a key role in human notions of subaquatic exploration, as seen in *Twenty Thousand Leagues Under the Sea* (1869), Jules Verne's popular science fiction novel about Captain Nemo and his Nautilus submarine.[13] Finally, the years after World War II saw a noticeable increase in the exploitation of ocean resources.[14]

Cousteau's films from this period foreground fascination and adventure, but colonisation and exploitation are never far away. In *World Without Sun*, we are not told that the money for realising the cost-intensive Conshelf II project was provided in part by the French oil industry, which was looking for places to drill in the Red Sea.[15] The relationship between exploitation and adventure is more explicit in the 1966 TV series episode *Conshelf Adventure*, in which a diver at Conshelf III is tasked with experimentally repairing an ocean-floor oil well at a depth of 100 metres. As the scholar Jon Crylen concludes, Cousteau's exploration is "in line with prevailing postwar Western sentiments toward the sea – that it was an enormous treasure chest waiting to be plundered – and at odds with the marine conservationism that Cousteau would eventually espouse."[16]

Cousteau's orchestration of the human relationship to the ocean is clearly expressed in his breakthrough film, *The Silent World* (1956), which is in the Louisiana's exhibition. In the famous opening sequence, the camera seamlessly tracks a group of divers descending into the abyss. The scholar Margaret Cohen has argued that the underwater flares carried by the divers, which make the scene so iconic, are used to accentuate the (re)conquering of the element our ancestors left. She compares it to the myth of Prometheus stealing fire from the gods on Mount Olympus and descending to the world of humans.[17] Fire is knowledge, technology and civilisation. In the myth of Prometheus, fire crosses the border between divine and human. In Cousteau's film, it opens the sea to *Homo aquaticus*.

Just as the flares dramatise the dive, so do the nearly nude, white bodies of the divers. Cohen calls it a "docudrama element," a stage effect. Usually, everyone would have worn a wetsuit to avoid losing body heat in the water. In Cohen's reading, the use of wetsuits would have obscured the connection between the divers' bodies and the ideal body of classical Greek statues.[18] In other words, Cousteau's aquatic man is, consciously or unconsciously, modelled on a classical white male body. This body inhabits practically all his films. As Crylen observes, *Homo aquaticus* stands in powerful "contrast to women and nonwhite native others."[19]

Western culture has harboured a centuries-old racist notion that native divers were closer to the animal kingdom, and so better able to handle themselves underwater, while white people, for their potential return to the sea, had to rely on technology and reason instead of nature.[20] Consciously or not, Cousteau's *Homo aquaticus* involves the white male body's conquest of the ocean, which would be colonised according to principles conforming to that body.

Black Atlantis

It may seem unlikely that a new oceanic myth would emerge from the electronic music scene of 1990s Detroit and infiltrate popular culture and contemporary art. Nonetheless, that is what happened from 1989 to 2002, thanks to the underground duo Drexciya. The duo, made up of the musicians James Stinson and Gerald Donald, did not perform in public or give interviews, keeping their identities a mystery.[21] Instead, the biographical void was filled with their musical expressions, titles and text fragments about a mythical underwater universe inhabited by a new race of Drexciyan underwater dwellers. Stinson and Donald never chronicled the myth systematically, though they did elaborate the narrative in the following liner notes for their 1997 compilation album *The Quest* (1997):

> Could it be possible for humans to breathe underwater? A fetus in its mother's womb is

certainly alive in an aquatic environment. During the greatest Holocaust the world has ever known, pregnant America-bound African slaves were thrown overboard by the thousands during labor for being sick and disruptive cargo. Is it possible that they could have given birth at sea to babies that never needed air? Recent experiments have shown mice able to breathe liquid oxygen. Even more shocking and conclusive was a recent instance of a premature human infant saved from certain death by breathing liquid oxygen through its underdeveloped lungs. These facts combined with reported sightings of gill men and swamp monsters in the coastal swamps of southeastern United States make the slave trade theory startlingly feasible. Are Drexciyans water-breathing, aquatically mutated descendants of those unfortunate victims of human greed? Have they been spared by God to teach us or terrorize us? Did they migrate from the Gulf of Mexico to the Mississippi river basin and on to the Great Lakes of Michigan? Do they walk among us? Are they more advanced than us and why do they make their strange music? What is their quest? These are many of the questions that you don't know and never will. The end of one thing ... and the beginning of another.
Out – The Unknown Writer

The anonymous writer describes how Drexciyan ocean people are descended from enslaved Africans cast overboard and mutated in the depths of the Atlantic Ocean and now migrating up America's rivers, possibly to seek revenge. In the Drexciyan universe, the feminine origin of the myth – pregnant women – is often contrasted with masculine song titles like "The Mutant Gillmen." The liner notes from *The Quest* are both speculative and pointed: the origin story draws on historical narratives mixed with science fiction and references to scientific research. The writer and cultural theorist Kodwo Eshun writes, "By reimagining the Transatlantic Slave Trade as a fiction of enforced mutation, the Drexciya mythos opened, and continues to open, a speculative space for the reimagining of the posthuman condition."[22]

A complex concept, "posthuman" typically refers to human evolution by means of new technology.[23] The posthuman person transcends traditional, physical and cognitive limitations, creating a hybrid of human anatomy and technology. In Cousteau's case, posthuman evolution depends on scientific and technological advances – such as surgically implanted gills accelerating the arrival of aquatic man. As he points out, "the new species could be created at birth in submarine clinics with a prompt operation to 'acclimatize' babies as early as possible. The infant, with its experience in the womb just behind it, would be a natural." But Eshun's use of the term "the posthuman condition" above does not refer to the application of technology to change humanity, highlighting a key difference between *Homo aquaticus* and Drexciyan sea people.

In both visions, we find the idea that newborn babies can breathe underwater because they come straight from the small sea of the womb. But while Cousteau turns to science, in the myth of Drexciya the process simply happens after pregnant women are cast overboard. Eshun calls this "enforced mutation." While Cousteau's *Homo aquaticus* is something towards which humanity can evolve, Drexciyan sea people have been around for centuries. As posthuman sea dwellers, Drexciyans are from the past, not the future.[25]

In a historical perspective, Cousteau's focus on science and technology arguably embodies the typical Western worldview that since the 18th century has regarded nature as a system of laws that humans can hack and exploit. Indeed, technological and scientific manipulation of human anatomy would return the white body to the sea. This same worldview also helped enable the European colonial powers to improve the efficiency of the transatlantic slave trade. In the 18th century, new navigation technologies, sophisticated ship constructions and logistics systems led to a boom in the slave trade.[26] In that light, white aquatic man is the product of the Western worldview, while Black sea dwellers are victims of it. As the historian Marcus Rediker writes, "If Europe, Africa and the Americas are haunted by the legacies of race, class and slavery, the slaver is the ghost ship of our modern consciousness."[27] Indeed, according to the liner notes from *The Quest*, Drexciyans are manifestations of ghosts walking among us.

Eshun's characterisation of Drexciya as a speculative, open space has made the myth an important theme for contemporary artists, including Ellen Gallagher, whose work is also in the Louisiana's exhibition.[28] The scholar Suzanna Chan describes Gallagher's use of the Drexciyan myth: "They feature the black Atlantic in countermemories that reinscribe the historical murder of African women through a myth of their survival and transformation into aquatic beings. The artworks defy contemporary eliminations of, and assaults on, black lives to claim a spectacular present and posthuman future."[29]

Gallagher's visual vocabulary is saturated with the sea. Her paintings often feature strange, fragmented ocean people floating among seaweed and aquatic organisms, their gender fluid and ambiguous. But there is clearly a powerful connection between these beings and their surroundings. They belong there, as if they had found a home in an underwater world beyond the reach of slavers. Replacing the masculine aspect of the original Drexciya myth, Gallagher focuses on the regenerative potential of the pregnant women and their transformation into aquatic beings.[30]

The Drexciya myth remains a posthuman vision; it deliberately does not strive for historical accuracy. Instead, fiction is used to generate alternative narratives about historical events that were fatal to millions of people abducted and shipped across the Atlantic. According to the scholar Austin Anderson, the Drexciya myth immerses "self-emancipated Africans deep into the hadalpelagic zone and imaginatively builds a Black Atlantis that offers Black people an oceanic space of possibility, belonging, and freedom."[31] In other words, Drexciya creates an underwater vision, in which the body that was removed from its homeland and robbed of its identity gains a new sense of belonging under the sea. Once a death zone, the Atlantic Ocean is now a Black Atlantis. Previously, the enslaved were dominated by white, Western culture, but as Drexciyan sea people, they can now create their own future underwater.

Oceanic rebirth

Comparing the technologically augmented white body and the mutated Black body makes it clear that they represent two very different ways for humans to return to the sea. With the help of science and technology, Cousteau seeks to create a future aquatic man, while Black sea dwellers grow out of one of the darkest chapters of Western colonialism. One aquatic being is from the future, the other from the past. But what, if anything, do they have in common?

The posthuman vision of the Drexciya myth and its many ramifications in art is infused with a feeling of belonging below the surface. It is about finding a new home in a situation where people have been forcibly displaced. The sea is a sanctuary and a place of possibility. The same is true with Cousteau, even if the historical circumstances are entirely different. Stripping away the underlying ideas of conquest and dominance, Cousteau's project is also about the sea as a space of freedom where metamorphosis can take place. In his 1953 book *The Silent World,* Cousteau describes the sensation of flying underwater: "To halt and hang attached to nothing, no lines or air pipe to the surface, was a dream. At night I often had visions of flying by extending my arms as wings. Now I flew without wings."[32]

The ocean is about transcendence, surpassing humanity, breathing underwater, flying without wings. However, Cousteau's aim of "bringing humanity full circle back into the sea" was a mistake. When exploration and exploitation go hand in hand, humanity and the sea both pay the price. From the late 1960s onwards, Cousteau was an unequivocal advocate for preserving and protecting the ocean environment. This is what he is best known for. Metaphorically, however, his vision of *Homo aquaticus* can be compared to the image of the decomposing marble bodies on the ocean floor off Antikythera.

Just as the white marble bodies can be connected to Cousteau's vision, the rebirth of Black aquatic people is embodied in the Ghanaian artist El Anatsui's *Akua's Surviving Children* (1996), which is also in the Louisiana's exhibition. The work is not derived specifically from Drexciya but from a similar idea of

Drexciyan wavejumper by Frankie Fultz. Detail from the cover art of the CD *The Quest*, 1997

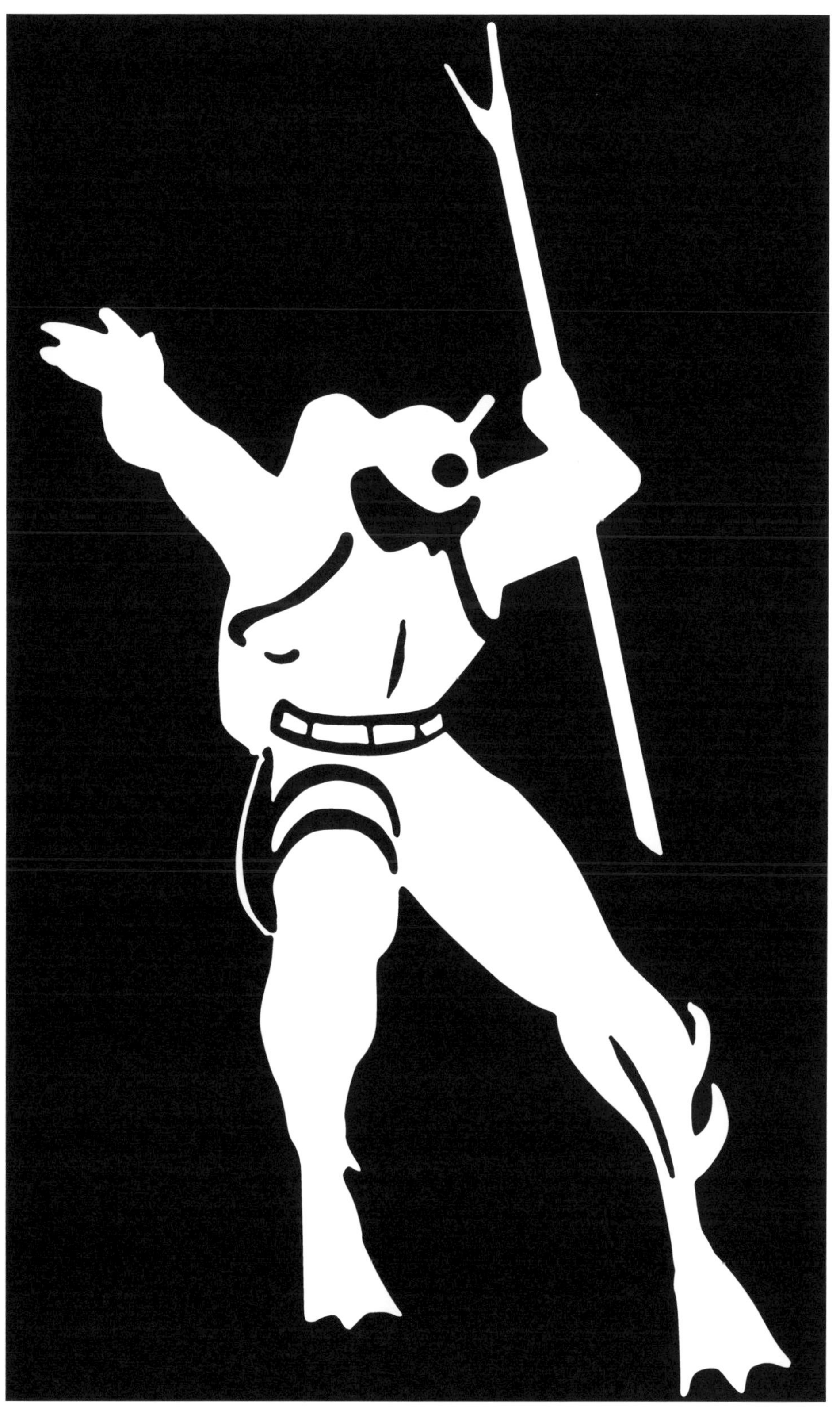

EL ANATSUI
Akua's Surviving Children, 1996

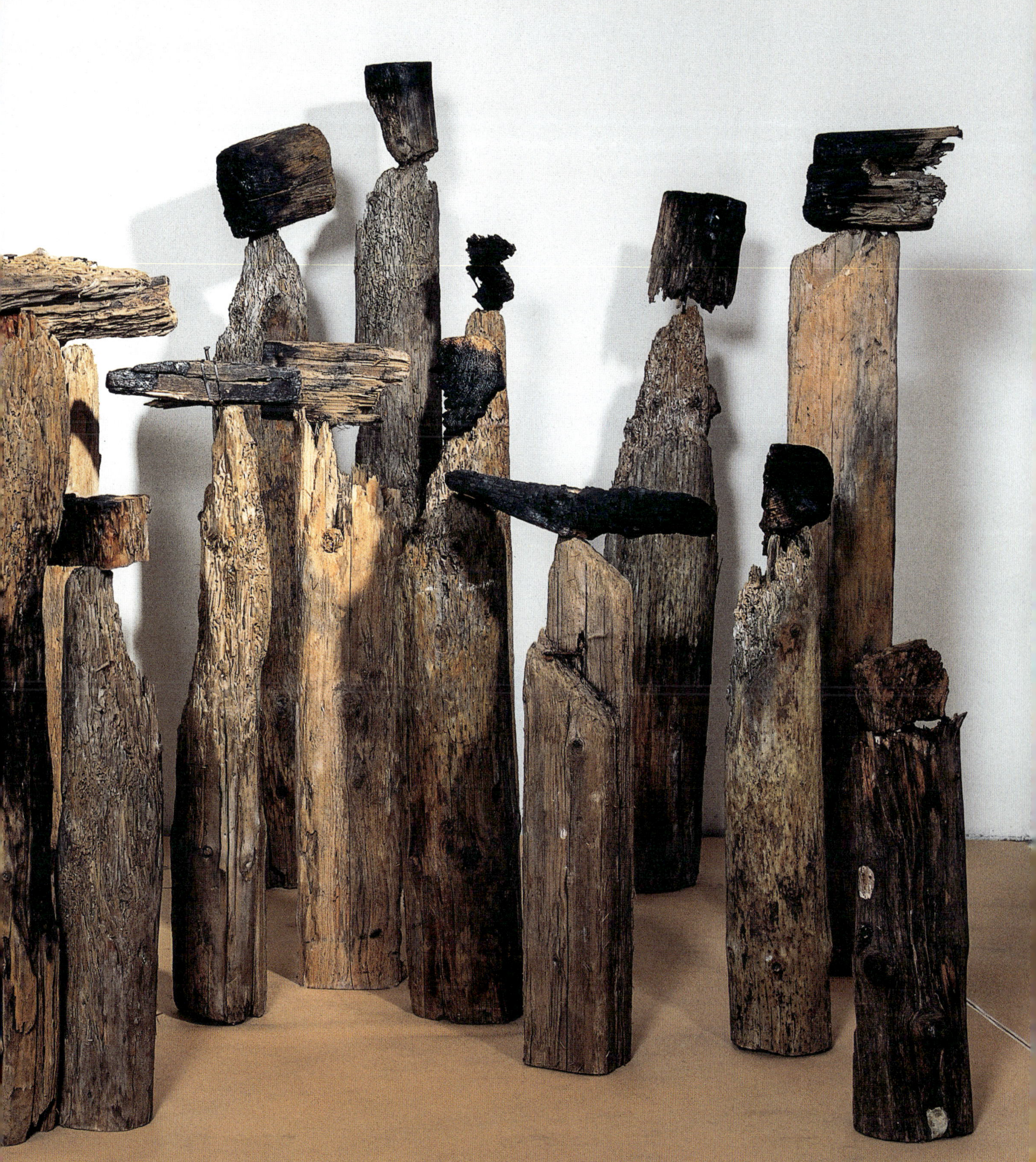

enslaved bodies returning from the sea. And just as the marble of the Antikythera statues makes it possible to talk about a white, disfigured body, El Anatsui uses driftwood, gathered on the beach at Hellebæk not far from the museum, to tell the story of Black bodies victimised by the Danish slave trade. Describing his process, El Anatsui says:

> I found a lone log lying on the beach of Hellebæk. When I descended the step dyke to the waterfront and stood it up, the telltale marks on it were very evocative. Apart from being tossed and shaped by the sea and weather over an apparently long period, it had a rusty iron stake or mooring stuck to it. I left it standing and went away. On a second visit to the same beach, two other logs had been washed ashore which I promptly raised up alongside this one. A clan of survivors began to build up. A connection which was hinted at earlier was reinforced, I think, from that point. I subsequently traversed several kilometres of the beach over some days, discovering close to 30 odd members of this clan, all of which were salvaged and brought to my workspace in the Hammermill for what I regard as rites of restitution: scorching on the furnace fire the faces of the heads which were fixed with nails handmade in the forge.[33]

In El Anatsui's work, the driftwood represents Black bodies that have returned from the sea. Like enslaved people, the wood was taken from its place of origin, transformed during its voyage across the sea and eventually returned to land, eroded and changed. The title, *Akua's Surviving Children*, refers to a Ghanaian fertility legend about a woman who carves a wooden figure of a child in order to get pregnant.[34] In El Anatsui's work, the mother might be the ocean that shaped its children and washed them ashore at Hellebæk. The artist completed the work by performing a purifying ritual in the Hammermill, which in centuries past made weapons for Danish slave traders.[35]

Thus, the Black sea people return, both in the myth of Drexciya and in the work of El Anatsui. Not as a technological vision of the future, but as a reminder that these new humans were created by historical circumstances centuries ago. Nor as partially disfigured marble bodies, but as a procession of driftwood – Black bodies shaped by and resurrected from the ocean.

At its heart, El Anatsui's work and much Drexciya-inspired art involve the ongoing processing of trauma. Art can transform the infinite pain of the past, providing alternative narratives that challenge ideas of politics, gender and race that lie just beneath the surface of Cousteau and others. Cousteau's view of the sea was shaped by a Western mindset that many of us still share. But art can also provide counter-narratives to the Western worldview, with the potential to open up new insight. The story of descendants of enslaved people living underwater, serving as reminders of the sins of the past, is frighteningly topical. Even though the nightmare of the slave trade is a thing of the past, thousands of people drown every year at the maritime borders of Europe. The sea dwellers in art are symbolic of historical human suffering – and of death, rebirth and life.

Kaspar Thormod holds a PhD and is an assistant curator on the *Ocean* exhibition. He is the author of the books *Artistic Reconfigurations of Rome: An Alternative Guide to the Eternal City, 1989-2014* (Brill: Leiden & Boston, 2018) and *Rom falder* (C&K Forlag, 2012).

1 There are many retellings of the circumstances around Stadiatis's discovery. See, e.g., Kenneth Mondschein, On Time: *A History of Western Timekeeping*, Baltimore: Johns Hopkins University Press, 2020, p. 1; Panos Valavanēs, Great Moments in Greek Archaeology, Los Angeles: J. Paul Getty Museum, 2007, p. 344; Nikos E. Kaltsas, Elena Vlachogianni and Polyxeni Bouyia, *The Antikythera Shipwreck: The Ship, the Treasures, the Mechanism*, Athens: Kapon Editions, 2012, p. 18.
2 Plato's *Phaedo*, 109a-b.
3 Rachel L. Carson, *The Sea Around Us*, New York: Oxford University Press, 1961, pp. 13-14.
4 Steve Mentz, *Ocean, Object Lessons*, London: Bloomsbury Academic, 2020, p. 4. In the first chapter of *Civilisation and Its Discontents* (1930), Sigmund Freud also discusses this oceanic feeling, a feeling of connection between oneself and the world that he traces back to the infant's primitive egoless state. See Sigmund Freud, *Civilization and Its Discontents*, London: Penguin UK, 2002.
5 Isak Dinesen, *Seven Gothic Tales*, Vintage International, 1991, p. 145.
6 Bradford Matsen, *Jacques Cousteau: The Sea King*, New York: Pantheon Books, 2009, pp. 160-161.
7 Kaltsas, Vlachogianni and Bouyia, *The Antikythera Shipwreck*, p. 32-34.
8 Jon Crylen, "Living in a World without Sun: Jacques Cousteau, Homo Aquaticus, and the Dream of Dwelling Undersea," in *Journal of Cinema and Media Studies* 58, No. 1, 2018, p. 4-5. See also Rozwadowski, "Bringing Humanity Full Circle Back into the Sea," p. 16; Graham Huggan:, *Nature's Saviours: Celebrity Conservationists in the Television Age*, London, New York: Routledge, 2013, pp. 67-69. Cousteau's speech has not been preserved but is quoted by his professional partner, the journalist James Dugan, and by Bradford Matsen. See James Dugan, "Portrait of Homo Aquaticus," *The New York Times*, 21 April 1963, https://www.nytimes.com/1963/04/21/archives/portrait-of-homo-aquaticus-a-noted-expert-jacquesyves-cousteau-the.html; Matsen, *Jacques Cousteau.*
9 Dugan, "Portrait of Homo Aquaticus," p. 38.
10 Matsen, *Jacques Cousteau*, p. 160.
11 "Conshelf I, II & III – Cousteau,'" viewed 25 May 2024, https://www.cousteau.org/legacy/technology/conshelf/. Cousteau's film fails to mention underwater habitats' dependence on having a ship on the surface, e.g. to pump down air.
12 Helen M. Rozwadowski, "Bringing Humanity Full Circle Back into the Sea: Homo Aquaticus, Evolution, and the Ocean," *Environmental Humanities* 14, No. 1, 2022, p. 5; Vaughn Scribner, "Mermaids and Tritons in the Age of Reason," The Public Domain Review, 29 September 2021, https://publicdomainreview.org/essay/mermaids-and-tritons-in-the-age-of-reason/; Celeste Olalquiaga, "The Missing Link," in Oceans, Pandora Syperek and Sarah Wade (eds.), *Documents of Contemporary Art Series*, London: Whitechapel Gallery, 2023, pp. 84-88; Natalie Deam, "The Great Melancholy Mother: Michelet's Evolutionary Ocean in 'The Sea,'" in *The Aesthetics of the Undersea*, Margaret Cohen and Killian Colm Quigley (eds.), London: Routledge Taylor et Francis Group, 2020, pp. 92-93.
13 "In Verne, focus is on technology's capacity to open up new outer worlds. Manmade technological inventions make humans into industrial masters of and consubstantial with a pliant world made transparent and communicative through science. In Verne, there are no uninhabitable spaces, only uninhabited ones." Søren Frank, *A Poetic History of the Oceans: Literature and Maritime Modernity*, Leiden: Brill, 2022, p. 265. See also the analysis of Jules Verne in Frits Andersen, *Underværker: fortællinger om havets vidundere*, Aarhus: Aarhus Universitetsforlag, 2023, pp. 105-121.
14 Rozwadowski, "Bringing Humanity Full Circle Back into the Sea," p. 2.
15 Crylen, "Living in a World without Sun," p. 15.
16 Ibid., p. 21.
17 Margaret Cohen, *The Underwater Eye: How the Movie Camera Opened the Depths and Unleashed New Realms of Fantasy*, Princeton, New Jersey: Princeton University Press, 2022, p. 110.
18 Ibid., p. 110-111.
19 Crylen, "Living in a World without Sun," pp. 18-19.
20 Rozwadowski, "Bringing Humanity Full Circle Back into the Sea," pp. 9-10.
21 Kodwo Eshun, "Drexciya as Spectre," in *Aquatopia: The Imaginary of the Ocean Deep*, Alex Farquarson and Martin Clark (eds.), Nottingham, London: Tate Publishing, 2013, p. 138-140.
22 Ibid., p. 138.
23 See Michele Farisco, "Posthuman Condition," in *Encyclopedia of Sciences and Religions*, Anne L. C. Runehov and Lluis Oviedo (eds.), Dordrecht: Springer Netherlands, 2013, p. 1815-1817.
24 Dugan, "Portrait of Homo Aquaticus," p. 63.
25 Eshun, "Drexciya as Spectre," p. 144.
26 See, e.g., Marcus Rediker, *The Slave Ship: A Human History*, New York: Viking, 2007; "Transatlantic Slave Trade: Timeline | Britannica," viewed 10 June 2024, https://www.britannica.com/summary/Transatlantic-Slave-Trade-Timeline; Paul Gilroy, *The Black Atlantic: Modernity and Double Consciousness*, Cambridge, Massachusetts: Harvard University Press, 1993.
27 Marcus Rediker, "History from below the Water Line: Sharks and the Atlantic Slave Trade," in Aquatopia: *The Imaginary of the Ocean Deep*, Alex Farquarson and Martin Clark (eds.), Nottingham, London: Tate Publishing, 2013, p. 118.
28 Another example of the dissemination of the Drexciya myth in contemporary art is found in *From the Deep: In the Wake of Drexciya with Ayana V. Jackson*, an exhibition that opened at the National Museum of African Art in Washington, D.C., 2023.
29 Suzanna Chan, "'Alive...Again.' Unmoored in the Aquafuture of Ellen Gallagher's 'Watery Ecstatic,'" *Women's Studies Quarterly* 45, No. 1/2, 2017, p. 246.
30 Ibid., p. 247; Robin D.G. Kelley, "Ellen Gallagher's Confounding Myths," in Oceans, Pandora Syperek and Sarah Wade (eds.), *Documents of Contemporary Art Series*, London: Whitechapel Gallery, 2023, pp. 80-81.
31 Austin Anderson, "Aquatic Knowledge for Those Who Know: Drexciya as Black Cultural Praxis," in *Bodies of Water in African American Literature, Music, and Film*, Sharon A. Lewis and Ama S. Wattley (eds.), Cambridge Scholars Publishing, 2023, p. 17.
32 Cited in Will Abberley (ed.), Underwater Worlds: *Submerged Visions in Science and Culture*, Newcastle upon Tyne: Cambridge Scholars Publishing, 2018, p. 7.
33 John Picton and El Anatsui, *El Anatsui: A Sculpted History of Africa*, London: Saffron Books, October Gallery, 1998, pp. 67-68. Original text in German, translated into English by October Gallery, London.
34 See "Asante Artist: Female Fertility Figure (Akuaba): Asante," Metropolitan Museum of Art, viewed 14 June 2024, https://www.metmuseum.org/art/collection/search/312279.
35 Picton and Anatsui, *El Anatsui*, pp. 68, 88.

Poetry is often indispensable in conveying information about the ocean. Exploring the intersection of art and science, the first part of the exhibition features illustrated books with spectacular images of underwater creatures alongside artfully crafted glass models of invertebrates which could not otherwise be preserved as specimens for scientific study. Also on display are exotic seashells acquired for staggering sums by collectors and shown and studied in cabinets of curiosities. Dreamlike films take us beneath the waves, revealing the ocean's secrets. The first section takes us from curiosities of 17th-century natural history to surrealist portraits of marine animals, from 18th-century scientific breakthroughs to today's deep-sea research.

1.

Poetic Science

JEAN PAINLEVÉ
Pieuvre tentacules (Octopus Tentacles), 1928

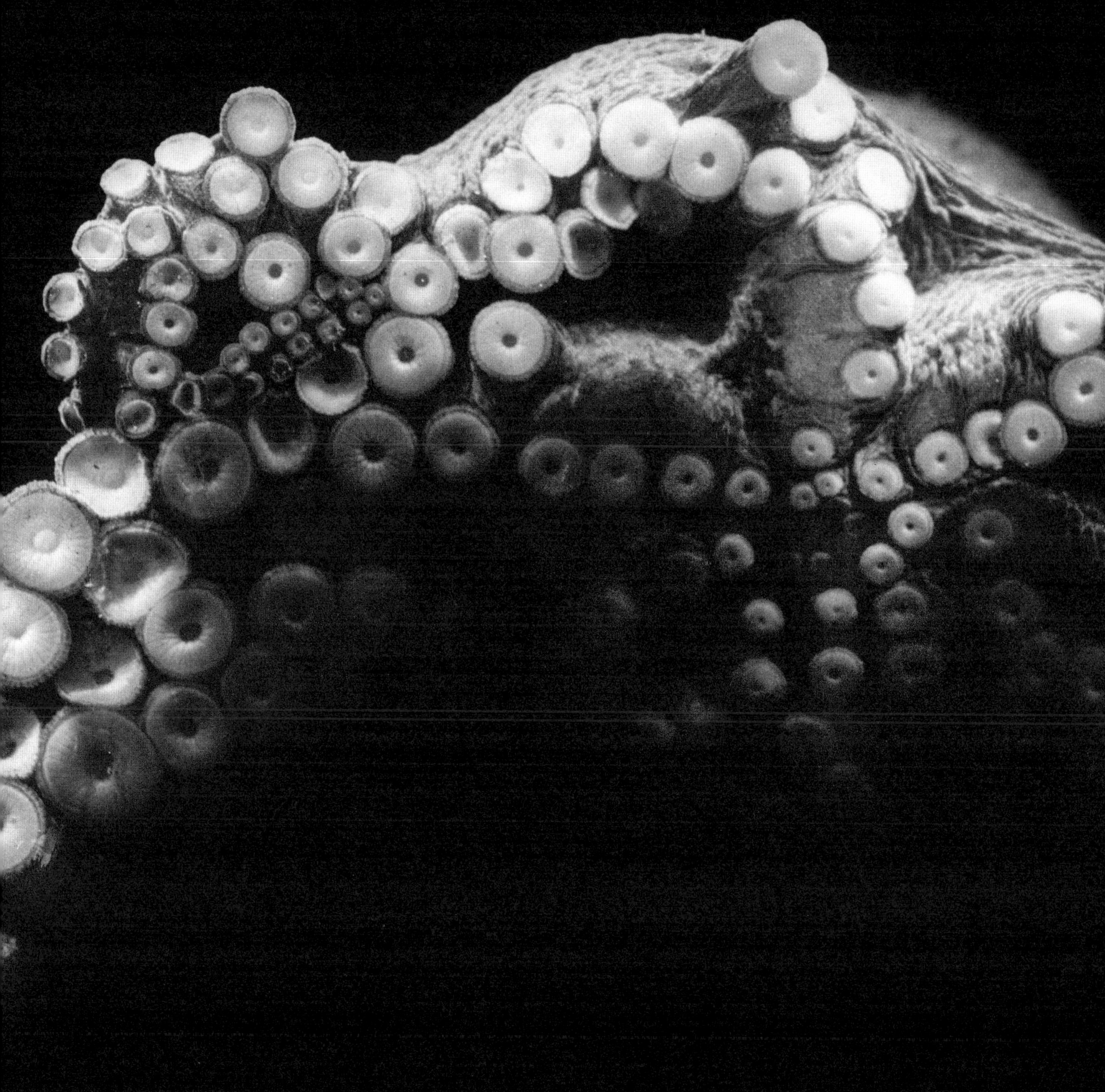

JEAN PAINLEVÉ: THE SEAHORSE (1935)

Mystery and miracle of secret waters, the seahorse gives its vertical gait, unique among ocean vertebrates, a lofty and rigid sadness, masking the strange suppleness with which, head suspended in the air as though freed of gravity, it winds its way through the algae. A surprising fact: giving birth is the male's act. In the course of multiple and graceful embraces, the female places about two hundred eggs in a pouch beneath the male's stomach, which he fertilizes. This pouch is not only protective, the constriction of its blood vessels contributes to the embryos' nutrition. The male undergoes a real and apparently extremely painful delivery five weeks after the wedding. Everything about this animal, a victim of contradictory forces, suggests that it has disguised itself to escape, and in warding off the fiercest fates, it carries away the most diverse and unexpected possibilities. To those who struggle ardently to improve their everyday luck, to those who wish for a companion who would forgo the usual selfishness in order to share their pains as well as their joys, this symbol of tenacity joins the most virile effort with the most maternal care.

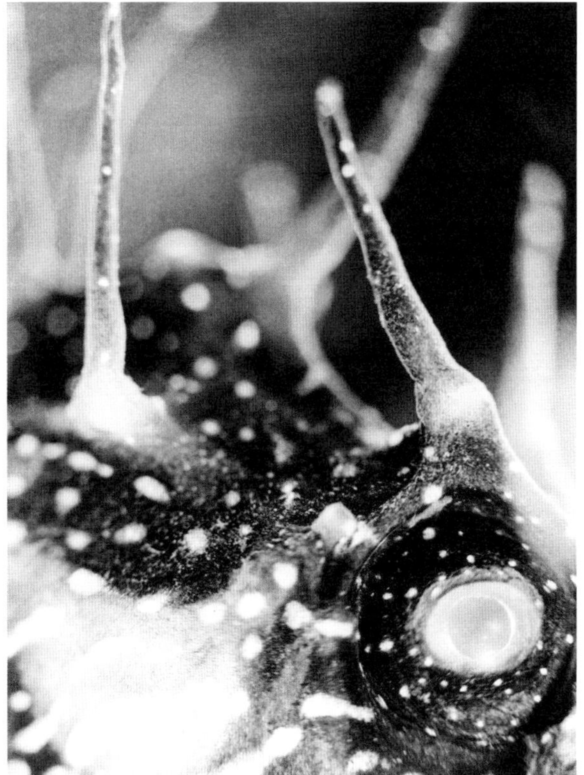

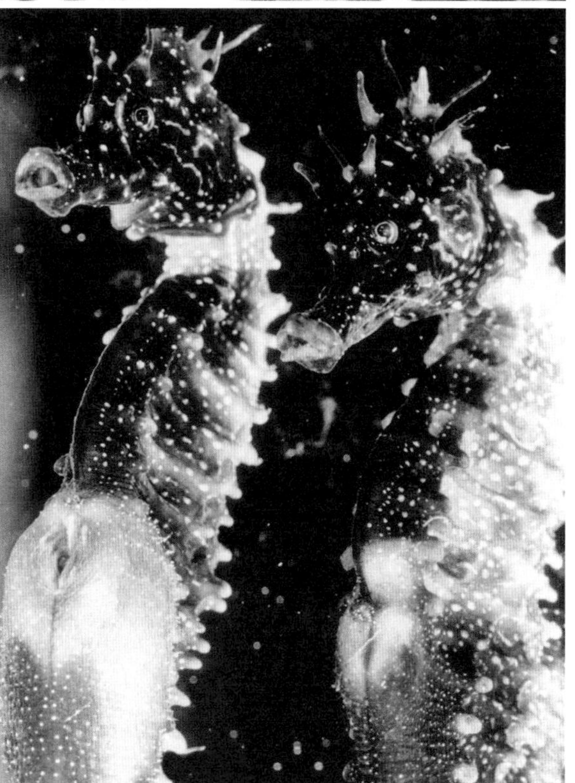

Top: *Tête d'hippocampe d'Arcachon* (Head of Arcachon Seahorse), 1931
Bottom: *Deux hippocampes mâles* (Two Male Seahorses), 1933

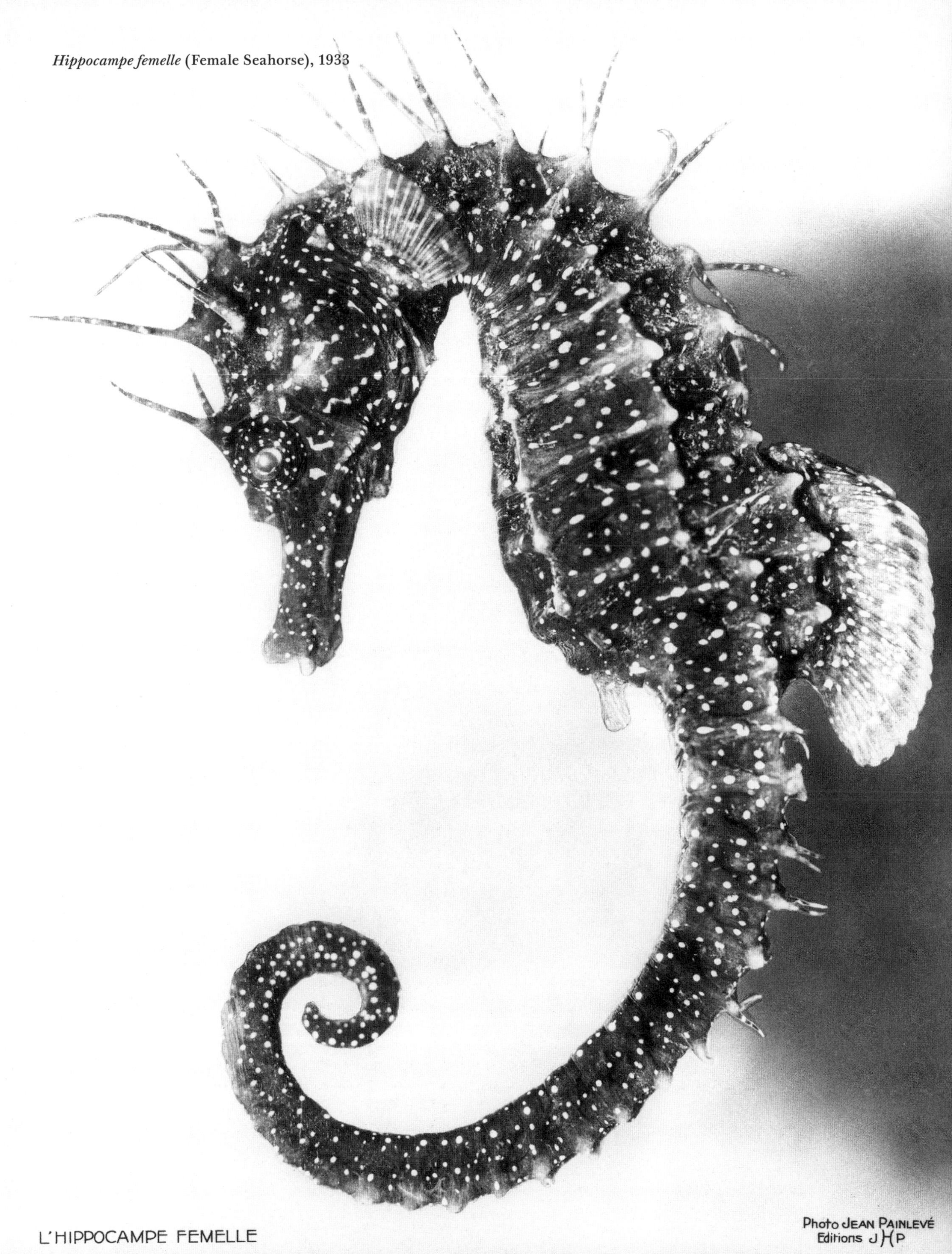

Hippocampe femelle (Female Seahorse), 1933

LEOPOLD & RUDOLF BLASCHKA
Top, from the left: Sea slug and cephalopods
Bottom, from the left: Sea anemone and radiolarian, all 1860-1890

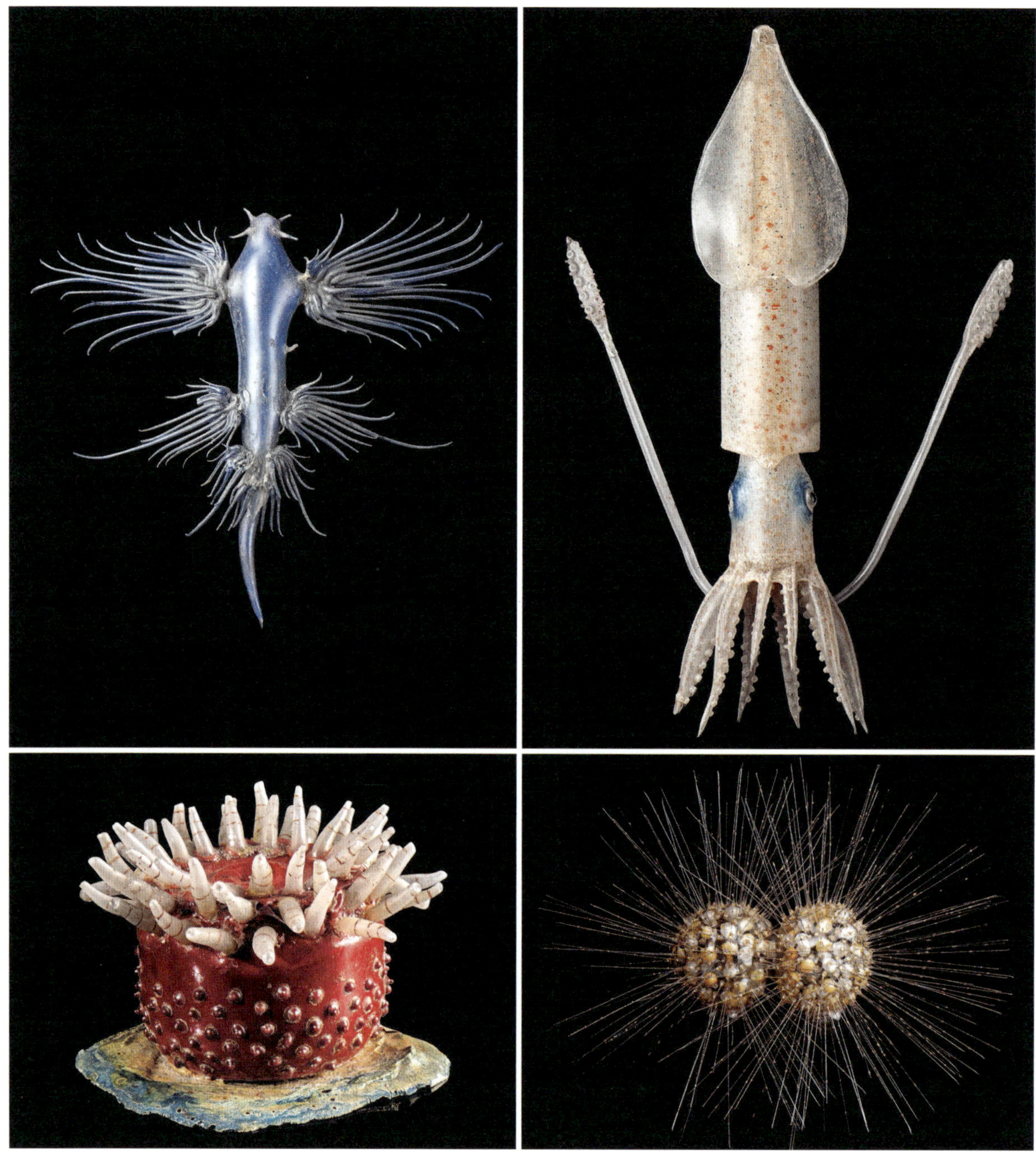

Opposite page: Cephalopod, 1860-1890

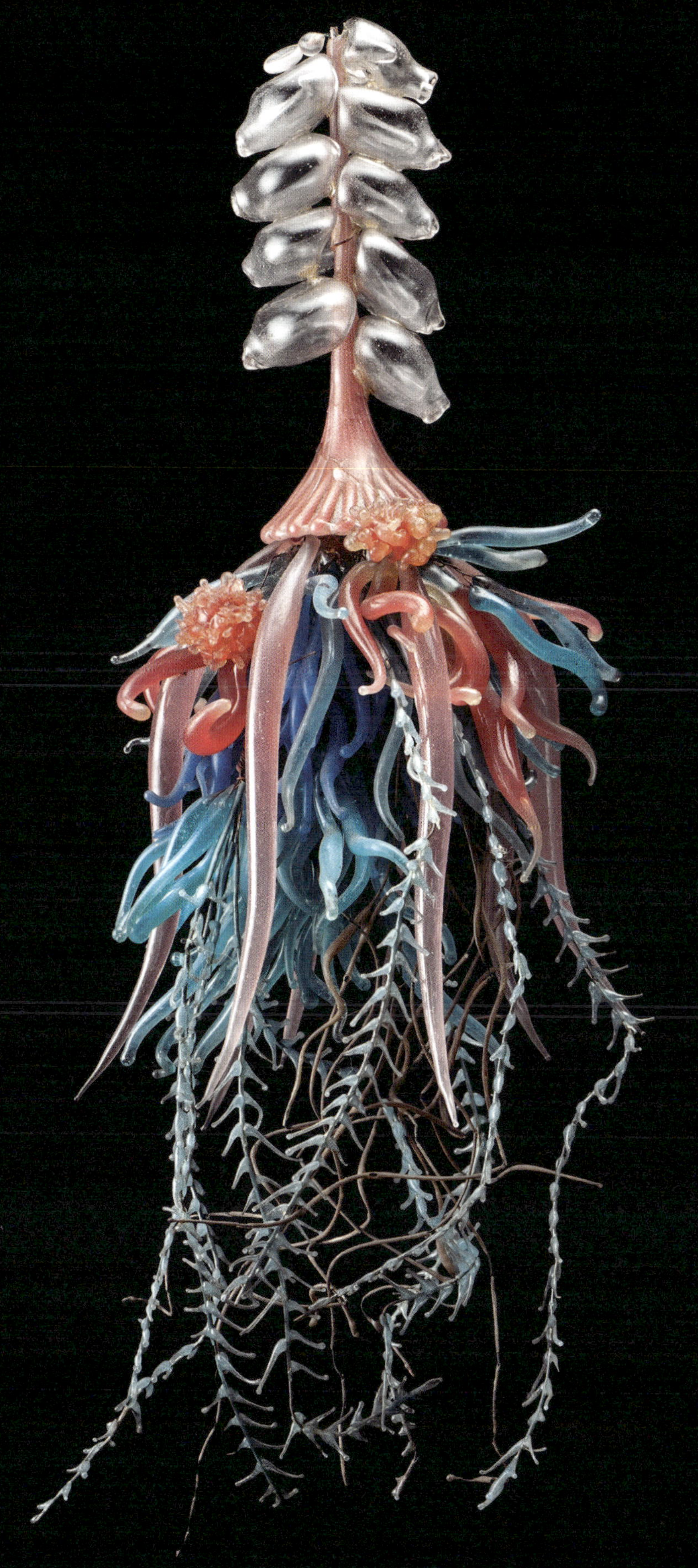

ERNST HAECKEL: Pages of the book *Kunstformen der Natur,* 1904
Opposite page: CARL CHUN: Pages of the book *Die Cephalopoden,* 1910-1915

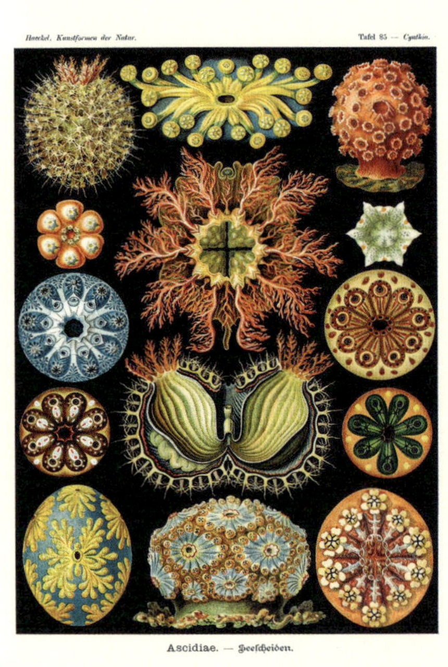

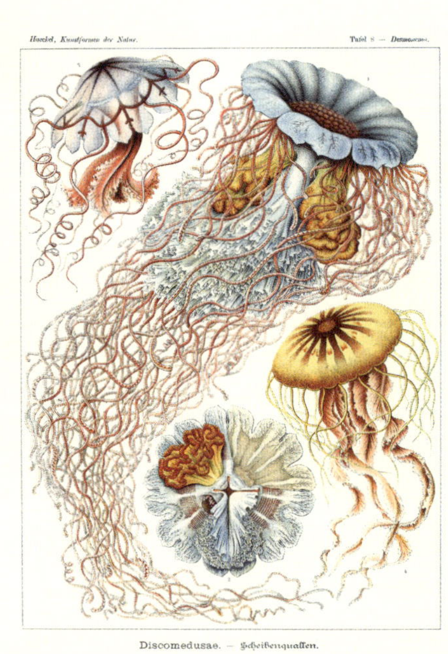

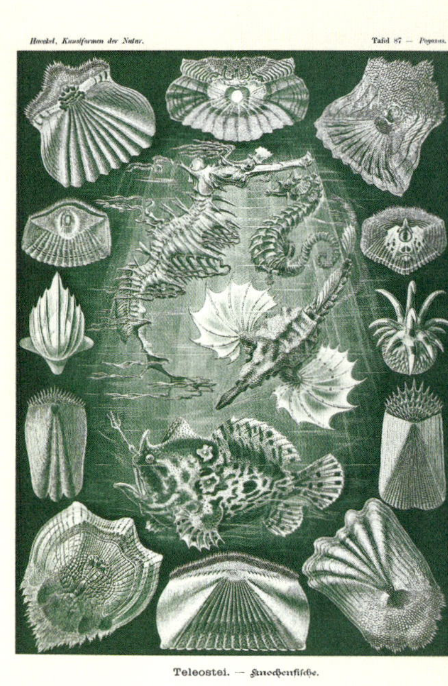

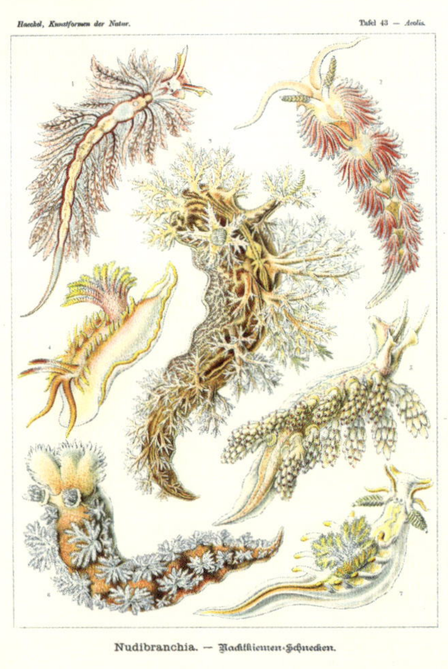

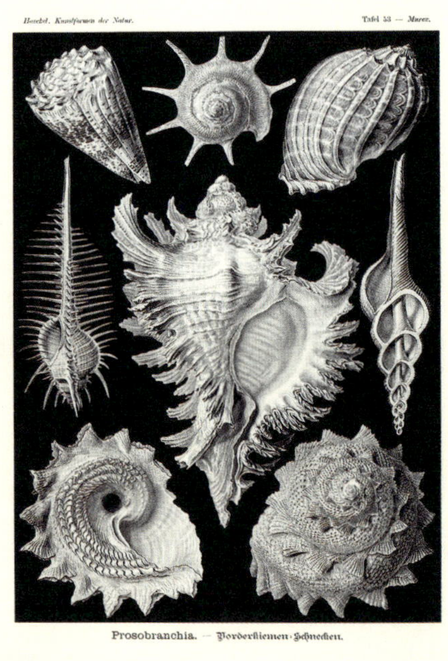

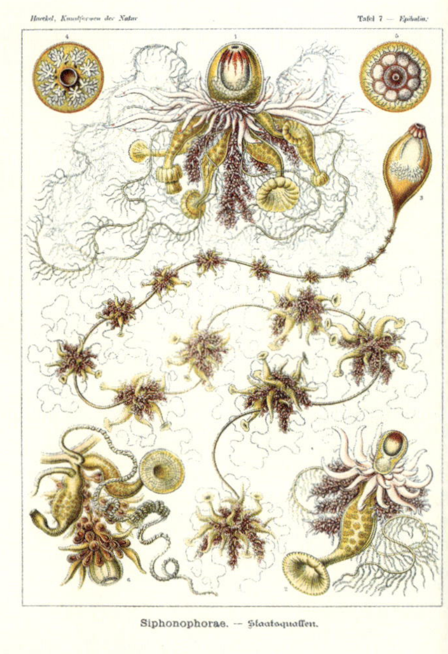

DEUTSCHE TIEFSEE-EXPEDITION 1898-99. Bd.XVIII. CHUN: CEPHALOPODA. TAF. LXXVI.

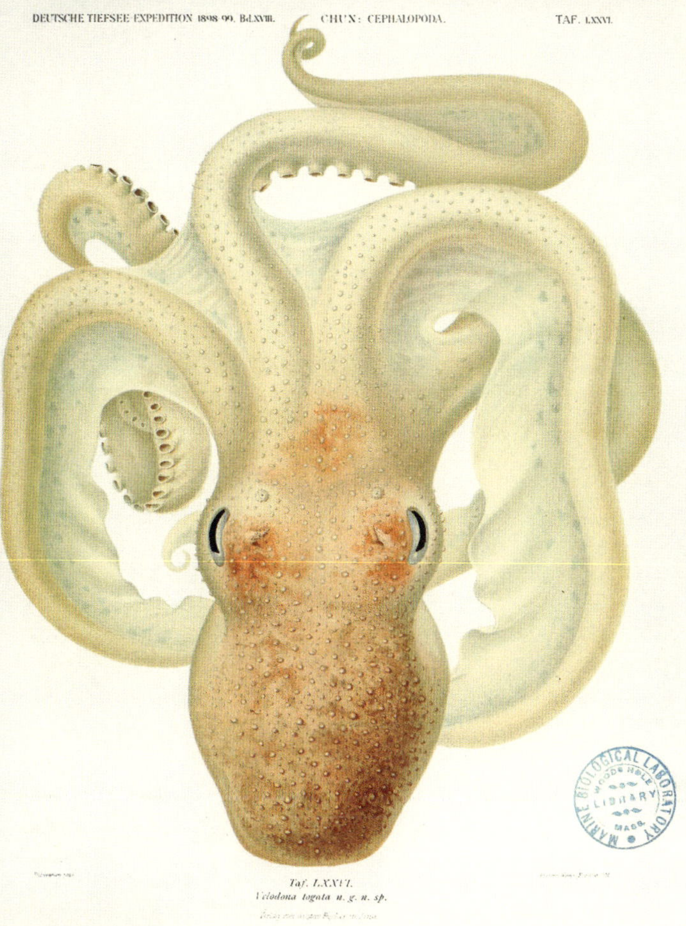

Taf. LXXVI.
Velodona togata n. g. n. sp.

DEUTSCHE TIEFSEE EXPEDITION 1898-99. Bd.XVIII. CHUN: CEPHALOPODA. TAF. XC.

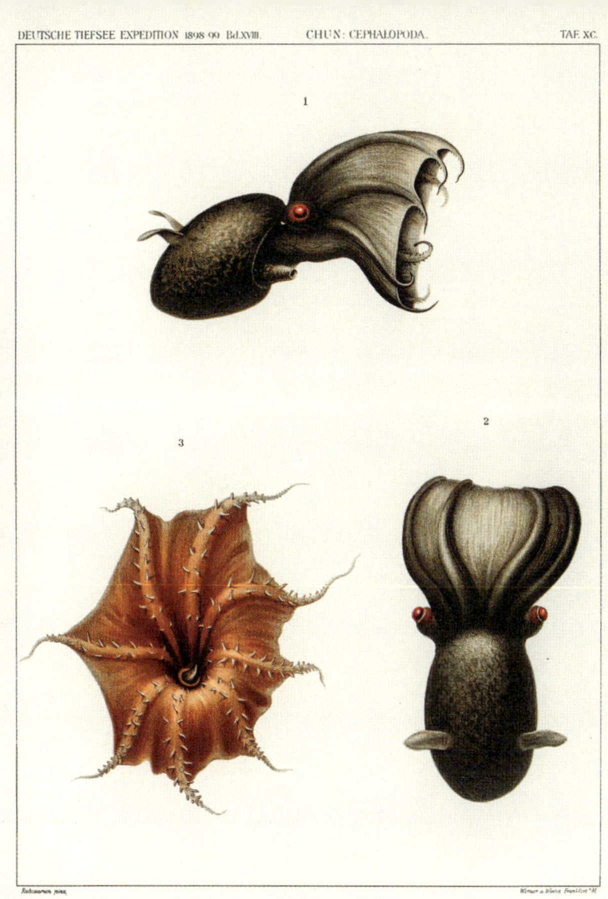

Rübsaamen pinx. Werner u. Winter, Frankfurt ᵃ/M.

Taf. XC.
Vampyroteuthis infernalis n. g. n. sp.

Verlag von Gustav Fischer in Jena.

DEUTSCHE TIEFSEE EXPEDITION 1898-99. Bd.XVIII. CHUN: CEPHALOPODA. TAF. LXXXII.

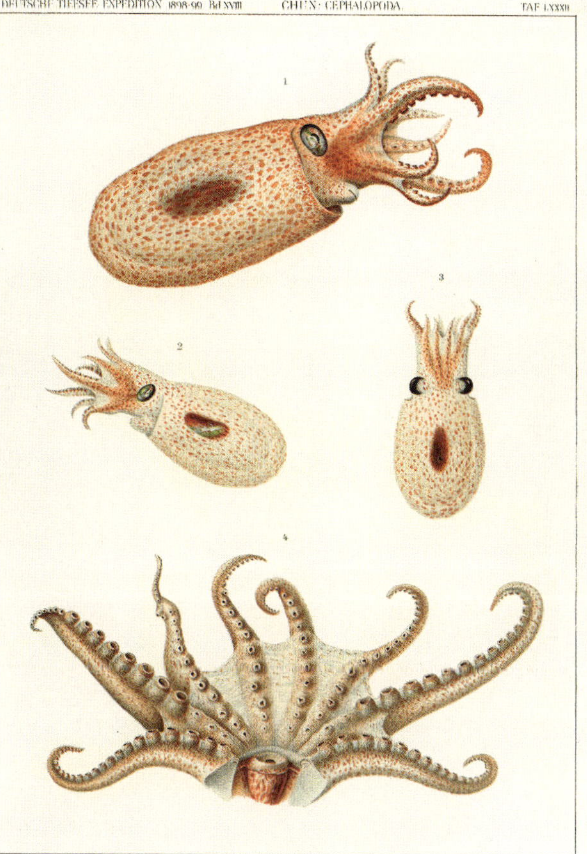

Taf. LXXXII.
Bolitaena diaphana Steenstr.

Verlag von Gustav Fischer in Jena.

DEUTSCHE TIEFSEE EXPEDITION 1898-99. Bd.XVIII. CHUN: CEPHALOPODA. TAF. LXXIX.

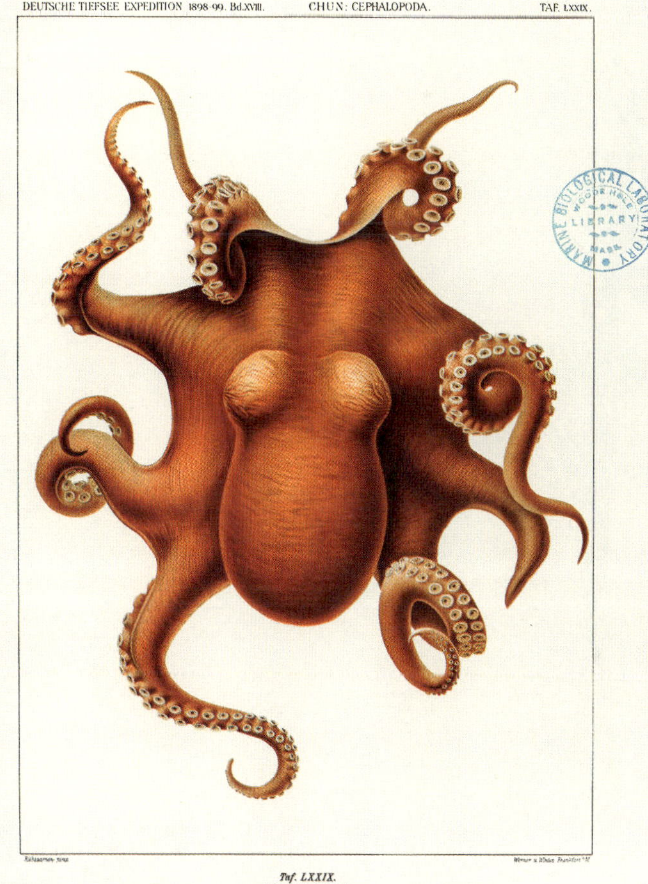

Rübsaamen pinx. Werner u. Winter, Frankfurt ᵃ/M.

Taf. LXXIX.
Polypus levis Hoyle.

Verlag von Gustav Fischer in Jena.

ÉTIENNE LACÉPÈDE: Pages of the book *Histoire naturelle des quadrupèdes ovipares, des serpents, des poissons et des cétacés,* 1836

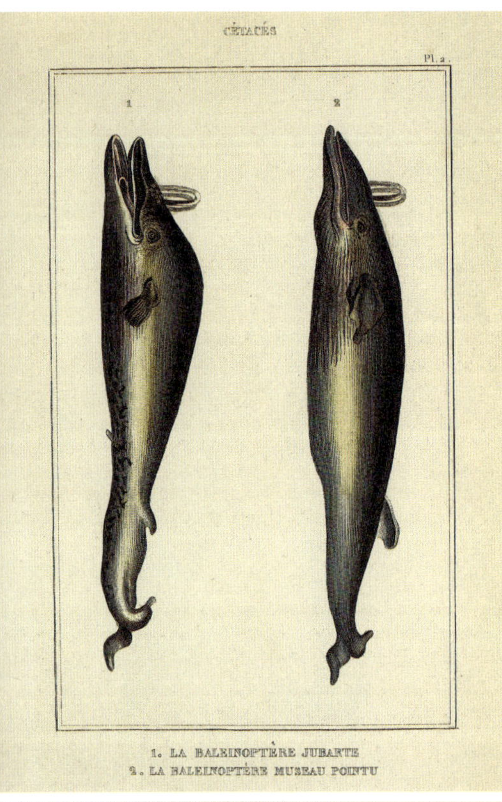

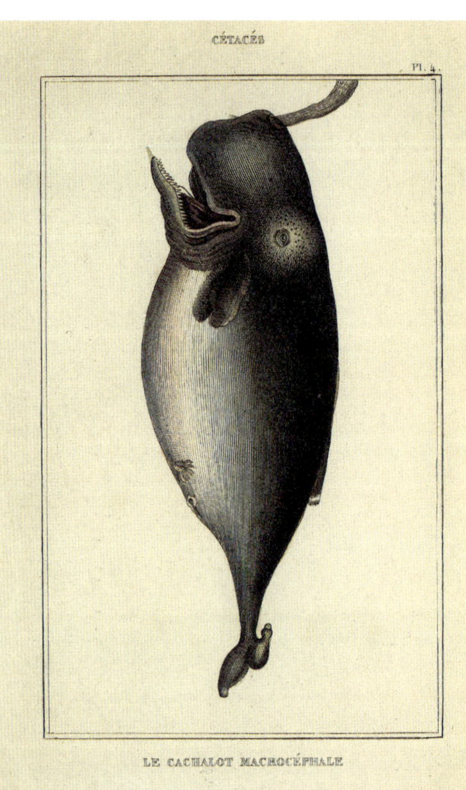

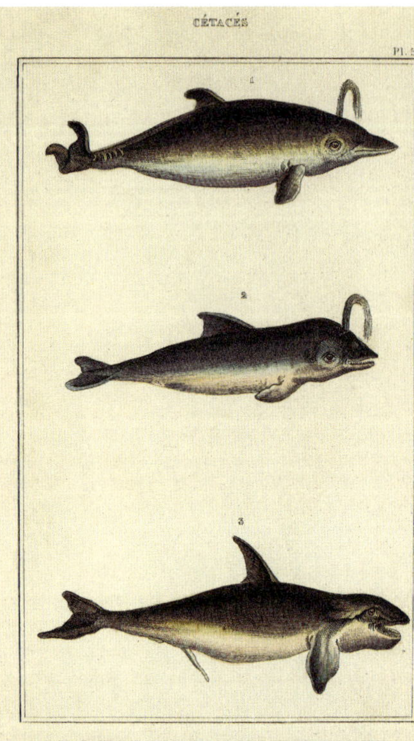

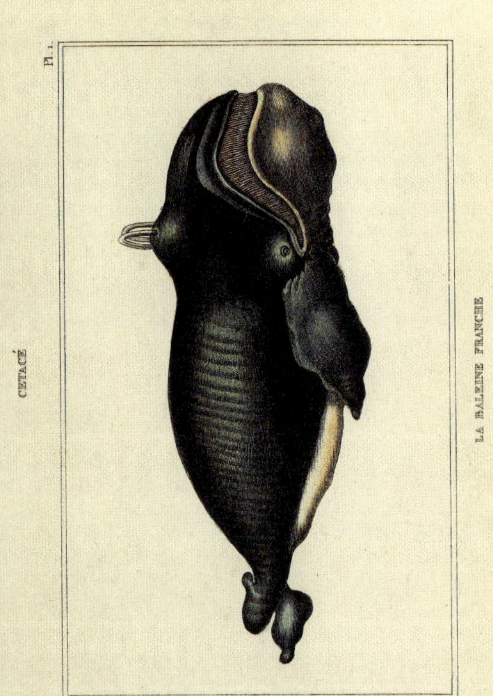

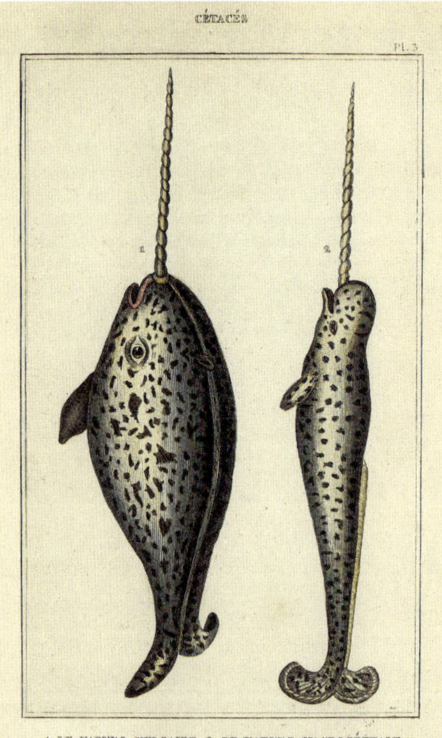

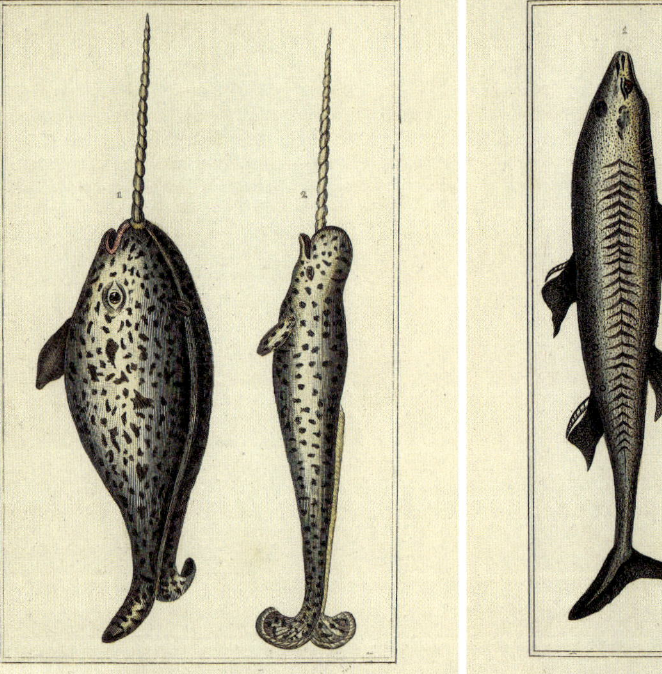

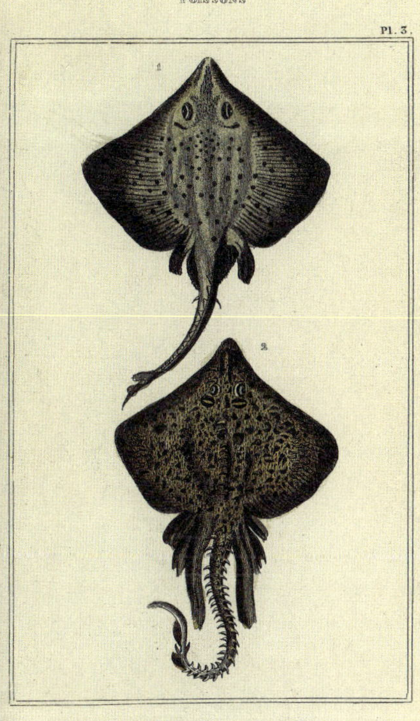

1. LA RAIE AIGLE. 2. LA RAIE TORPILLE

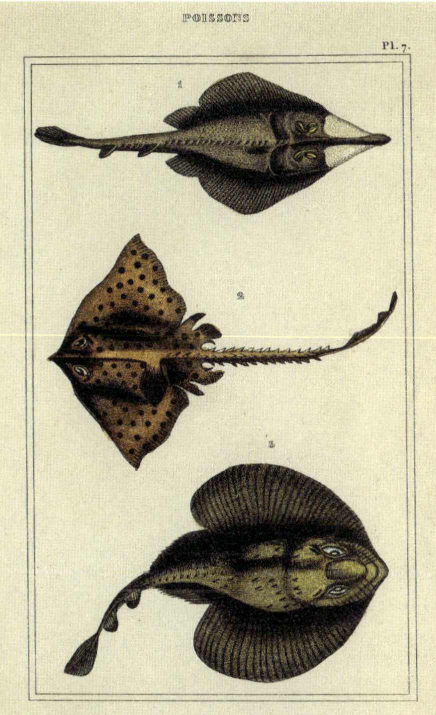

1. LA RAIE THOUIN. 2. LA RAIE CUVIER
3. LA RAIE CHINOISE

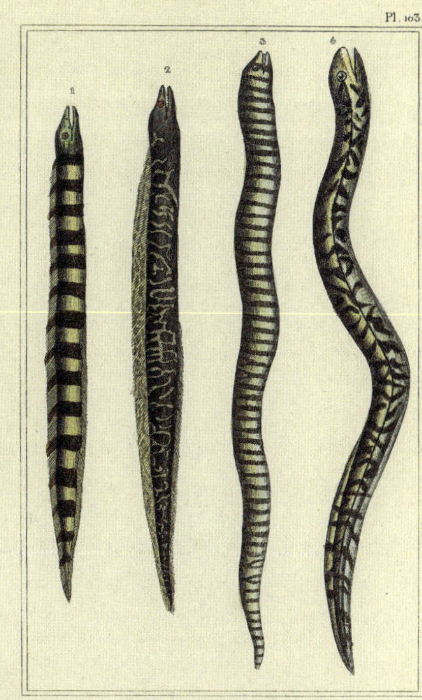

1. LA MURÉNOPHIS COLUBRINE. 2. LA MURÉNOPHIS ONDULÉ
3. LA GYMNOMURÈNE CERCLÉE. 4. L'UNIBRANCHAPERTURE MARBRÉE

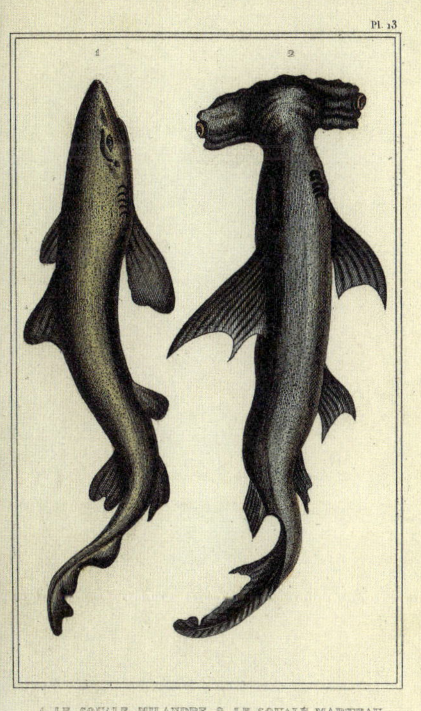

1. LE SQUALE MILANDRE. 2. LE SQUALE MARTEAU.

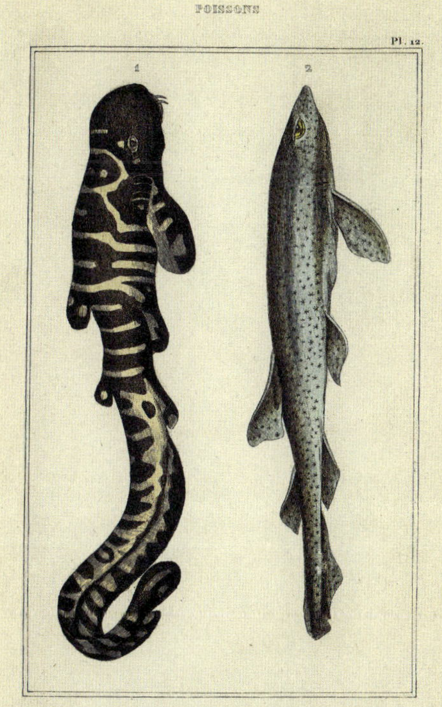

1. LE SQUALE BARBU. 2. LE SQUALE ROCHIER

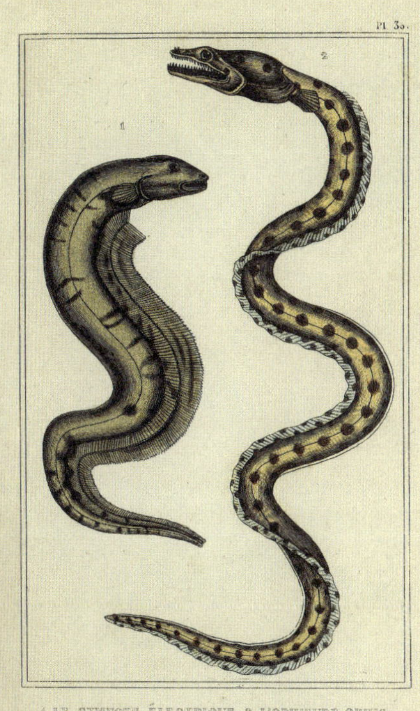

1. LE GYMNOTE ÉLECTRIQUE. 2. L'OPHISURE OPHIS.

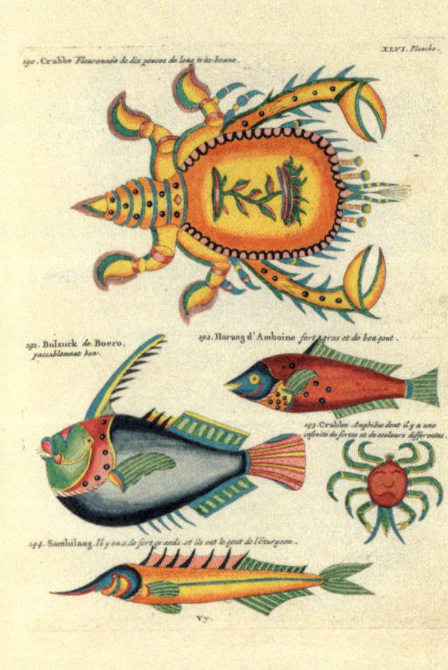
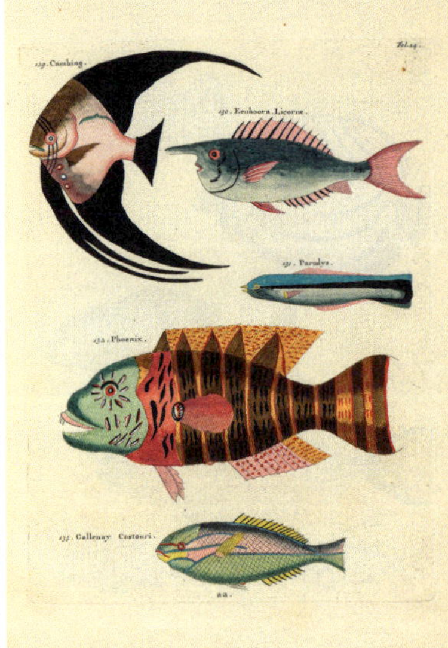
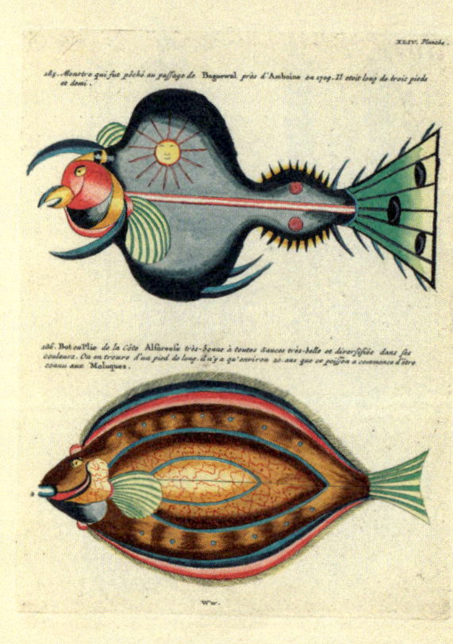
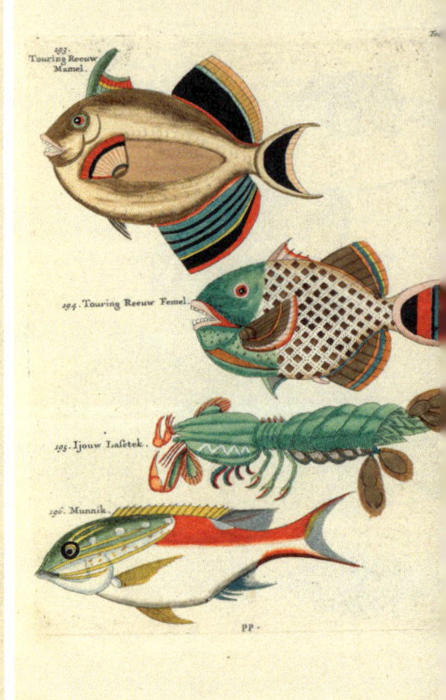
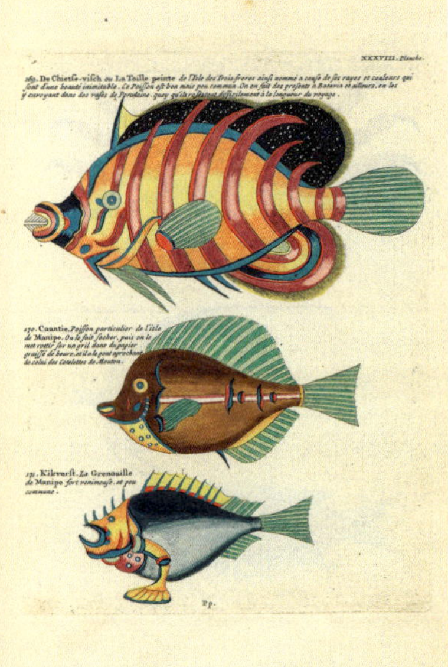
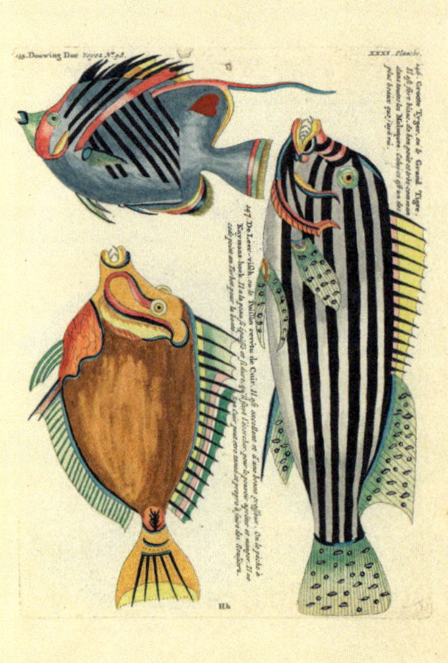
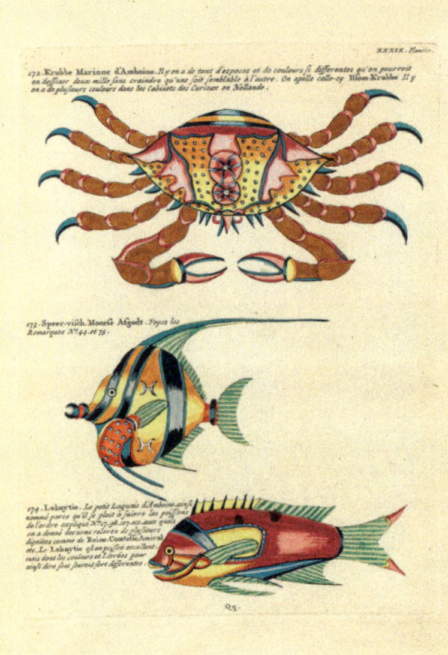
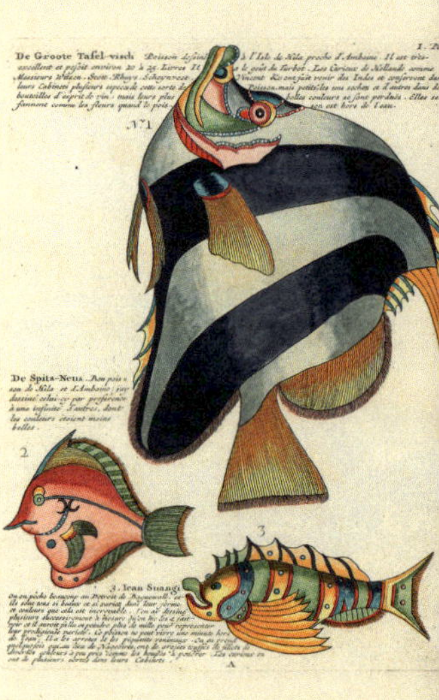
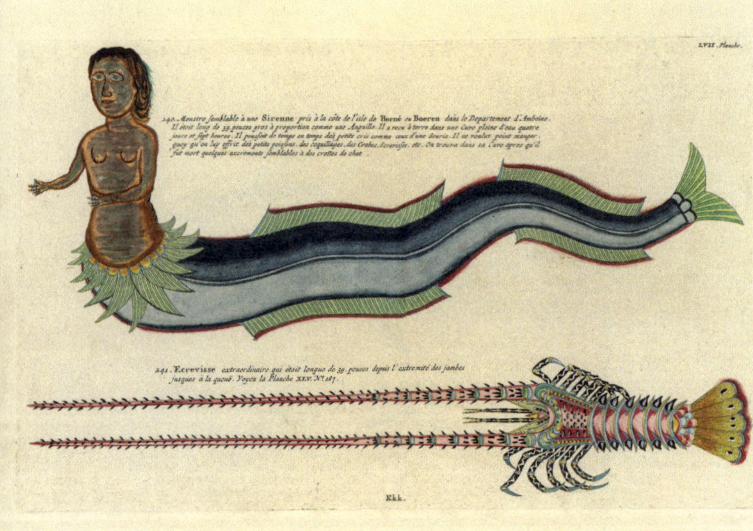
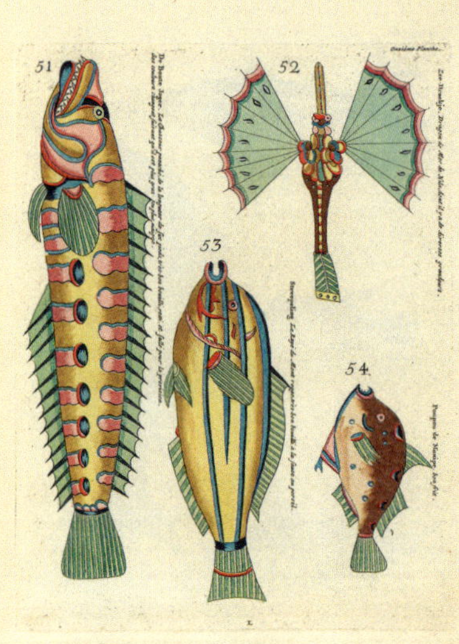
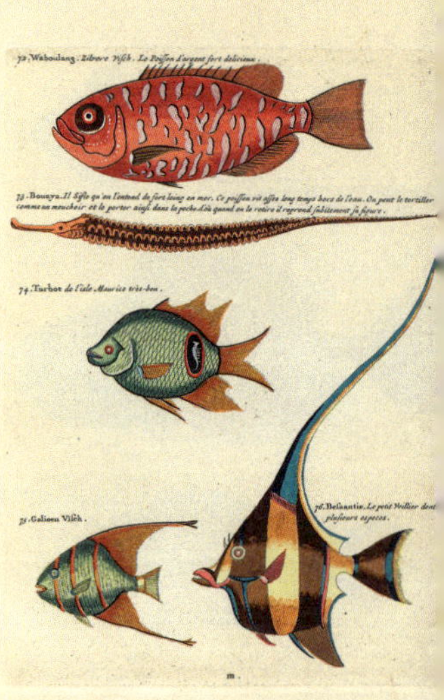

NICCOLÒ GUALTIERI: Pages of the book *Index testarum conchyliorum quae adservantur in museo Niccolo Gualtieri,* 1742
Opposite page: LOUIS RENARD: Pages of the book *Poissons, ecrevisses et crabes, de diverses couleurs et figures extraordinaires, que l'on trouve autour des isles Moluques et sur les côtes des terres Australes,* 1754

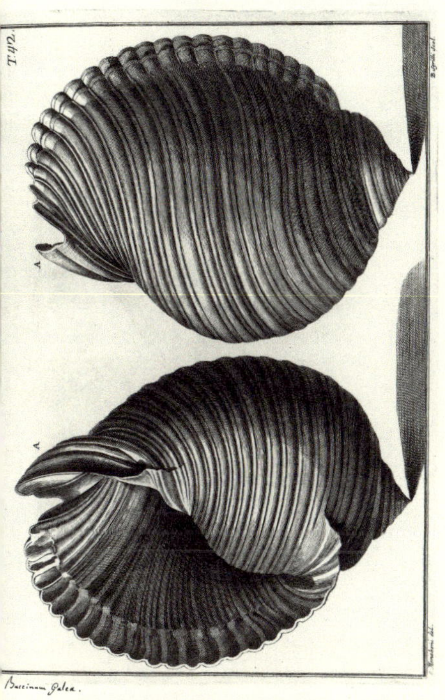

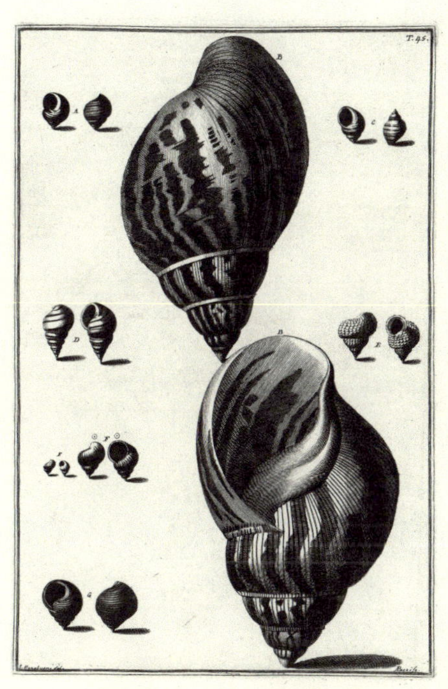

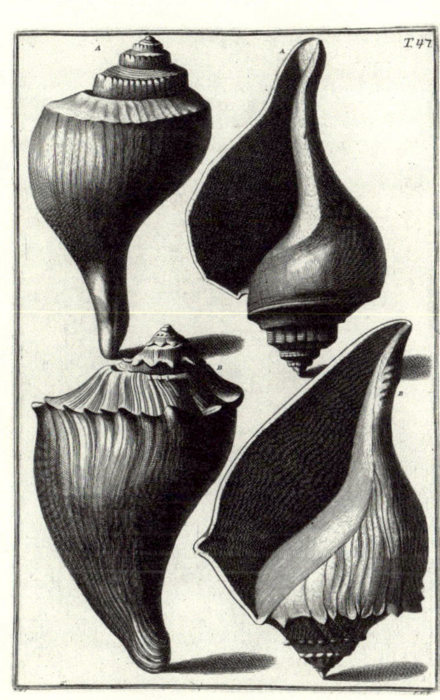

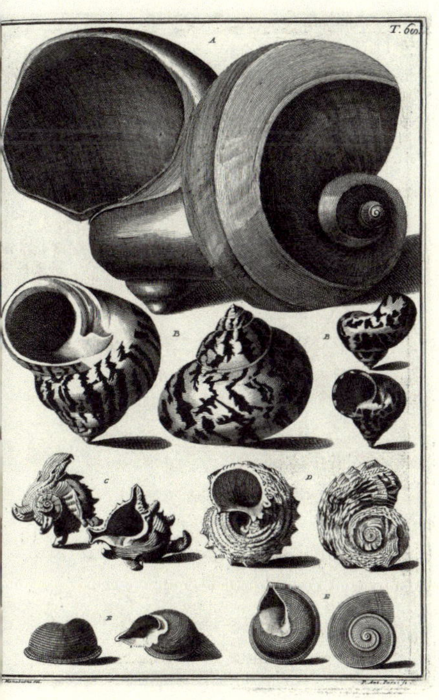

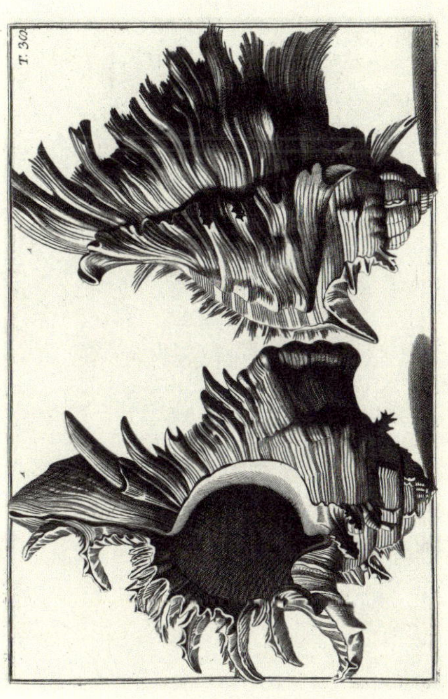

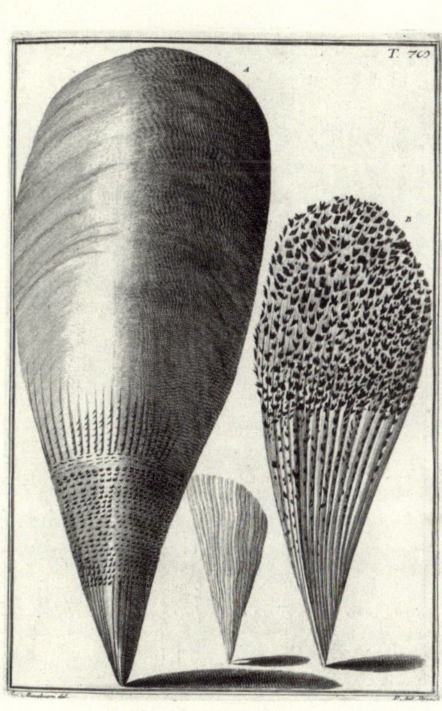

HENDRICK GOLTZIUS

Portrait of the Haarlem Shell Collector Jan Govertsen van der Aer, 1603

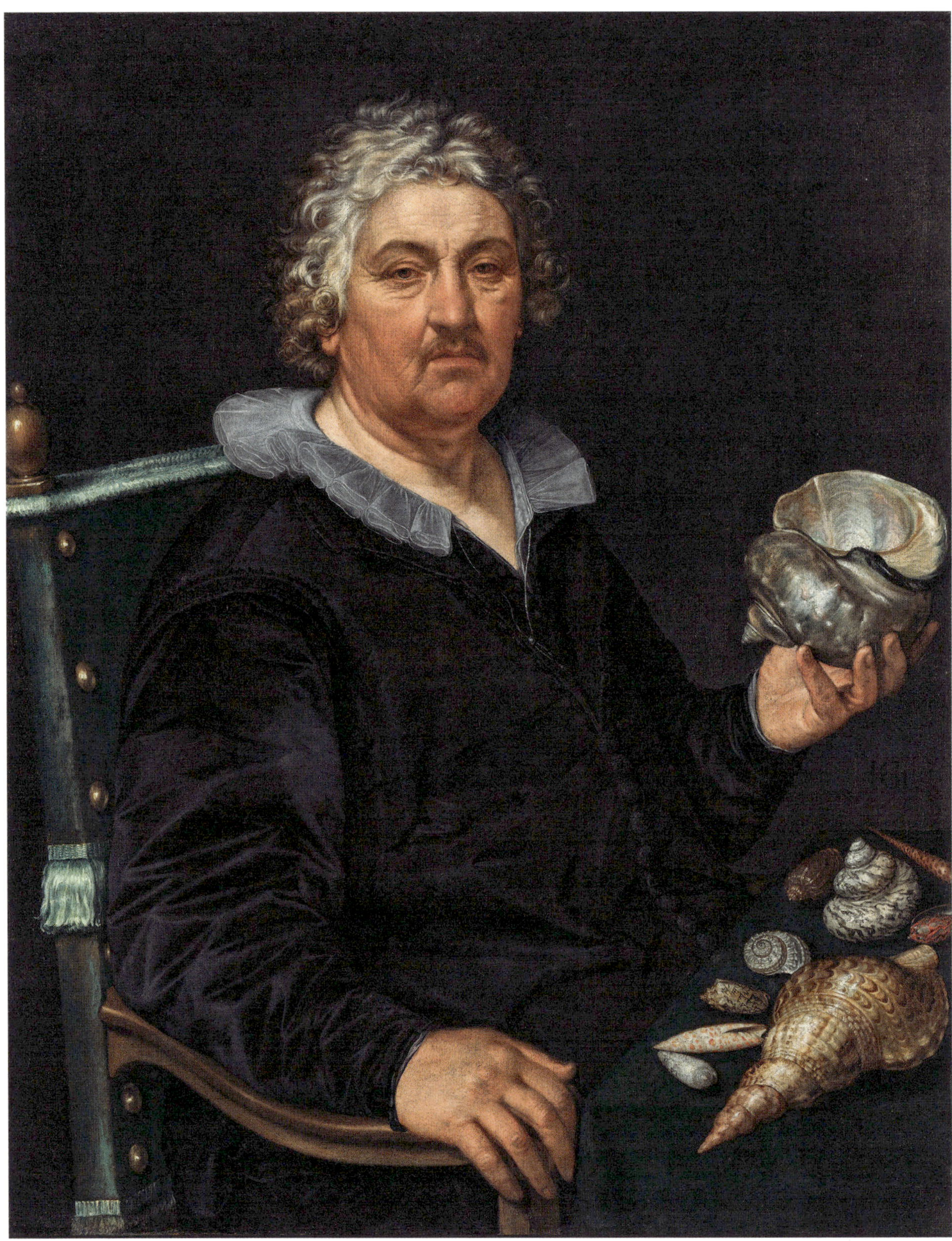

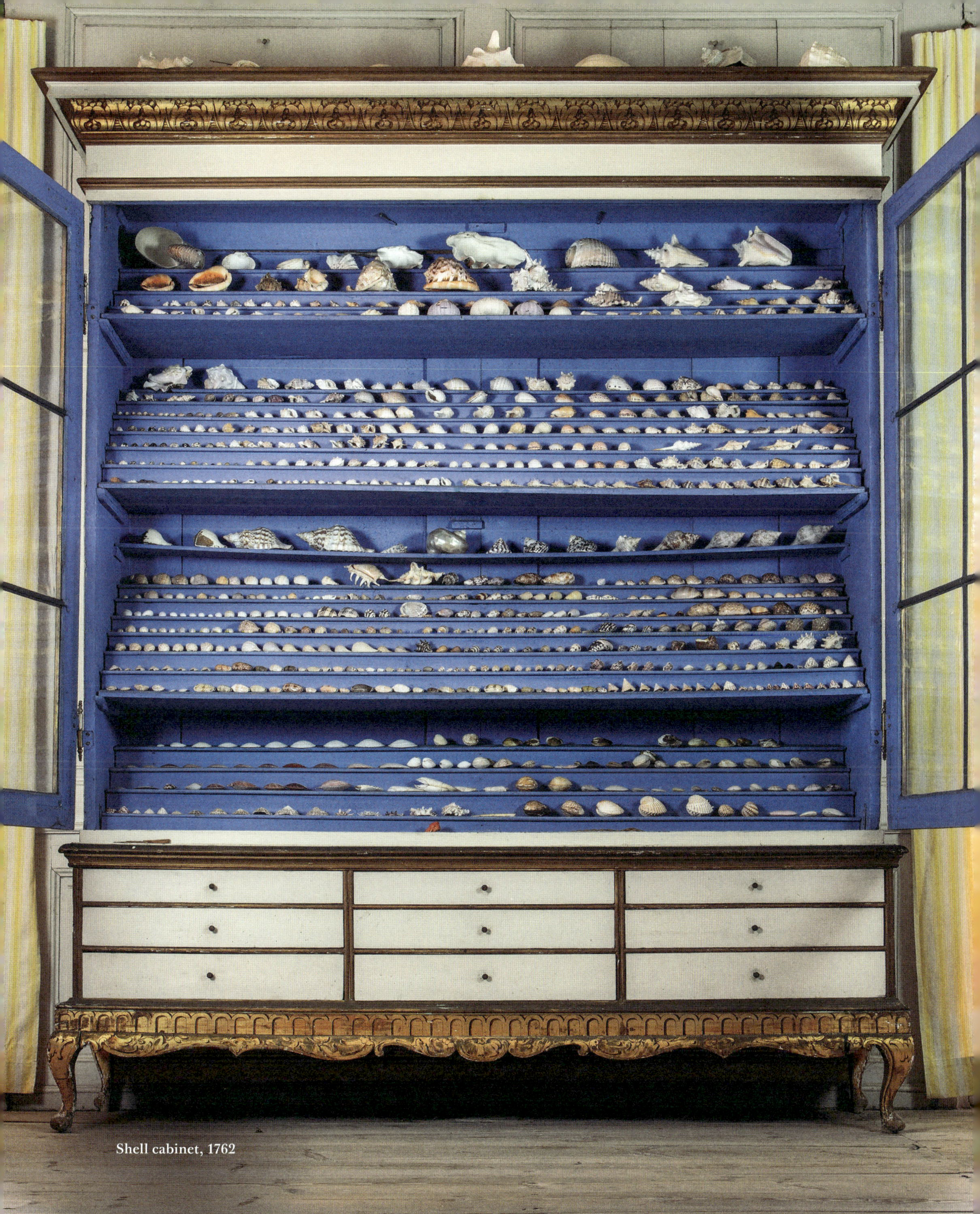

Shell cabinet, 1762

CORNELIS VAN HAARLEM
Neptune and Amphidrite, c. 1616/1617

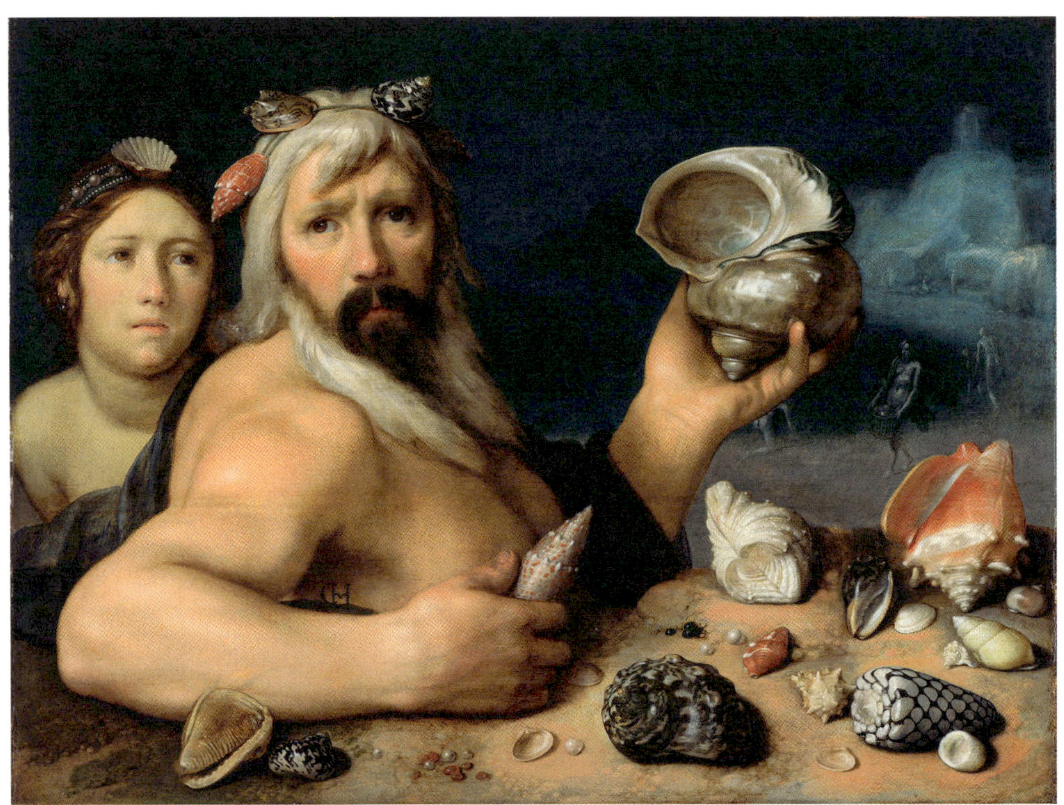

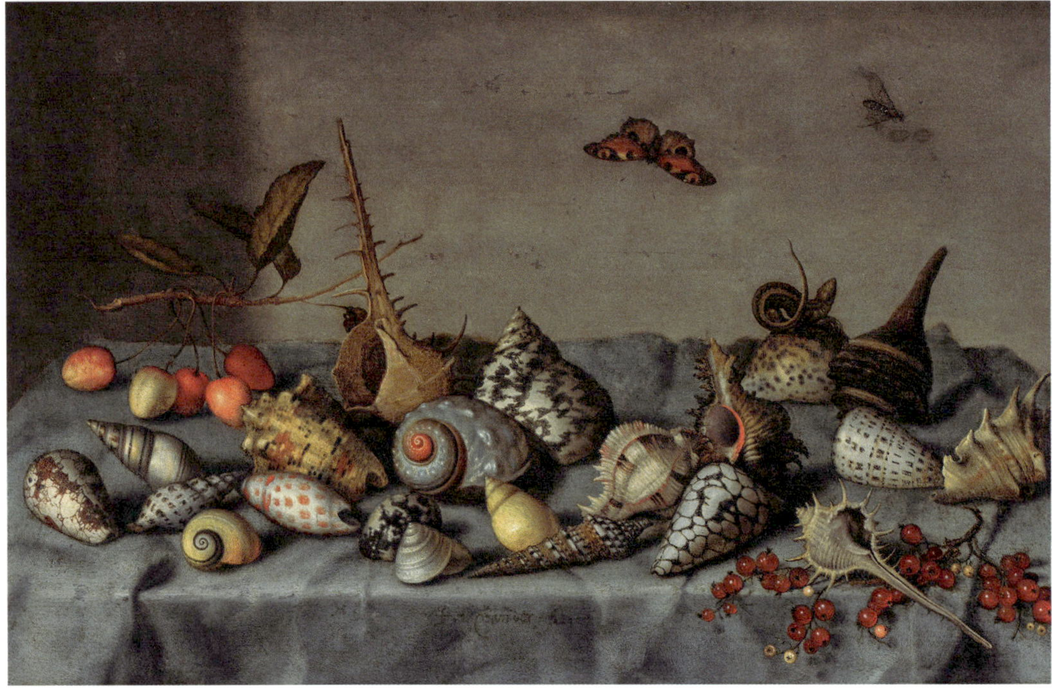

BALTHASAR VAN DER AST
Still life with Shells, c. 1640

ADRIAEN COORTE
Shells on a Stone Plinth, 1698

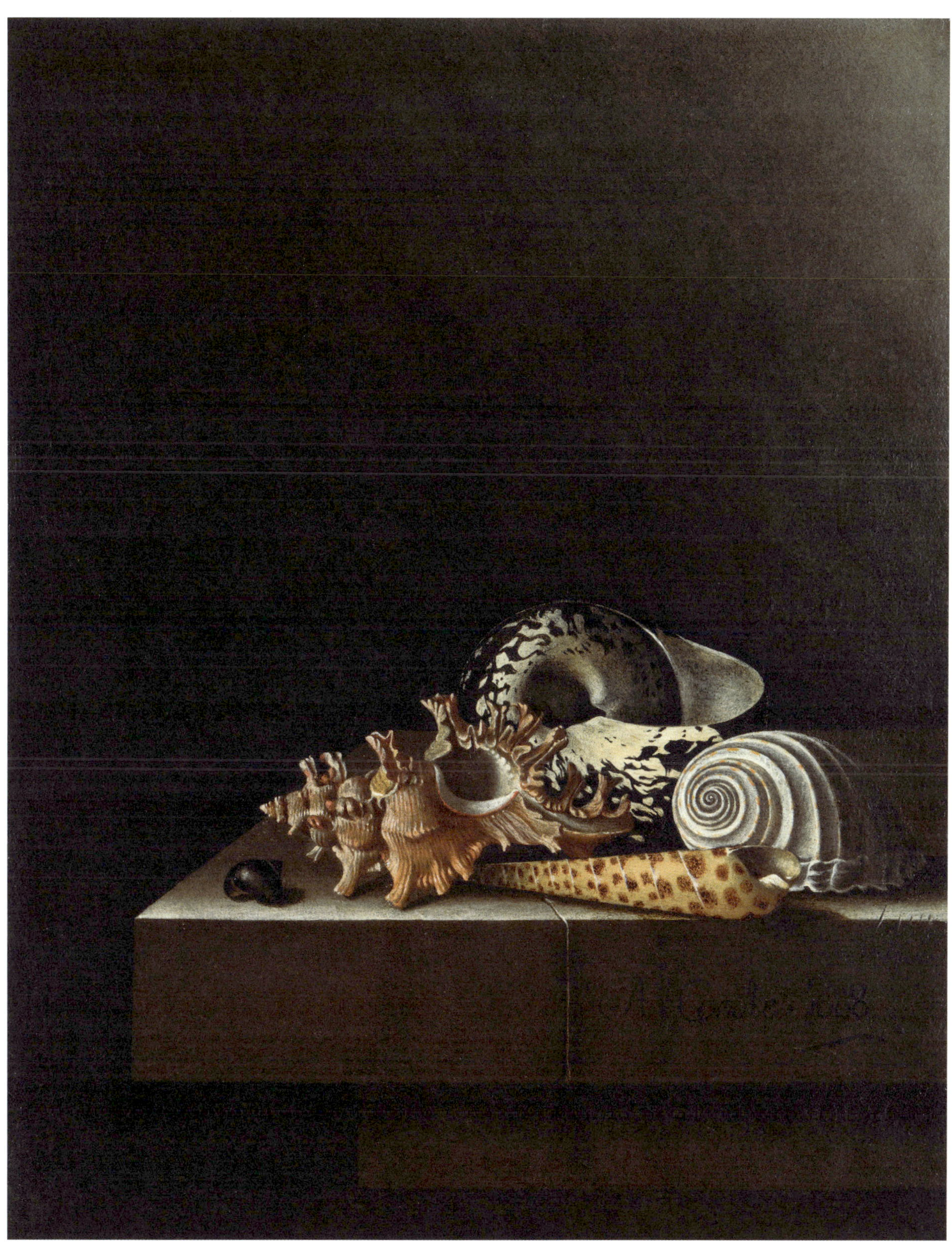

FRANCESCA WOODMAN
Untitled, 1978
Bottom, from the left: *Anguilla #2* (from *Eel series*), 1978,
Untitled (from *Eel series*), 1978, and *Untitled* (from *Eel series*), 1978

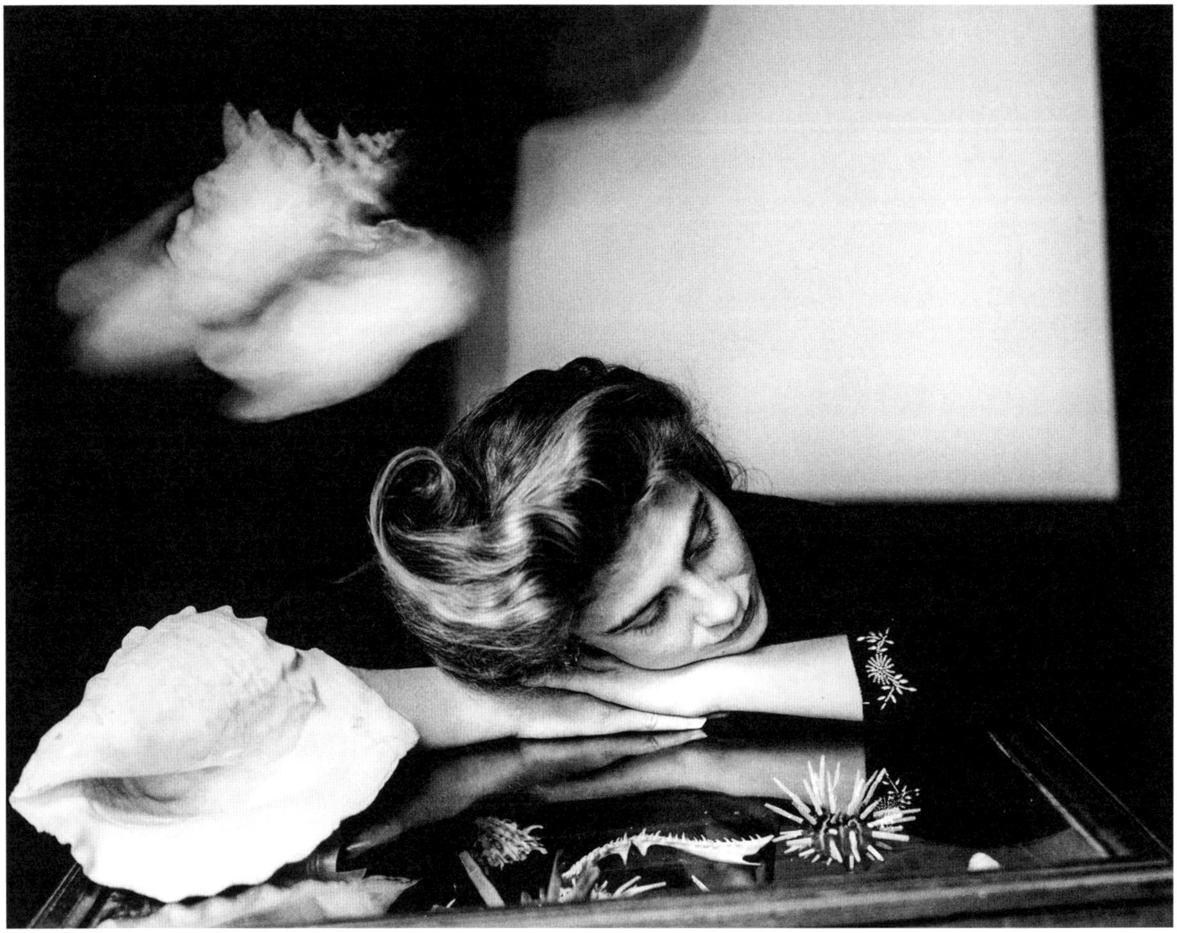

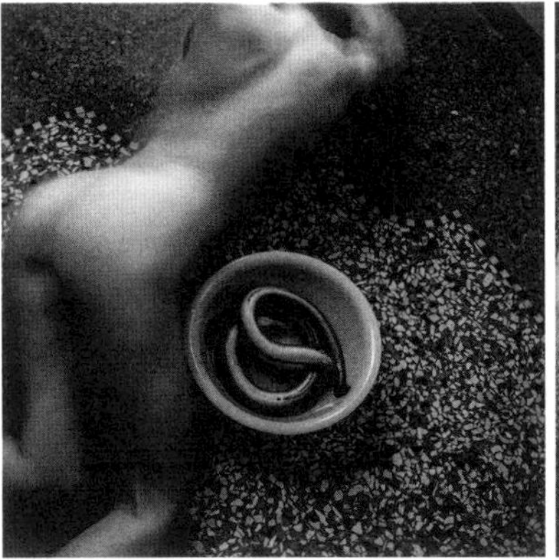

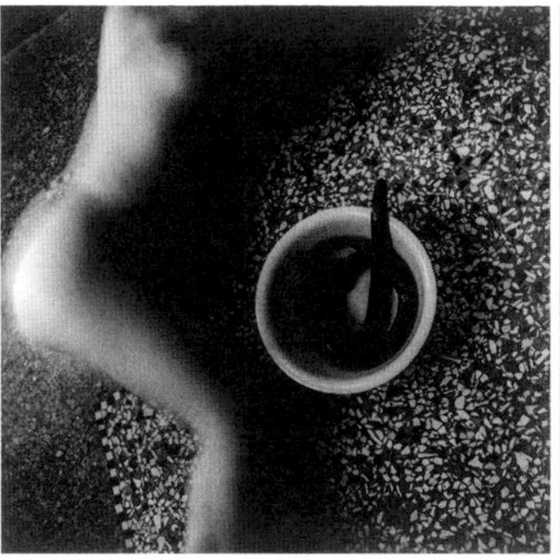

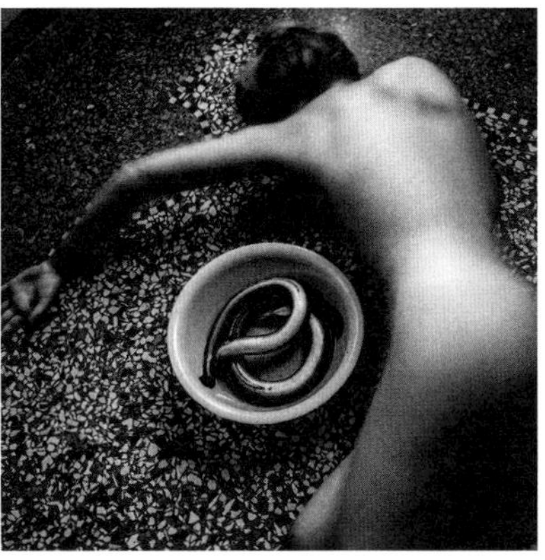

GEORGIA O'KEEFFE
Closed Clam Shell, 1926
Open Clam Shell, 1926

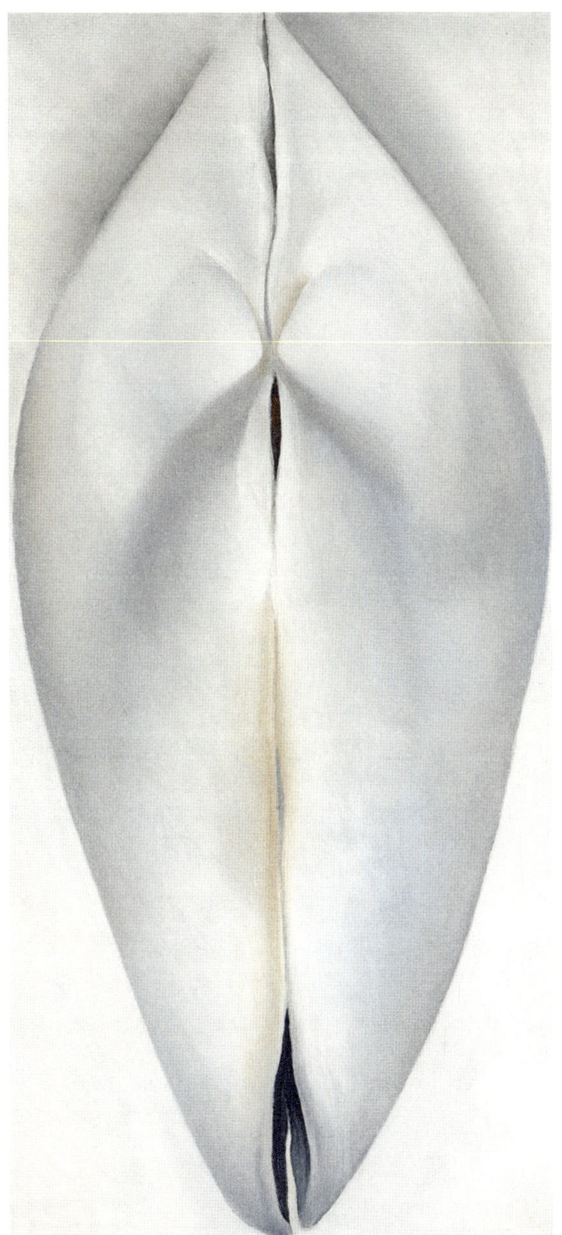

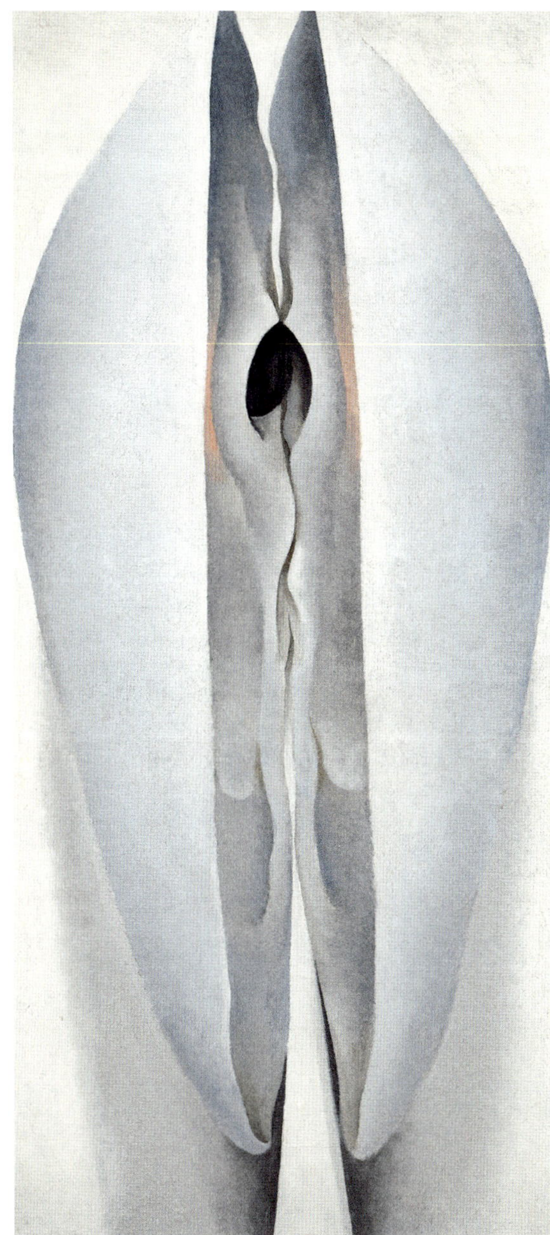

Who has known the ocean? Neither you nor I, with our earth-bound senses, know the foam and surge of the tide that beats over the crab hiding under the seaweed of his tide pool home; or the lilt of the long, slow swells of mid-ocean, where shoals of wandering fish prey and are preyed upon, and the dolphin breaks the waves to breathe the upper atmosphere. Nor can we know the vicissitudes of life on the ocean floor, where the sunlight, filtering through a hundred feet of water, makes but a fleeting, bluish twilight, in which dwell sponge and mollusk and starfish and coral, where swarms of diminutive fish twinkle through the dusk like a silver rain of meteors, and eels lie in wait among the rocks. Even less is it given to man to descend those six incomprehensible miles into the recesses of the abyss, where reign utter silence and unvarying cold and eternal night.

To sense this world of waters known to the creatures of the sea we must shed our human perceptions of length and breadth and time and place, and enter vicariously into a universe of all-pervading water. For to the sea's children nothing is so important as the fluidity of their world. It is water that they breathe; water that brings them food; water through which they see, by filtered sunshine from which first the red rays, then the greens, and finally the purples have been strained; water through which they sense vibrations equivalent to sound. And indeed it is nothing more or less than sea water, in all its varying conditions of temperature, saltiness, and pressure, that forms the invisible barriers that confine each marine type within a special zone of life – one to the shore line, another to some submarine chasm on the far slopes of the continental shelf, and yet another, perhaps, to an imperceptibly defined stratum at mid-depths of ocean.

There are comparatively few living things whose shifting pattern of life embraces both land and sea. Such are creatures of the tide pools among the rocks and of the mud flats sloping away from dune and beach grass to the water's edge. Between low water and the flotsam and jetsam of the high-tide mark, land and sea wage a never-ending conflict for possession.

Undersea

Rachel Carson

As on land the coming of night brings a change over the face of field and forest, sending some wild things into the safe retreat of their burrows and bringing others forth to prowl and forage, so at ebb tide the creatures of the waters largely disappear from sight, and in their place come marauders from the land to search the tide pools and to probe the sands for the silent, waiting fauna of the shore.

Twice between succeeding dawns, as the waters abandon pursuit of the beckoning moon and fall back, foot by foot, periwinkle and starfish and crab are cast upon the mercy of the sands. Every heap of brine-drenched seaweed, every pool forgotten by the retreating sea in recess of sand or rock, offers sanctuary from sun and biting sand.

In the tide pools, seas in miniature, sponges of the simpler kinds encrust the rocks, each hungrily drawing in through its myriad mouths the nutriment-laden water. Starfishes and sea anemones are common dwellers in such rock-grit pools. Shell-less cousins of the snail, the naked sea slugs are spots of brilliant rose and bronze, spreading arborescent gills to the waters, while the tube worms, architects of the tide pools, fashion their conical dwellings of sand grains, cemented on against another in glistening mosaic.

On the sands the clams burrow down in search of coolness and moisture, and oysters close their all-excluding shells and wait for the return of the water. Crabs crowd into damp rock caverns, where periwinkles cling to the walls. Colonies of gnome-like shrimps find refuge under dripping strands of brown, leathery weed heaped on the beach.

Hard upon the retreating sea press invaders from the land. Shore birds patter along the beach by day, and legions of the ghost crab shuffle across the damp sands by night. Chief, perhaps, among the plunderers is man, probing the soft mud flats and dipping his nets into the shallow waters.

At last comes a tentative ripple, then another, and finally the full, surging sweep of the incoming tide. The folk of the pools awake – clams stir in the mud. Barnacles open their shells and begin a rhythmic sifting of the waters. One by one, brilliant-hued flowers blossom in the shallow water as tubeworms extend cautious tentacles.

The ocean is a place of paradoxes. It is the home of the great white shark, two-thousand-pound killer of the seas, and of the hundred-foot blue whale, the largest animal that ever lived. It is also the home of living things so small that your two hands might scoop up as many of them as there are stars in the Milky Way. And it is because of the flowering of astronomical numbers of these diminutive plants, known as diatoms, that the surface of waters of the ocean are in reality boundless pastures. Every marine animal, from the smallest to the sharks and whales, is ultimately dependent for its food upon these microscopic entities of the vegetable life of the ocean. Within their fragile walls, the sea performs a vital alchemy that utilizes the sterile chemical elements dissolved in the water and welds them with the torch of sunlight into the stuff of life. Only through this little-understood synthesis of proteins, fats, and carbohydrates by myriad plant “producers” is the mineral wealth of the sea made available to the animal “consumers” that browse as they float with the currents. Drifting endlessly, midway between the sea of air above and the depths of the abyss below, these strange creatures and the marine inflorescence that sustains them are called “plankton” – the wanderers.

Many of the fishes, as well as the bottom-dwelling mollusks and worms and starfish, begin life as temporary members of this roving company, for the ocean cradles their young in its surface waters. The sea is not a solicitous foster mother. The delicate eggs and fragile larvae are buffeted by storms raging across the open ocean and preyed upon by diminutive monsters, the hungry glass worms and comb jellies of the plankton.

These ocean pastures are also the domain of vast shoals of adult fishes: herring, anchovy, menhaden, and mackerel, feeding upon the animals of the plankton and in their turn preyed upon; for here the dogfish hunt in packs, and the ravenous bluefish, like roving buccaneers, take their booty where they find it.

Dropping downward a scant hundred feet to the white sand beneath, an undersea traveler would discover a land where the noonday sun is swathed in twilight blues and purples, and where the blackness of midnight is eerily aglow with the cold phosphorescence of living things. Dwelling among the crepuscular shadows of the ocean floor are creatures whose terrestrial counterparts are drab and commonplace, but which are themselves invested with delicate beauty by the sea. Crystal cones form the shells of pteropods or winged snails that drift downward from the surface to these dim regions by day; and the translucent spires of lovely *ianthina* are tinged with Tyrian purple.

Other creatures of the sea's bottom may be fantastic rather than beautiful. Spine-studded urchins, like rotund hedgehogs of the sea, tumble over the sands, where mollusks lie with slightly opened shells, busily straining the water for debris. Life flows on monotonously for these passive sifters of the currents, who move little or not at all from year to year. Among the rock ledges, eels and cunners forage greedily, while the lobster feels his way with nimble wariness through the perpetual twilight.

Farther out on the continental shelf, the ocean floor is scarred with deep ravines, perhaps the valleys of drowned rivers, and dotted with undersea plateaus. Hosts of fish graze on these submerged islands, which are richly carpeted with sluggish or sessile forms of life. Chief among the ground fish are haddock, cods, flounders and their mightier relative, the halibut. From these and shallower waters man, the predator, exacts a yearly tribute of nearly thirty billion pounds of fish.

If the underwater traveler might continue to explore the ocean floor, he would traverse miles of level prairie lands; he would ascend the sloping sides of hills; and he would skirt deep and ragged crevasses yawning suddenly at his feet. Through the gathering darkness, he would come at last to the edge of the continental shelf. The ceiling of the ocean would lie a hundred fathoms above him, and his feet would rest upon the brink of a slope that drops precipitously another mile, and then descends more gently into an inky void that is the abyss.

What human mind can visualize conditions in the uttermost depths of the ocean? Increasing with every foot of depth, enormous pressures reach, three thousand fathoms down, the inconceivable magnitude of three tons to every square inch of surface. In these silent deeps a glacial cold prevails, a bleak iciness which never varies, summer or winter, years melting into centuries, and centuries into ages of geologic time. There, too, darkness reigns – the blackness of primeval night in which the ocean came into being, unbroken, through eons of succeeding time, by the gray light of dawn.

It is easy to understand why early students of the ocean believed these regions were devoid of life, but strange creatures have now been dredged from the depths to bear mute and fragmentary testimony concerning life in the abyss.

The "monsters" of the deep sea are small, voracious fishes with gaping, tooth-studded jaws, some with sensitive feelers serving the function of eyes, other bearing luminous torches or lures to search out or entice their living prey. Through the night of the abyss, the flickering lights of these foragers move to and fro. Many of the sessile bottom dwellers glow with a strange radiance suffusing the entire body, while other swimming creatures may have tiny, glittering lights picked out in rows and patterns.

The deep-sea prawn and the abyssal cuttlefish eject a luminous cloud, and under cover of this pillar of fire escape from their enemies.

Monotones of red and brown and lusterless black are the prevailing colors in the deep sea, allowing the wearers to reflect the minimum of the phosphorescent gleams, and to blend into the safe obscurity of the surrounding gloom.

On the muddy bottom of the abyss, treacherous oozes threaten to engulf small scavengers as they busily sift the debris for food. Crabs and prawns pick their way over the yielding mud on stilt-like legs; sea spiders creep over sponges raised on delicate stalks above the slime.

Because the last vestige of plant life was left behind in the shallow zone penetrated by the rays of the sun, the inhabitants of these depths contrast strangely with the self-supporting assemblage of the surface waters. Preying one upon another, the abyssal creatures are ultimately dependent upon the slow rain of dead plants and animals from above. Every living thing of the ocean, plant and animal alike, returns to the water at the end of its own life span the materials that had been temporarily assembled to form its body. So there descends into the depths a gentle, never-ending rain of the disintegrating particles of what once were living creatures of the sunlit surface waters, or of those twilight regions beneath.

Here in the sea mingle elements which, in their long and amazing history, have lent life and strength and beauty to a bewildering variety of living creatures. Ions of calcium, now free in the water, were borrowed years ago from the from the sea to form part of the protective armor of a mollusk, returned to the main reservoir when their temporary owner had ceased to have need of them, and later incorporated into the delicate statuary of a coral reef. Here are atoms of silica, once imprisoned in a layer of flint in the subterranean darkness; later, within the fragile shell of a diatom, tossed by waves and warmed by the sun; and again entering into the exquisite structure of a radiolarian shell, that miracle of ephemeral beauty that might be the work of a fairy glass-blower with a snowflake as his pattern.

Except for the precipitous slopes and regions swept bare by the submarine currents, the ocean floor is covered with primeval oozes which have been accumulating for eons deposits of varied origins; earth-born materials freighted seaward by rivers or worn from the shores of continents by the ceaseless grinding of waves; volcanic dust transported long distances by wind, floating lightly on the surface and eventually sinking into the depths to mingle with the products of no less mighty eruptions of submarine volcanoes; spherules of iron and nickel from interstellar space; and substances of organic origin – the siliceous skeletons of Radiolaria and the frustules of diatoms, the limey remains of algae and corals, and the shells of minute Foraminifera and delicate pelagic snails. While the bottoms near the shore are covered with detritus from the land, the remains of the floating and swimming creatures of the sea prevail in the deep waters of the open ocean. Beneath tropical seas, in depths of 1000 to 1500 fathoms, calcareous oozes cover nearly a third of the ocean floor; while the colder waters of the temperate and polar regions release to the underlying bottom the siliceous remains of diatoms and Radiolaria. In the red clay that carpets the great deeps at 3000 fathoms or more, such delicate skeletons are extremely rare. Among the few organic remains not dissolved before they reach these cold and silent depths are the ear bones of whales and the teeth of sharks.

Thus we see the parts of the plan fall into place: the water receiving from earth and air the simple materials, storing them up until the gathering energy of the spring sun wakens the sleeping plants to a burst of dynamic activity, hungry swarms of planktonic animals growing and multiplying upon the abundant plants, and themselves falling prey to the shoals of fish; all, in the end, to be redissolved into their component substances when the inexorable laws of the sea demand it. Individual elements are lost to view, only to reappear again and again in different incarnations in a kind of material immortality. Kindred forces to those which, in some period inconceivably remote, gave birth to that primeval bit of protoplasm tossing on the ancient seas continue their mighty and incomprehensible work. Against this cosmic background the life span of a particular plant or animal appears, not as a drama complete in itself, but only as a brief interlude in a panorama of endless change.

Rachel Carson (1907-1964) was an American marine biologist and author, known as the mother of the environmental movement. She is the author of the sea trilogy *Under the Sea-Wind* (1941), *The Sea Around Us* (1951) and *The Edge of the Sea* (1955), as well as *Silent Spring* (1962), a groundbreaking account of the countless ways pesticides harm the environment and threaten human health. Her fifth book, *The Sense of Wonder*, was published posthumously in 1965. This text, "Undersea," was originally published in a pamphlet by the U.S. Bureau of Fisheries in 1935 under the title "The World of Waters." When it was printed as an essay in *The Atlantic Monthly* two years later, it marked Carson's literary debut.

Throughout history, the unfathomable power of the sea has fuelled the human imagination. Waves were believed to be animated by spirits, and tales were spun of sea gods and goddesses. The vast, overwhelming sea has served as a mirror of existential longing and emotion. Romantic art featured solitary figures looking out over endless horizons, shipwrecks and waves crashing against the shore. The second part of the exhibition embraces ocean mythologies and the Romantic cultivation of the sublime. The ocean as a mythological space has appeared in art since prehistoric times. Classical, Renaissance and Baroque images abound with sea creatures and gods. The same is true in other cultures, from Haiti to Ghana and Japan, while the darkest chapters of colonialism have spawned myths that give a voice to the oppressed.

2.

Facing the Unknown

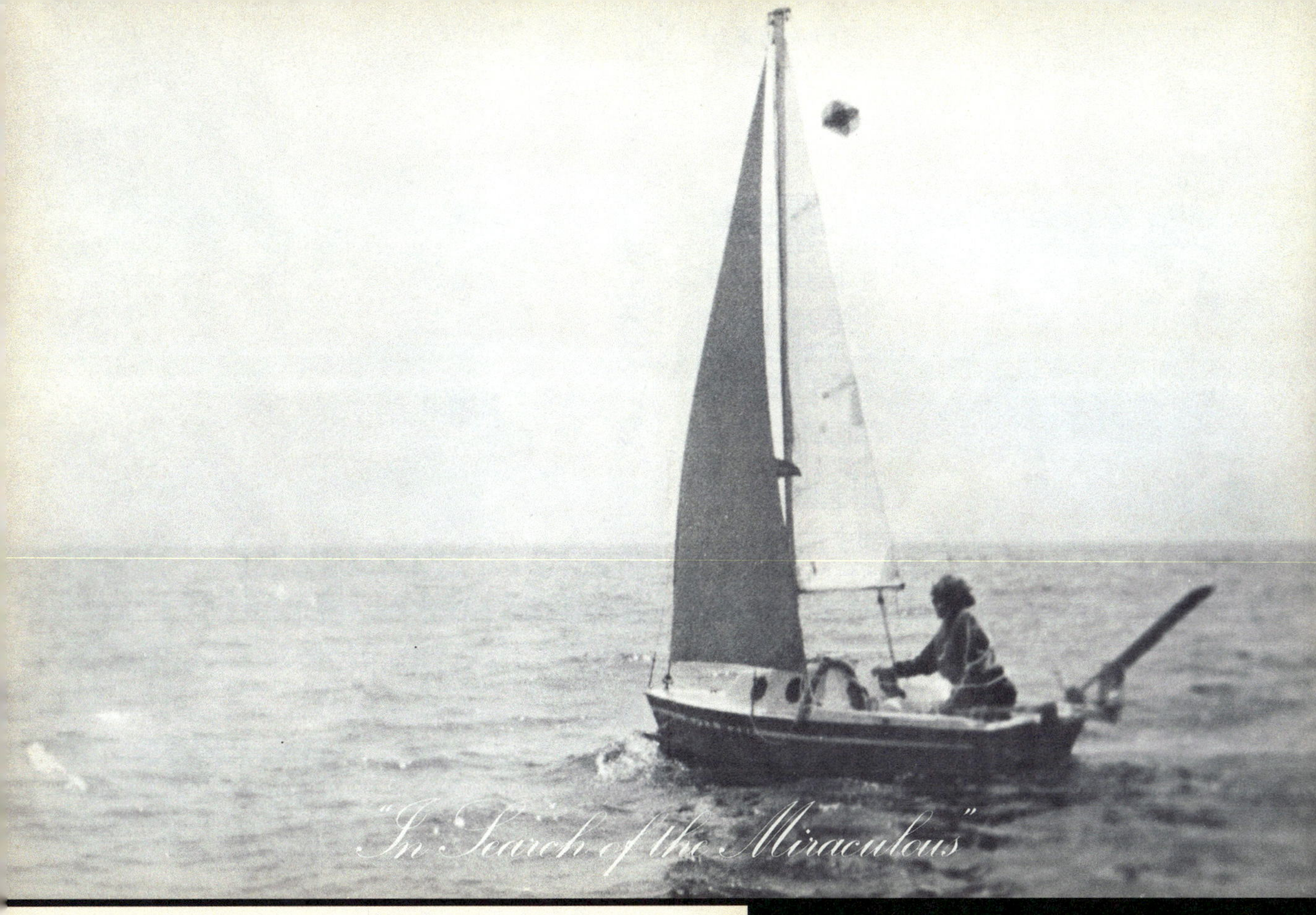

A Life On The Ocean Wave

Allegro

HENRY RUSSELL

1. A life on the o-cean wave, A home on the roll-ing deep, Where the scattered wa-ters rave, And the winds their rev-els keep! Like an ea-gle caged, I pine On this dull, un-chang-ing shore; Oh, give me the flash-ing brine, The spray and the tem-pest roar! A life on the o-cean wave, A home on the roll-ing deep! Where the scat-tered waters rave, And the winds their rev-els keep! The winds, the winds, the winds their revels keep, the winds, the winds, the winds their revels keep.

2. Once more on the deck I stand Of my own swift-gliding craft, Set sail! fare-well to the land, The gale fol-lows far a-baft: We shoot thro' the sparkling foam, Like an o-cean bird set free; Like the o-cean birds, our home We'll find far out on the sea! A life on the o-cean

art & project

bulletin 89

1007 amsterdam
willemsparkweg 36
(020) 713991

drukwerk aan
printed matter to

bas jan ader

"in search of the miraculous"
(songs for the north atlantic; july 1975 -)

in cooperation with the claire s. copley gallery, los angeles, usa, and the groninger museum, groningen, holland

BAS JAN ADER

Bulletin 89: In Search of the Miraculous (Songs for the North Atlantic), 1975

The Dutch conceptual and performance artist Bas Jan Ader (1942-1975) disappeared at sea in 1975. For his project *In Search of the Miraculous*, he attempted to sail solo across the Atlantic from the United States to Europe. In several of his works, Ader consciously played the role of a tragic and sublime hero. The magazine sheet with a photo on the front cover and a sea shanty on the back is part of the project. A total of 800 copies were printed.

HIROSHI SUGIMOTO
From the left:
Channel, Weston Cliff, 1994
Marmara Sea, Silivli, 1991
Tyrrhenian Sea, Conda, 1994

AUGUST STRINDBERG
Storm in the Skerries. "The Flying Dutchman", Dalarö, 1892
Opposite page: *The Wave V,* 1901

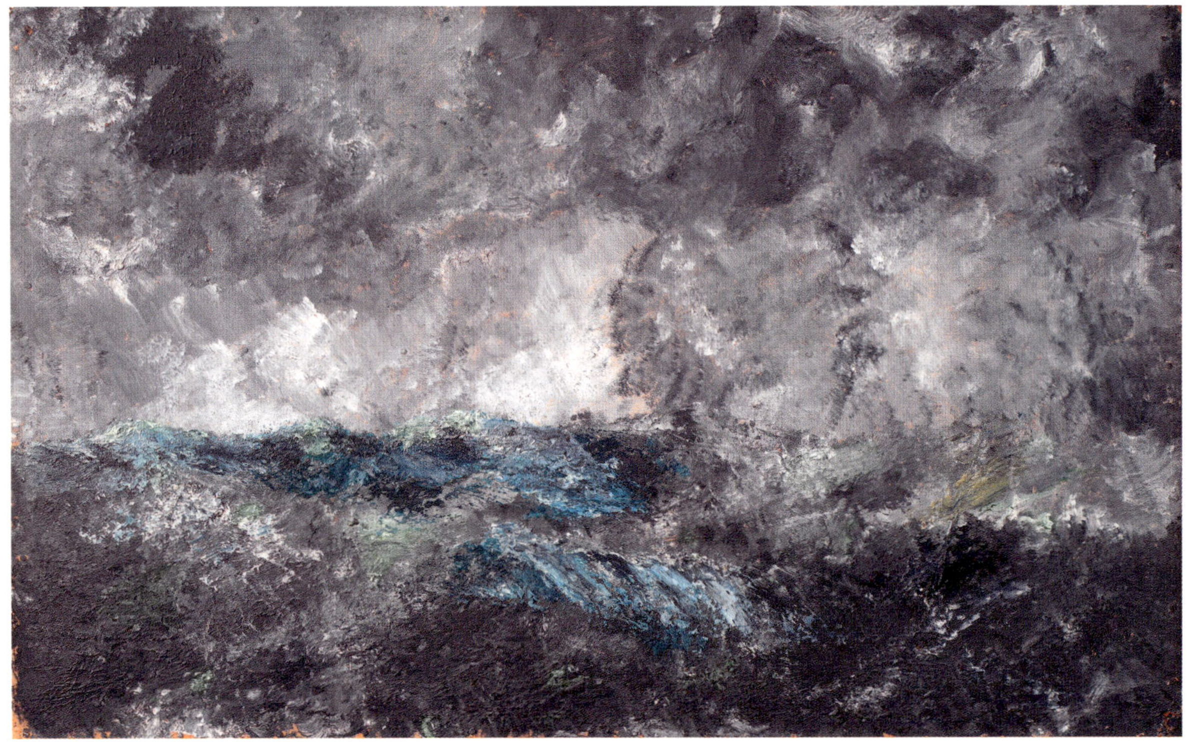

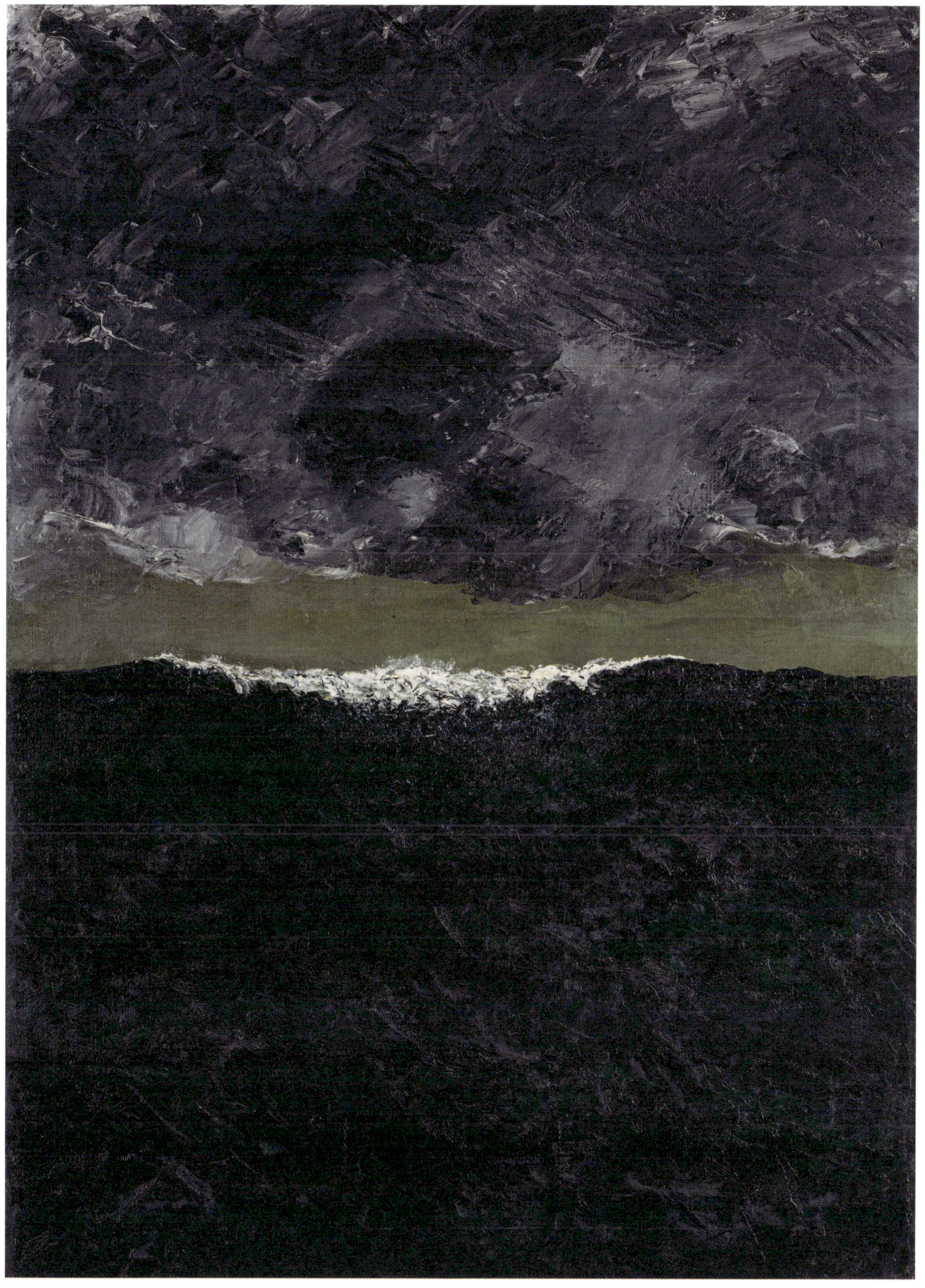

PEDER BALKE
Top, from the left: *Vessel in Rough Sea* and *Rough Sea*
Middle, from the left: *North Cape* and *Rough Sea with Steamboat and Sailing Ship*
Bottom, from the left: *Shipwreck*, *North Cape* and *Seascape*, all 1860s-1870s

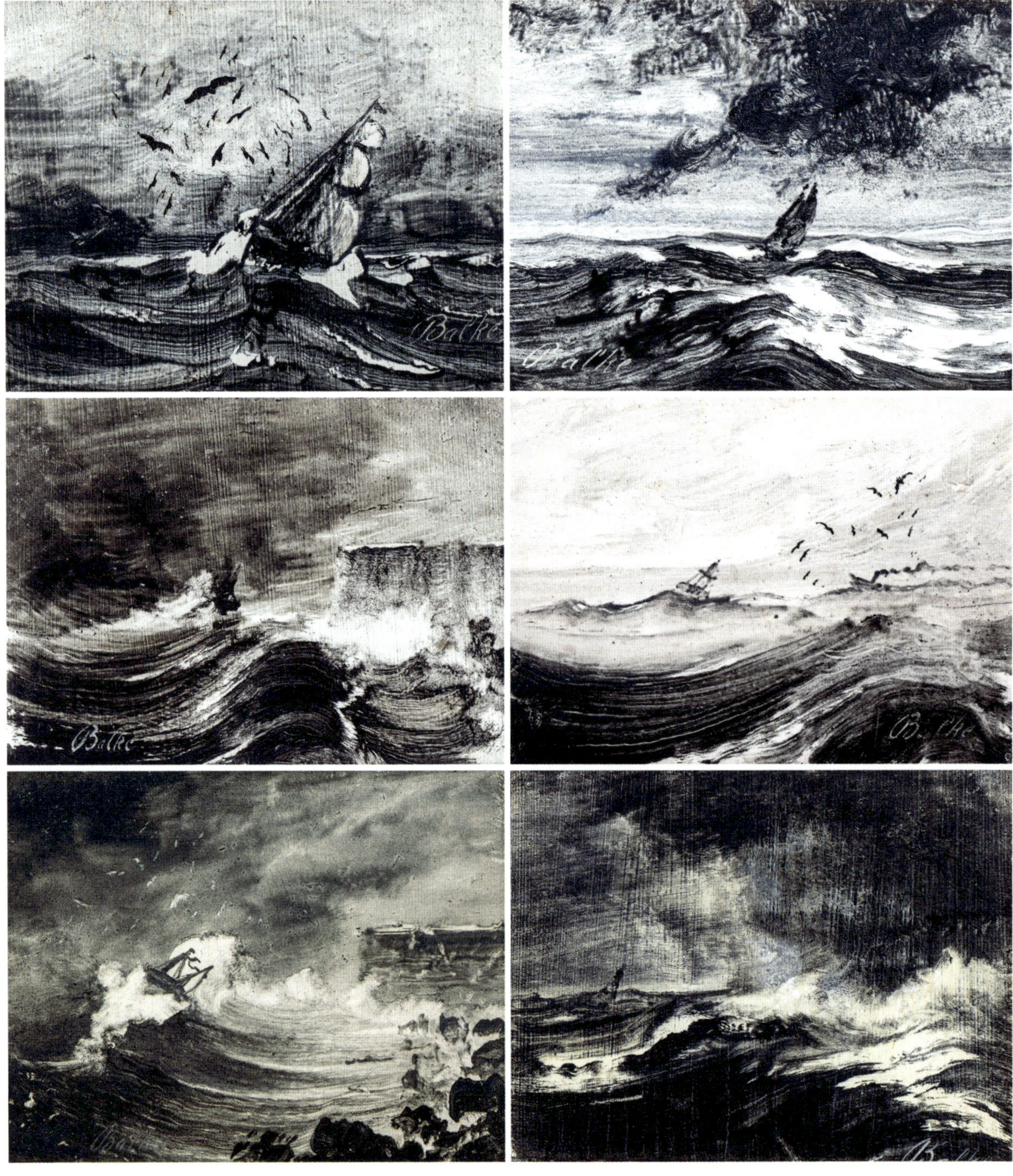

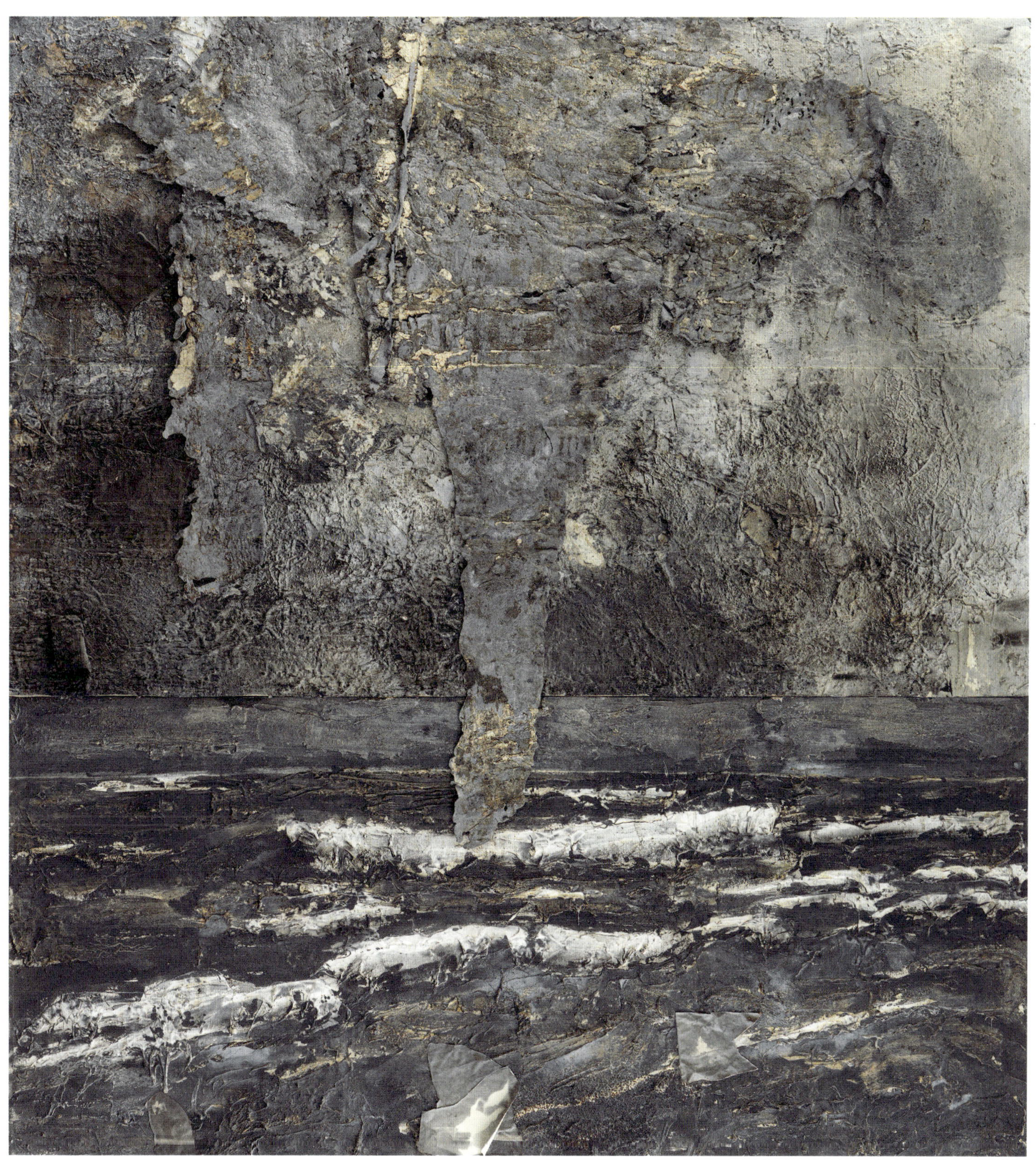

ANSELM KIEFER
Inflammation, 1983-1986

SUSAN HILLER

On the Edge, 2015

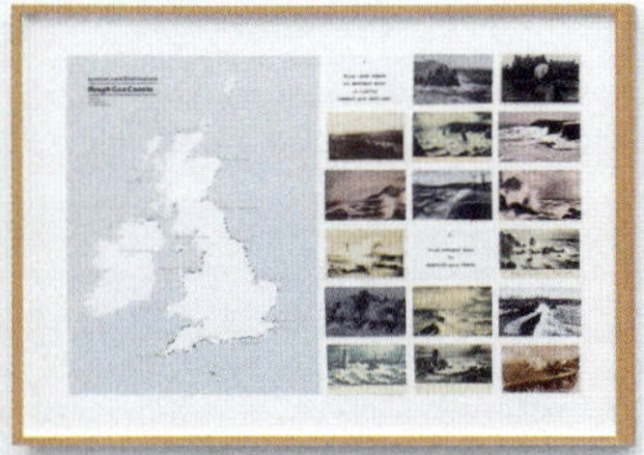
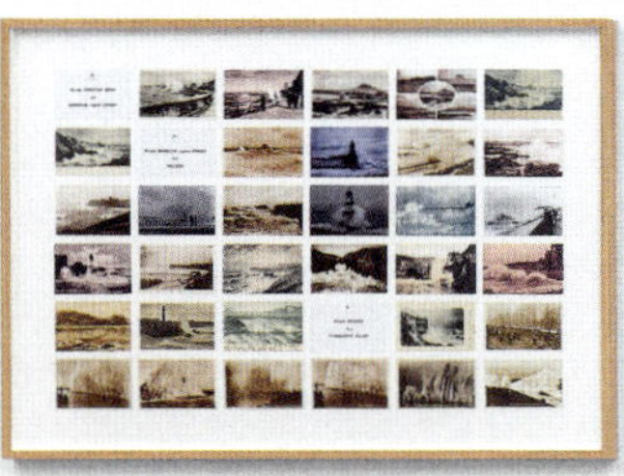
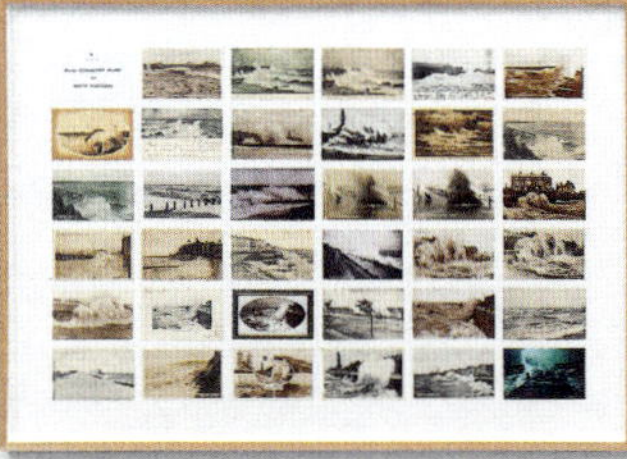
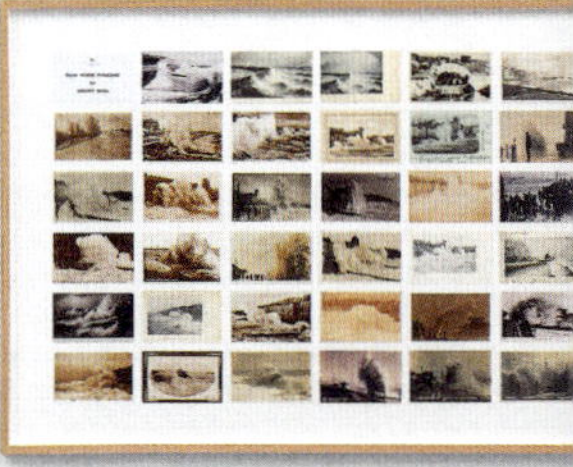
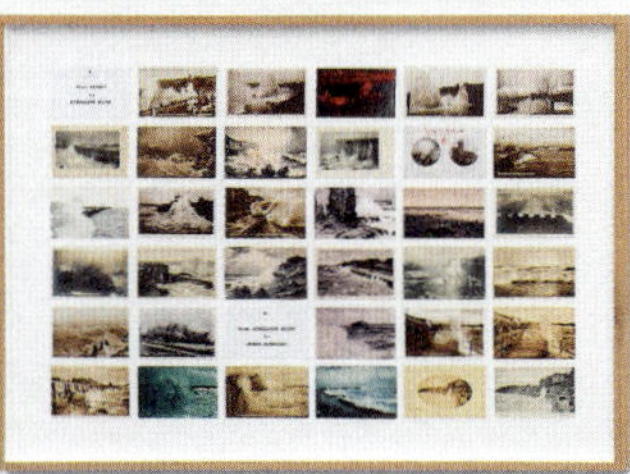
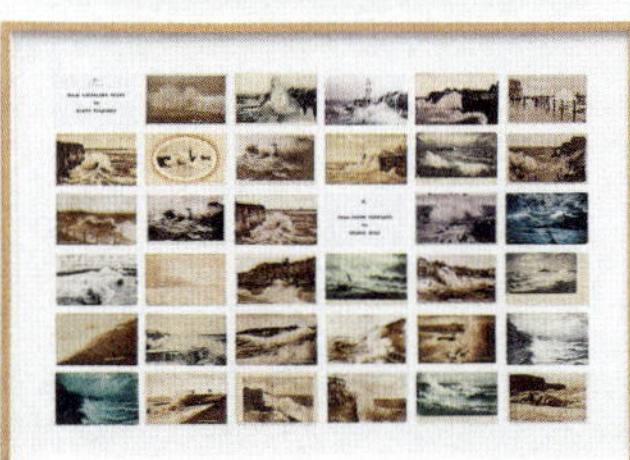
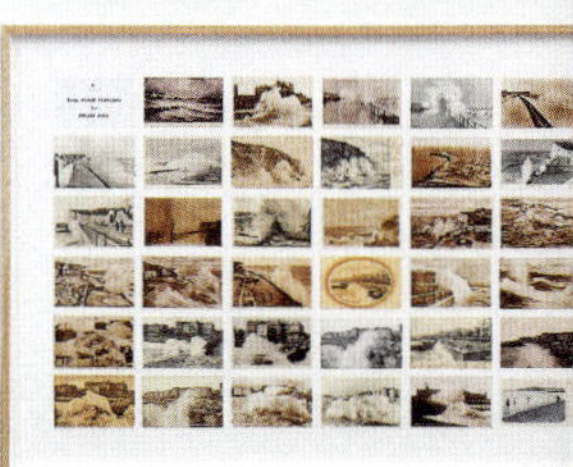

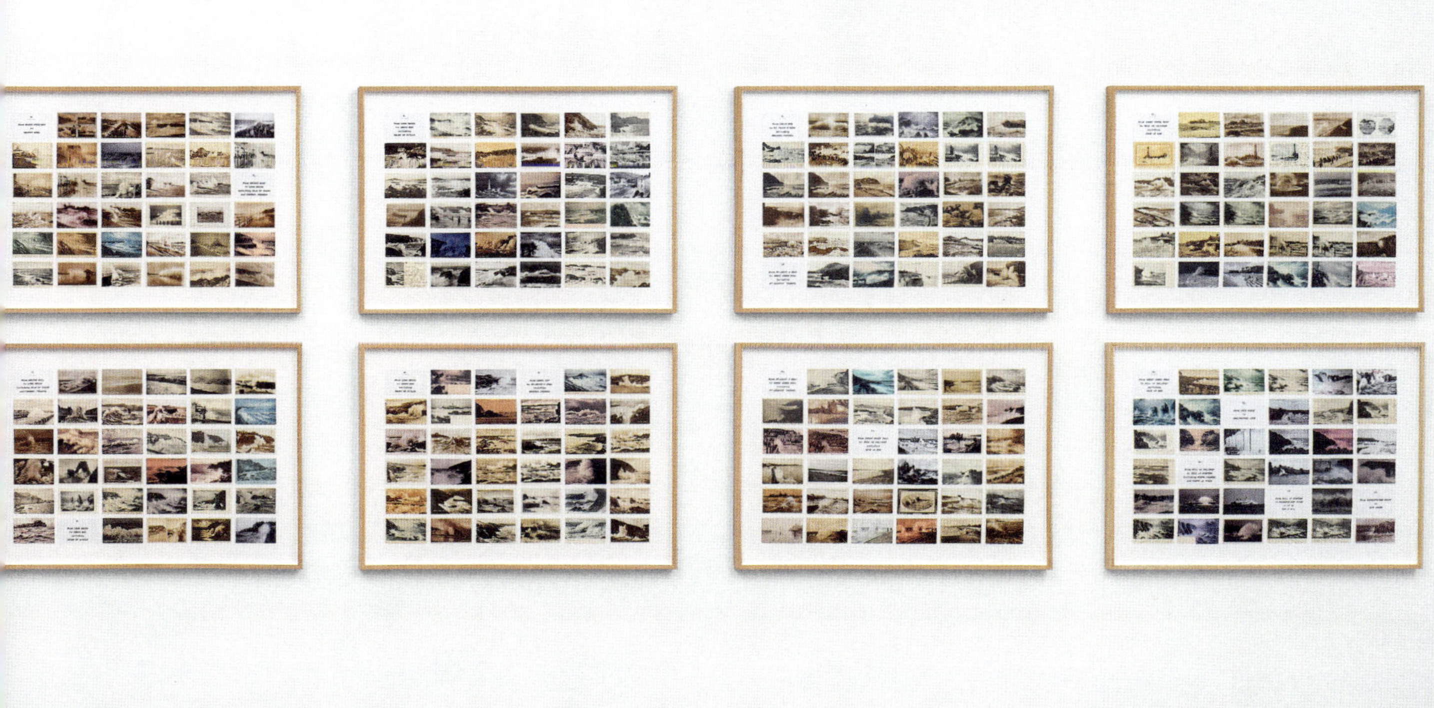

CASPAR DAVID FRIEDRICH
After the Storm, 1817

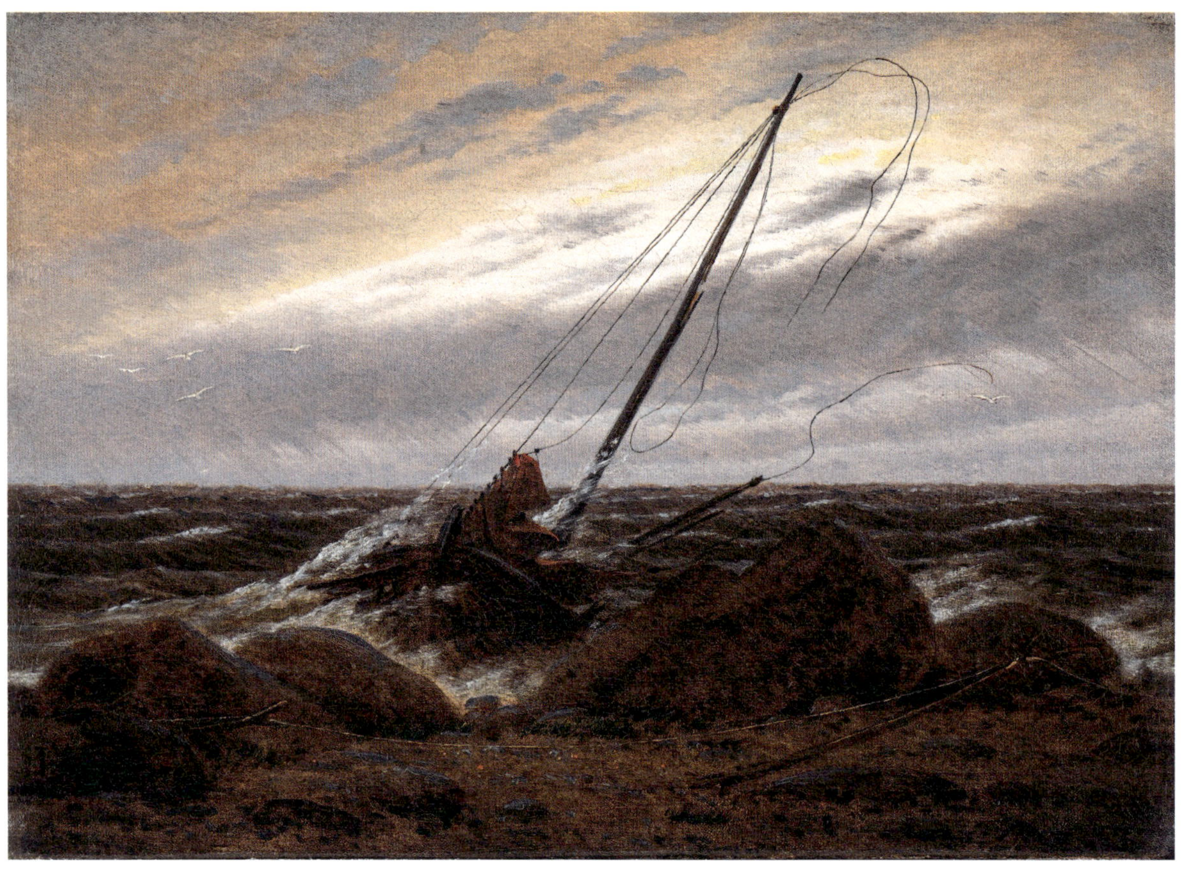

JOHAN CHRISTIAN DAHL

Seascape with Wreck, 1831

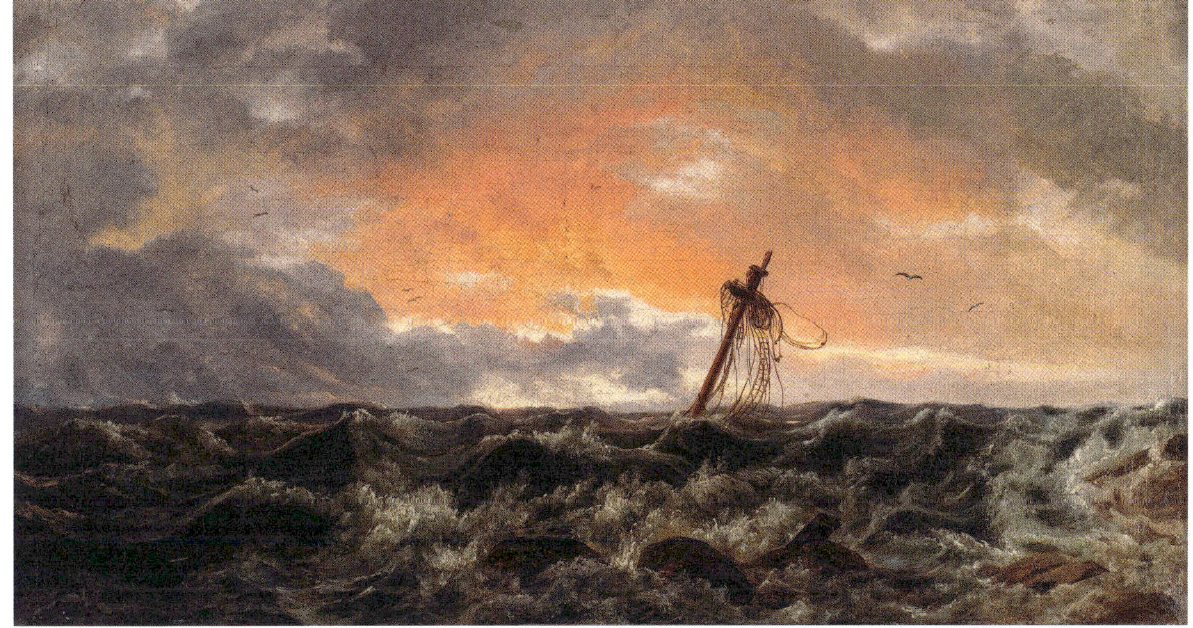

UTAGAWA KUNIYOSHI
Calming the Waves at Kakuta on the Way to Exile at Sado Island, 1835-1836
Bottom: *Yoshitsune attacked by Taira ghosts,* 1853
Opposite page: UTAGAWA HIROSHIGE
Awa Province, Naruto Rapids, 1855

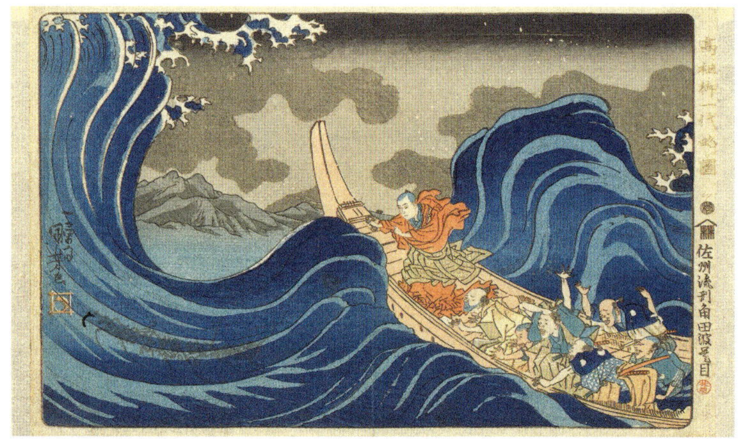

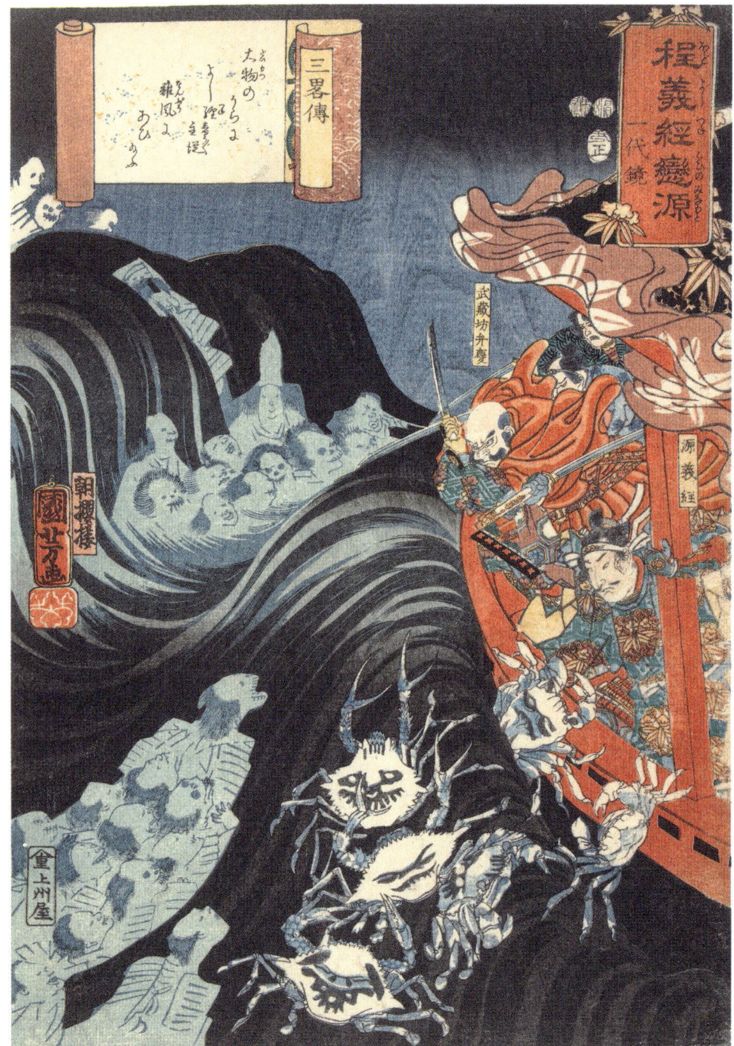

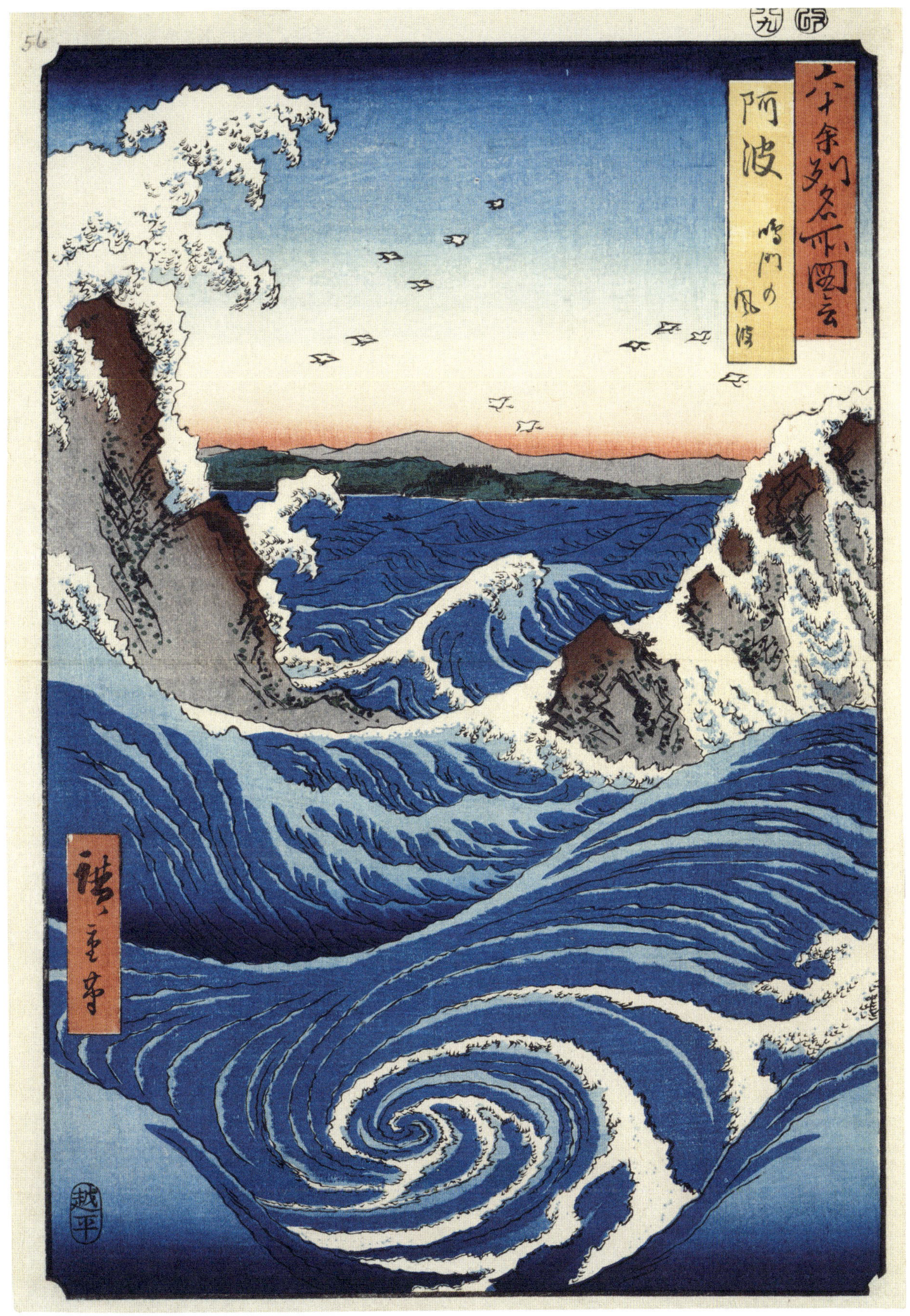
六十余州名所図会
阿波
鳴門の風波
廣重筆

UTAGAWA KUNIYOSHI

Diver Recovers Jewel from the Palace of the Dragon King, 1847-1848

Opposite page: *Tamakazura, the Diver Brings Back the Pearls.* From the series *Comparison of Scenes from the Tale of Genji and the Floating World,* 1843-1847

Bottom: UTAGAWA KUNISADA I: *The scrap dealer Jiemon and the carpenter Rokusaburo,* 1854-1859

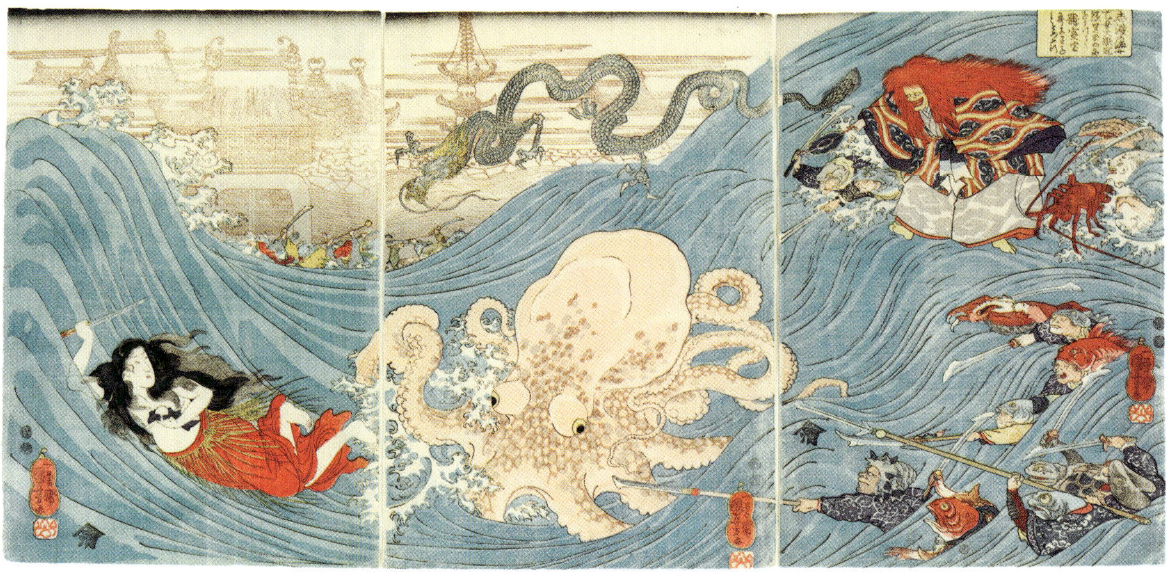

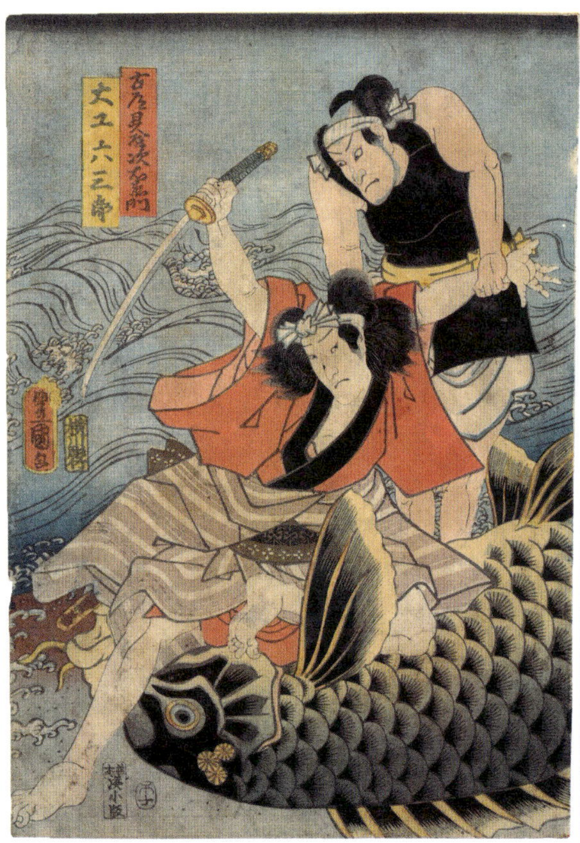

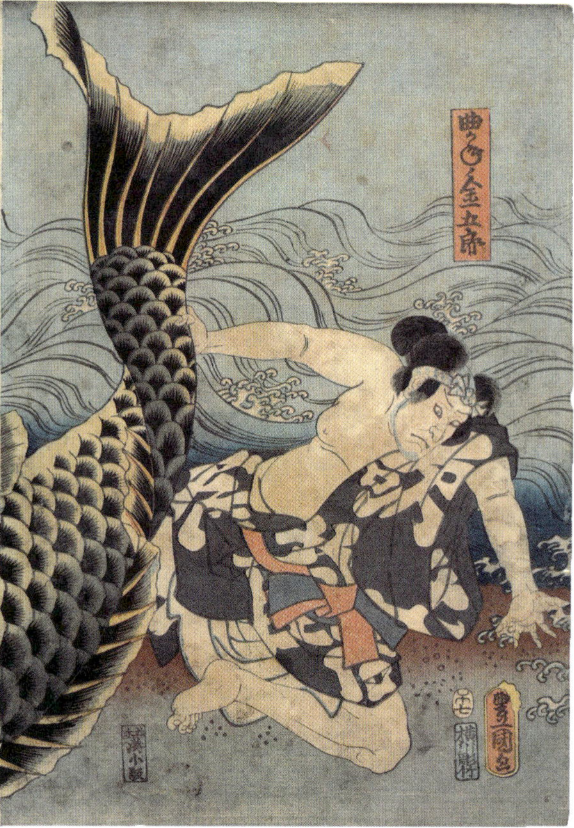

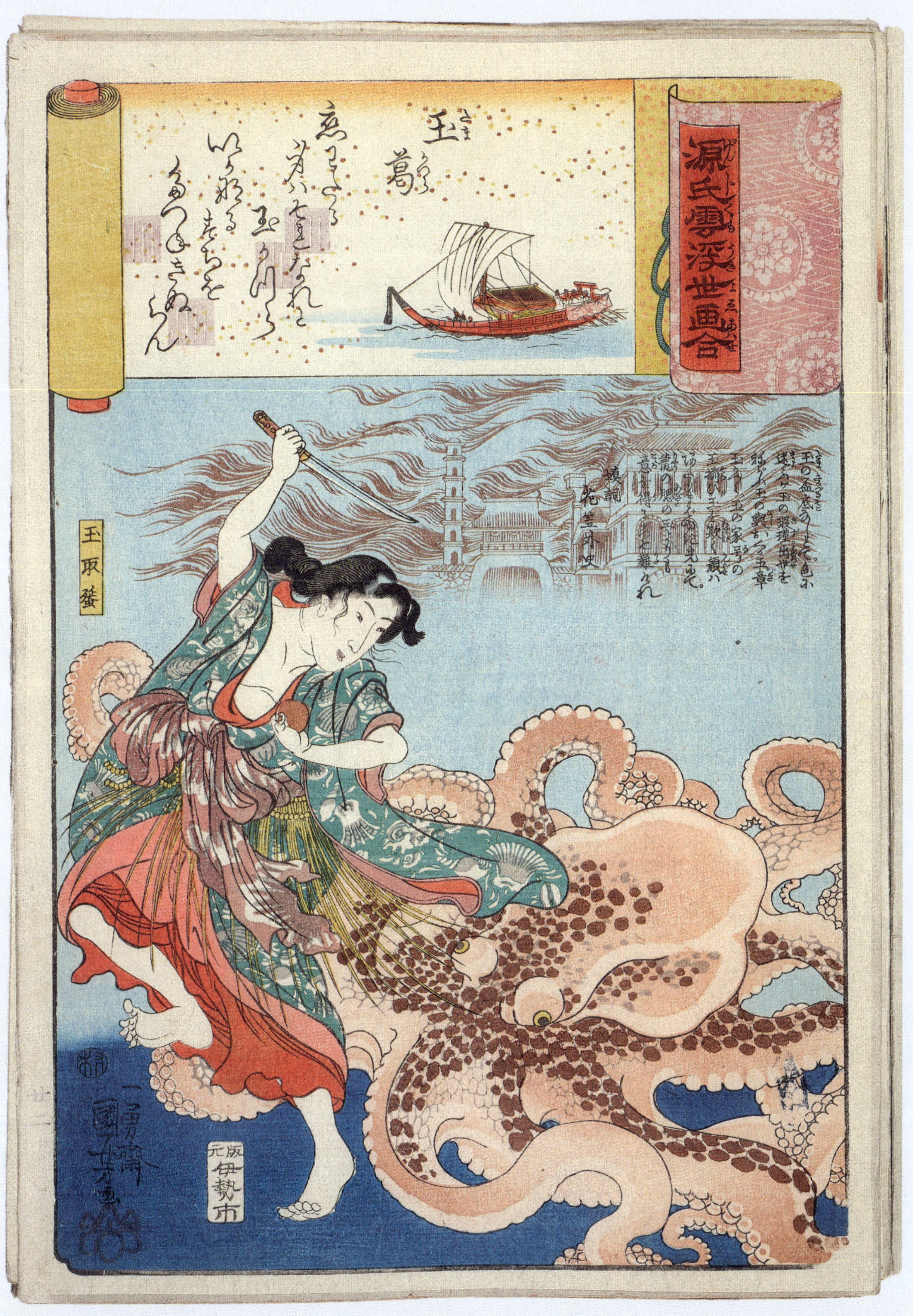
源氏雲浮世画合
玉蔓
玉取蜑
一勇斎國芳画
版元
伊勢市

ANDREA MANTEGNA
Battle of the Sea Gods, left and right half, c. 1470-1500

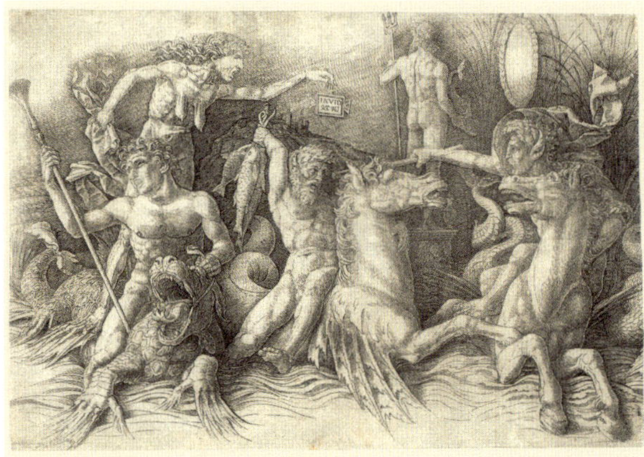

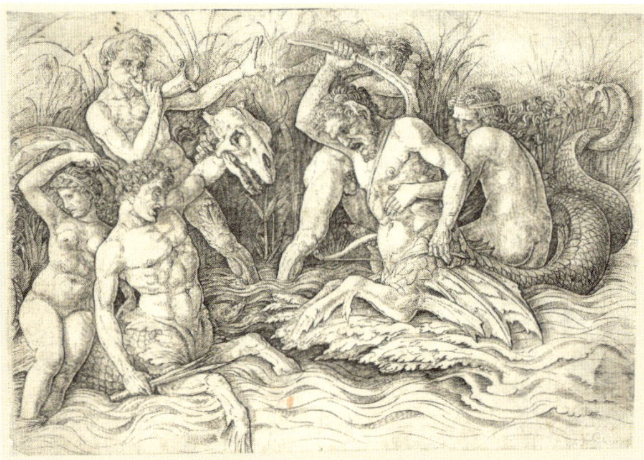

JACOB MATHAM
Neptune and Thetis, 1611-1614

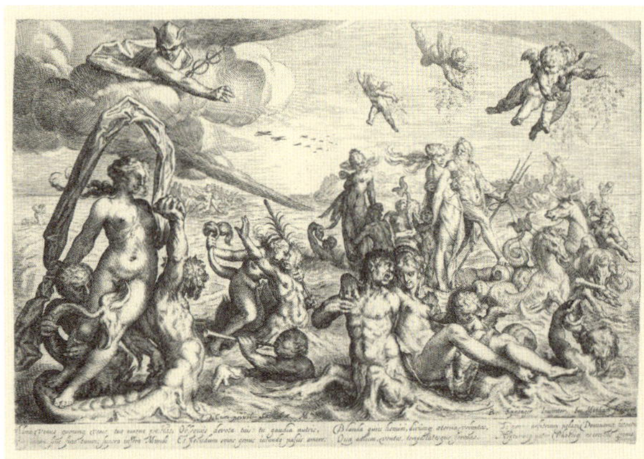

PIETER DE JODE II
The Birth of Venus (after Peter Paul Rubens), 1606-1674

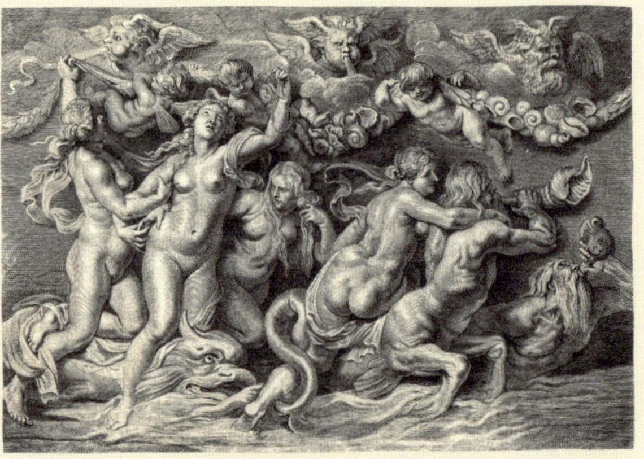

Opposite page:
WILLEM VAN SWANENBURGH
Neptune Riding on two Dolphins, 1603-1607

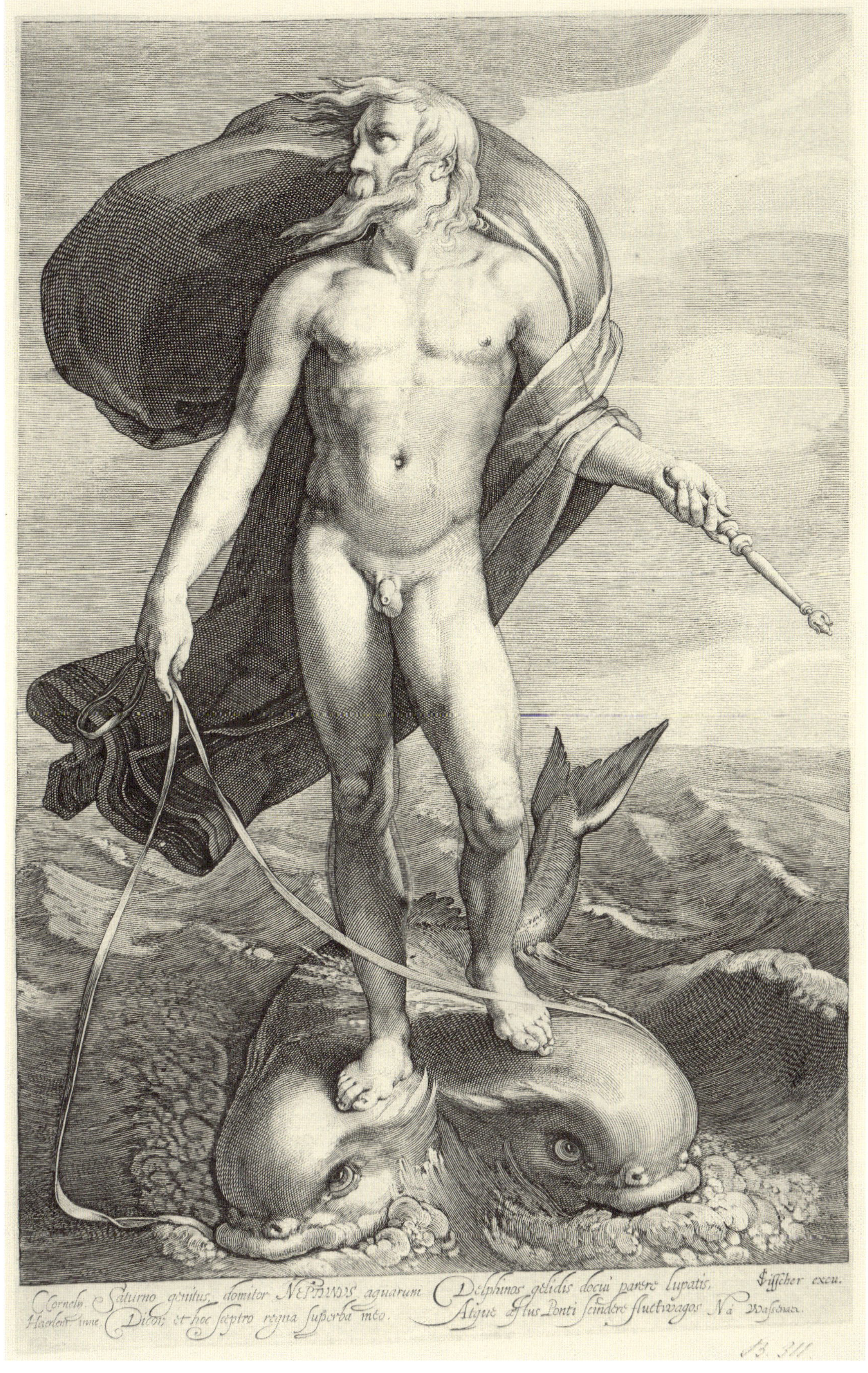
Corneliu. Haerlem. inue.
Saturno genitus, domitor NEPTVNVS aquarum
Dicor, et hoc sceptro regna superba meo.
Delphinos gelidis docui parere lupatis,
Atque æstus Ponti scindere fluctivagos
Visscher excu.
N. à Wassenaer.
B. 311.

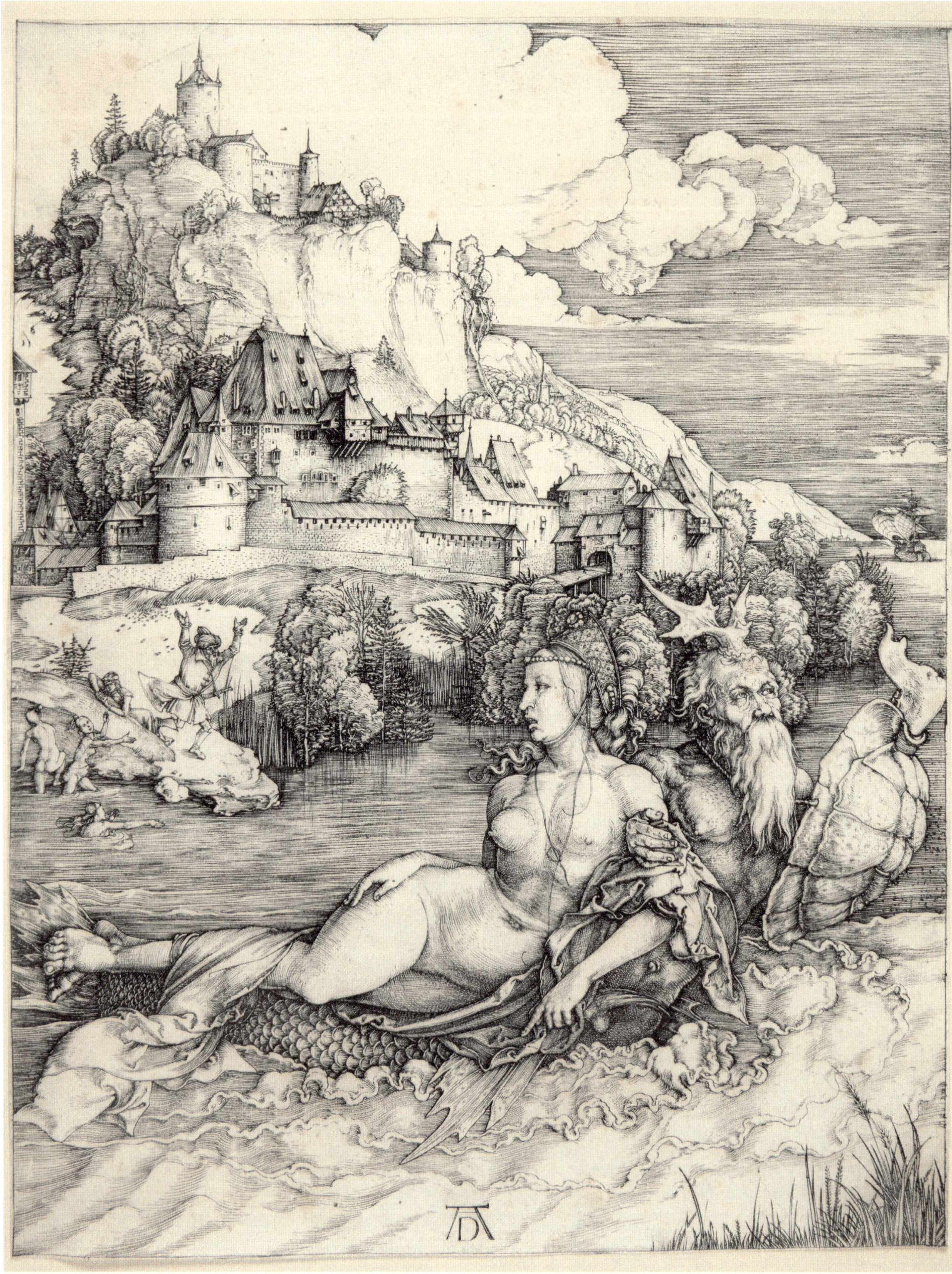

ELISABETH JERICHAU BAUMANN
Havfrue (Mermaid), 1863

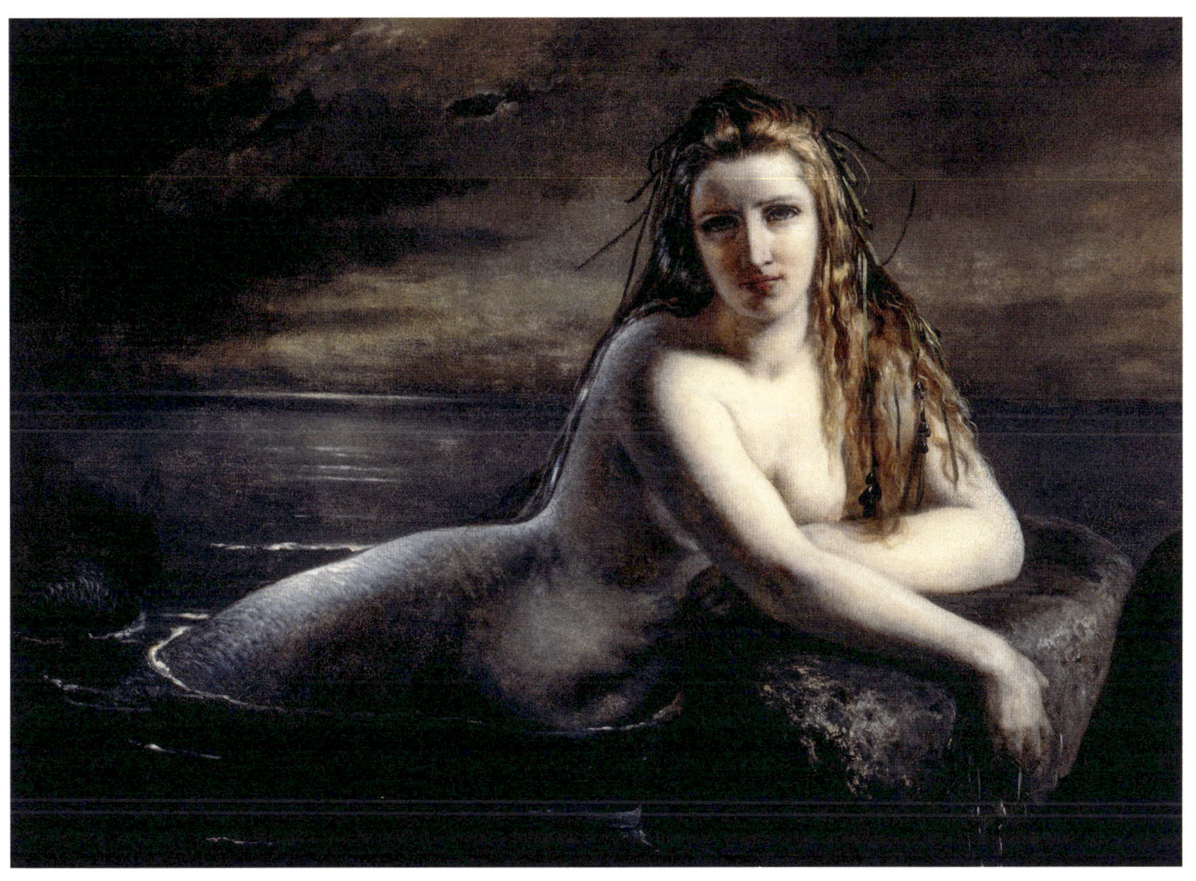

Opposite page:
ALBRECHT DÜRER
The Sea Monster, c. 1498

WERNER VAN DEN VALCKERT
Galathea, 1619
Neptune, 1609

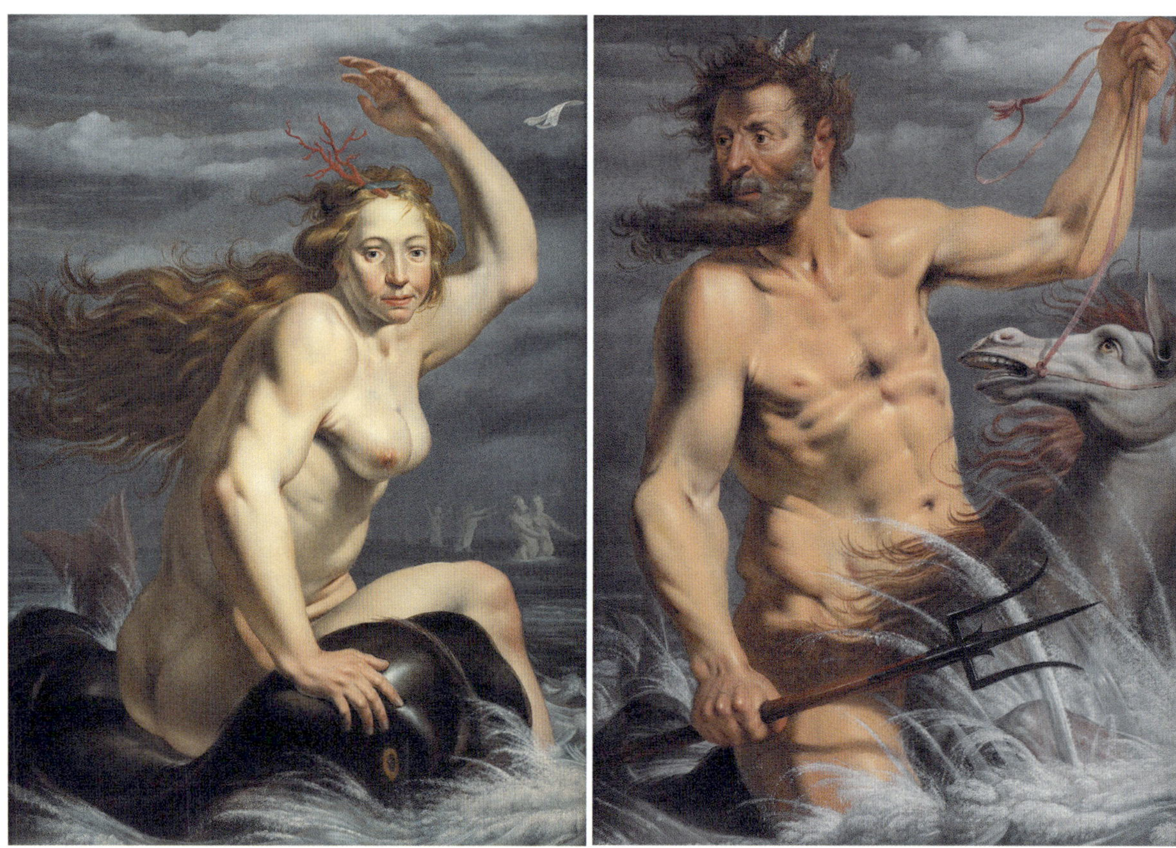

Opposite page:
Statue of a wrestler, early 1st century BC.

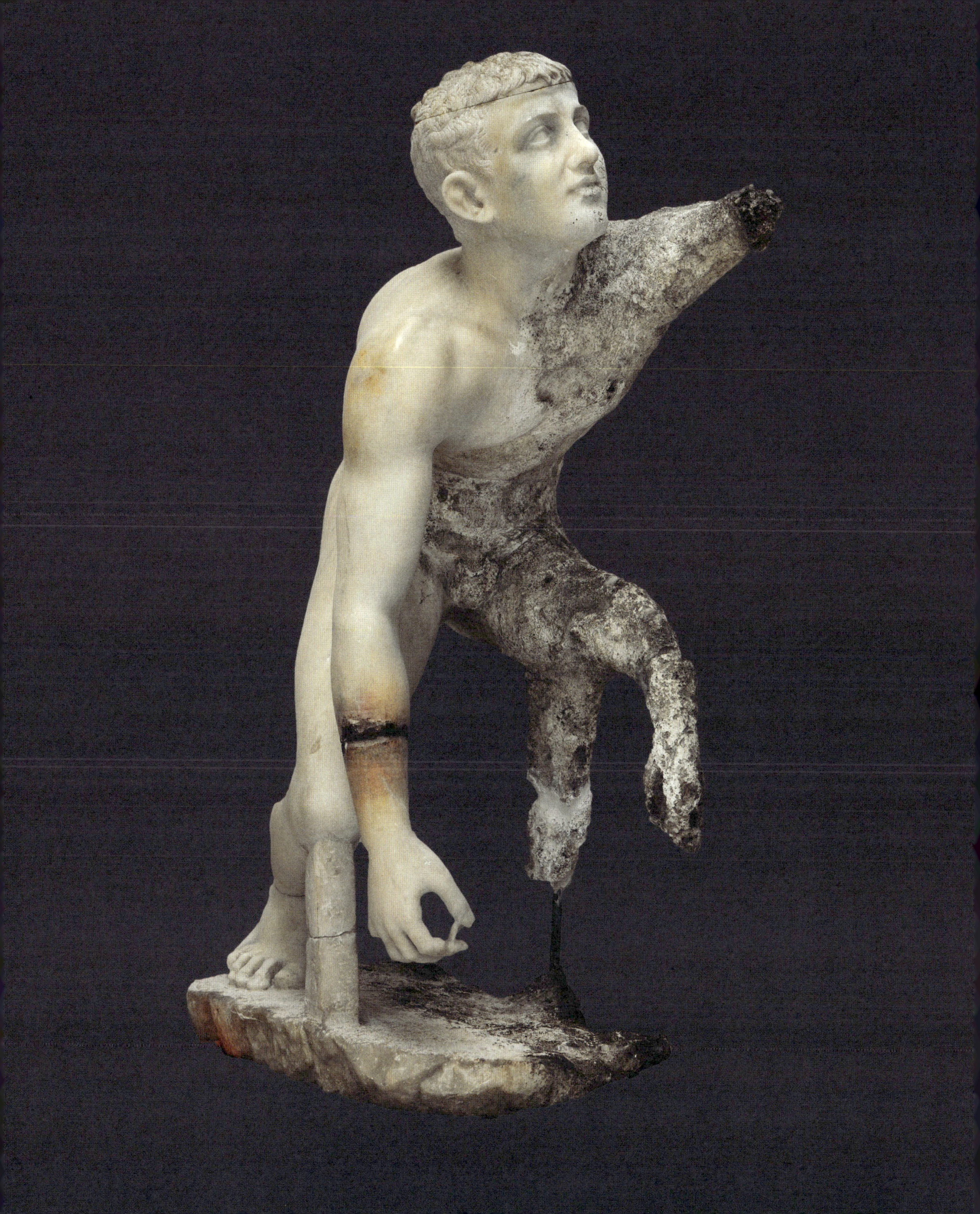

FRANTZ ZÉPHIRIN
Indian Spirits Facing Colonization, 2000
Bottom: *The Slave Ship Brooks,* 2007

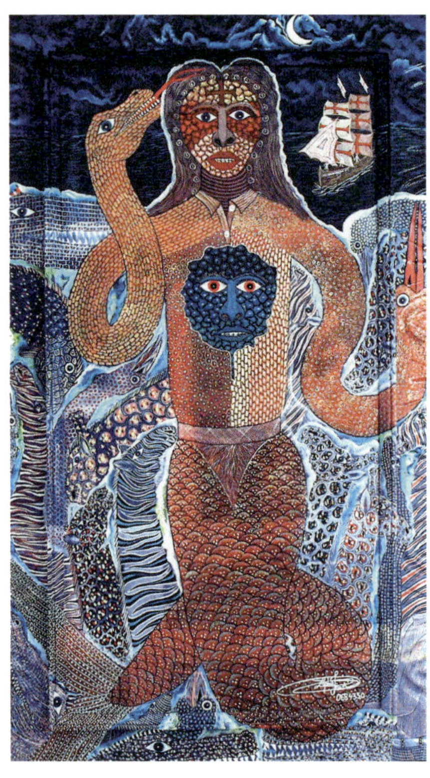

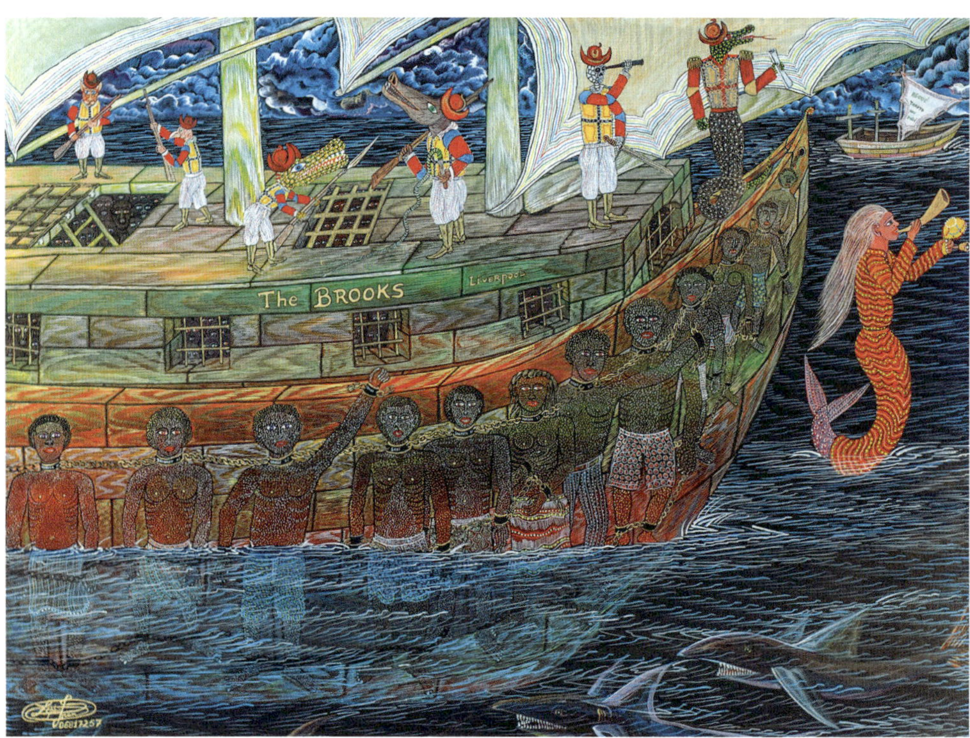

JEANNETTE EHLERS
Atlantic (Endless Row), 2009

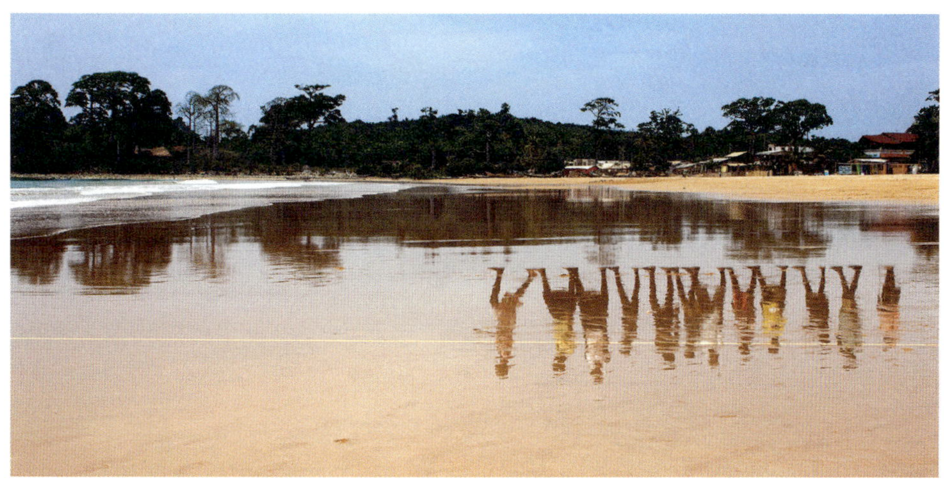

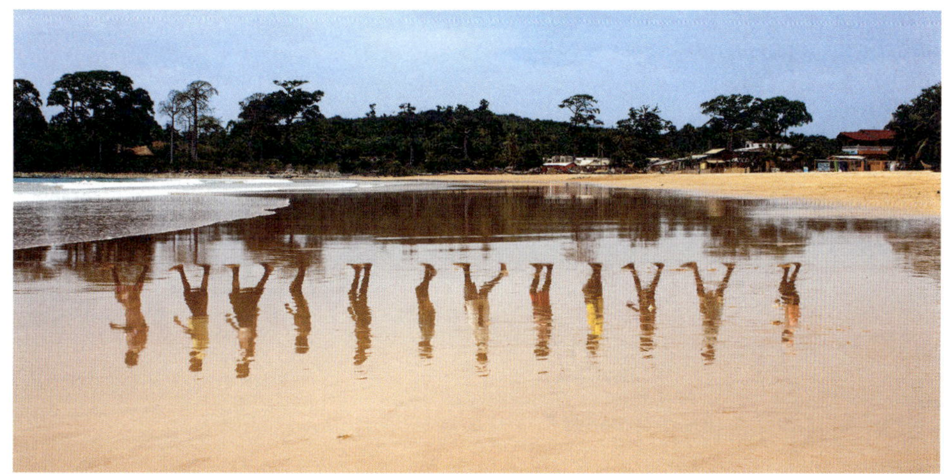

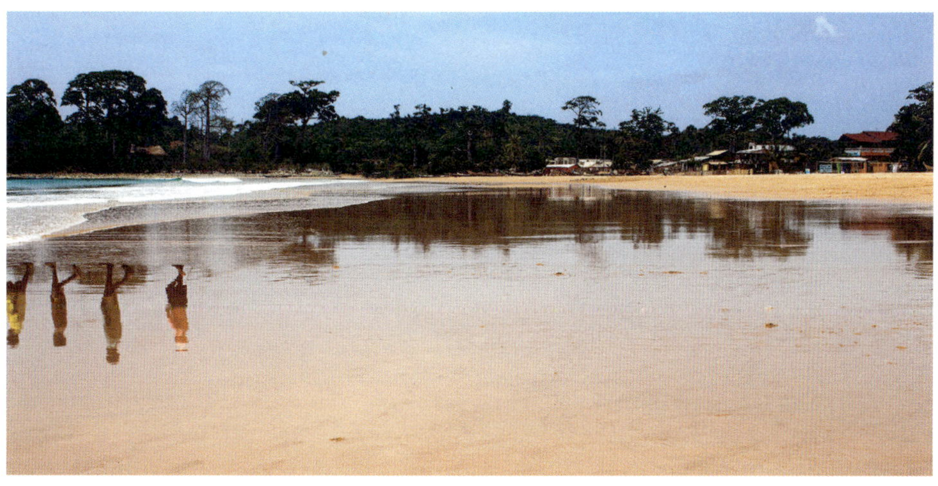

ELLEN GALLAGHER
Fast-Fish and Loose-Fish, 2023

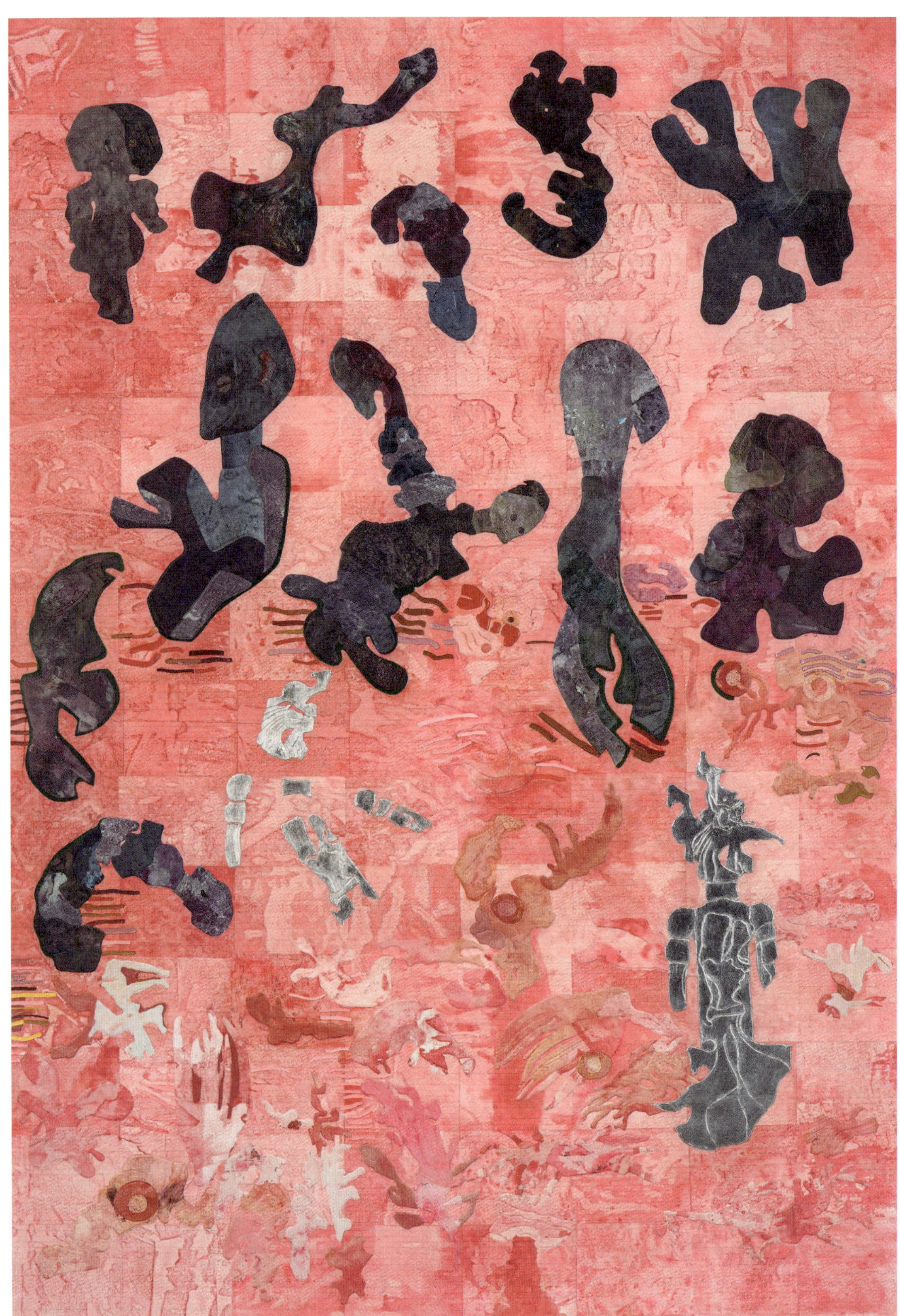

ELLEN GALLAGHER
Fast-Fish and Loose-Fish, 2023

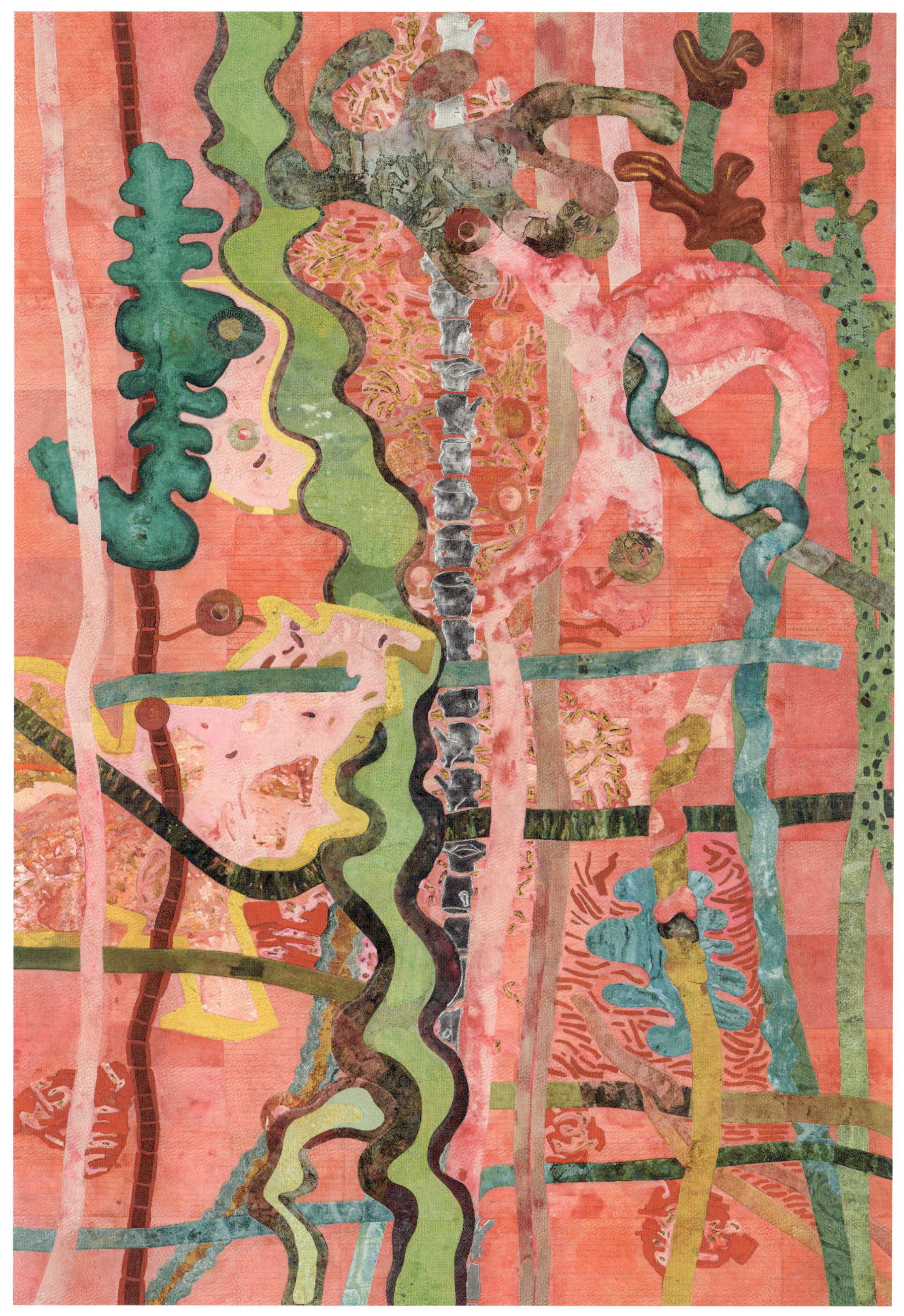

KARA WALKER

Rift of the Medusa, 2017

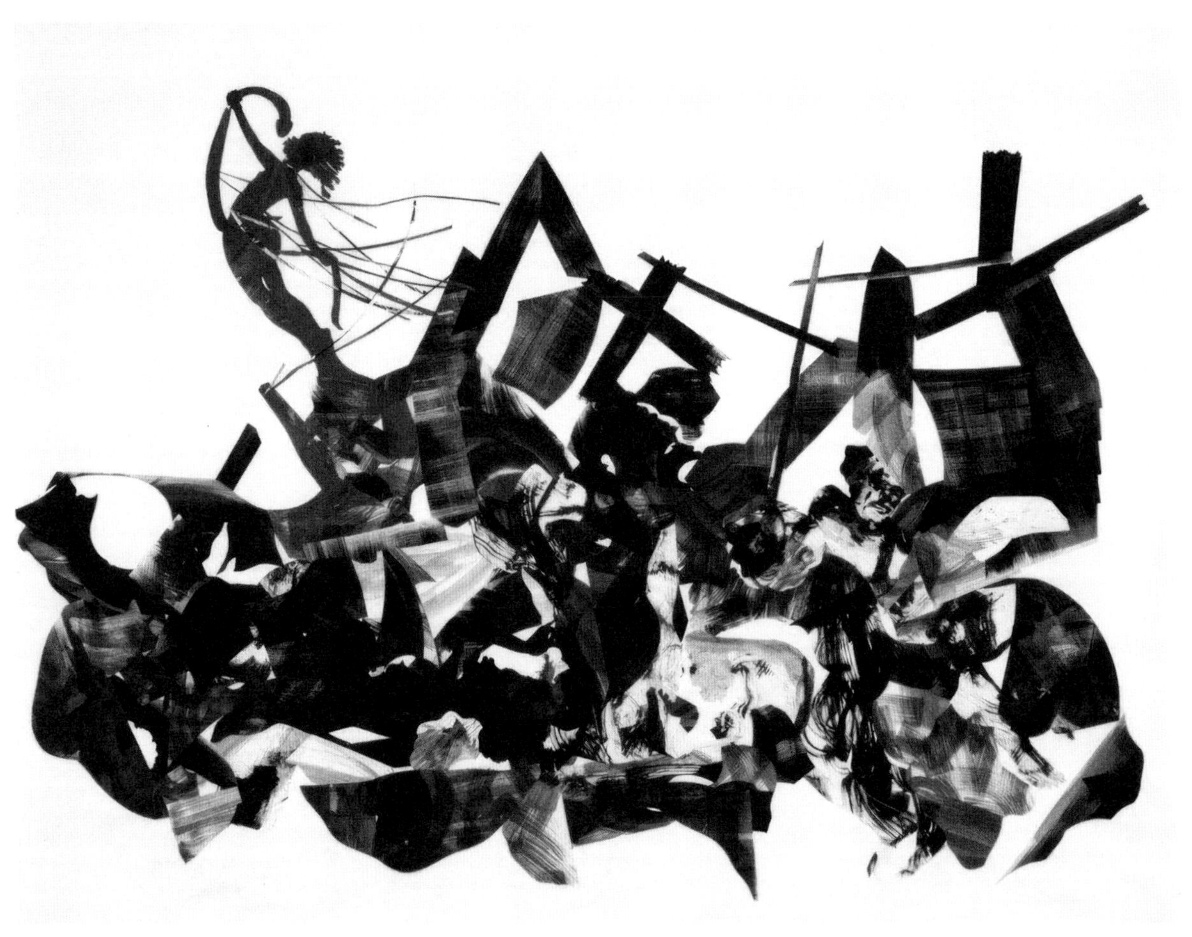

MARK BRADFORD

Playing with the Ocean's Ceiling, 2014

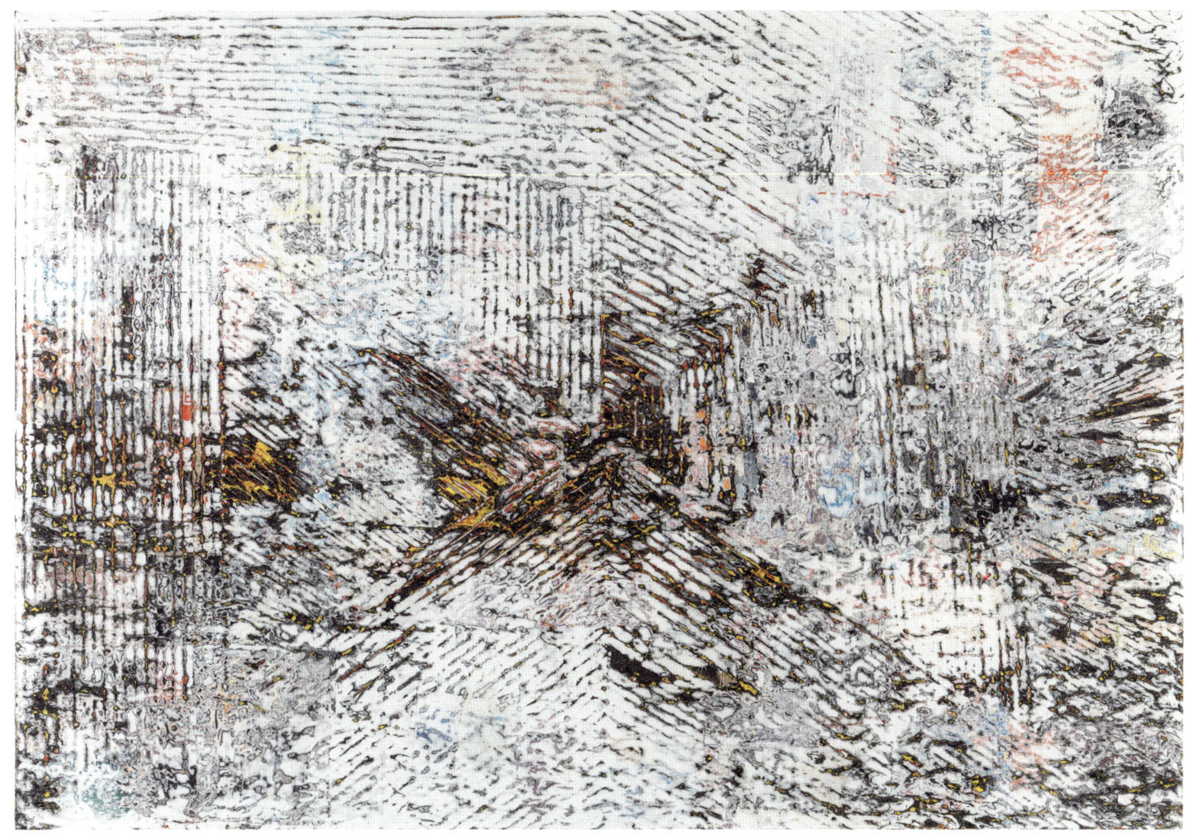

Our Existence Depends on the Ocean

Katherine Richardson

There is nothing that one can long for like the sea. Man's love for the sea is selfless. We cannot cultivate it, we cannot drink its water, in its bosom we die. And yet, when we are away from the sea, we feel that something of our own soul is drying up within us, disappearing like a washed-up jellyfish in the dry sand.

Isak Dinesen (Karen Blixen),
Seven Gothic Tales (1935)

Were we to be cast into the ocean so far from shore that we could not swim or wade to land, our future would look very bleak, indeed. We would lose body heat to the surrounding water and expend valuable energy to keep our heads above water to breathe. We wouldn't have access to freshwater or food and, at least in some parts of the ocean, there would be the very real danger of becoming dinner for an ocean resident. We are nevertheless drawn to the ocean. Nowhere is our enchantment with the sea better captured than in the above quote from the famous Danish author Karen Blixen.

For the most part, our consideration of the ocean is confined to this enchantment, i.e., to what we feel or can touch although we, of course, also acknowledge the ocean's direct economic contributions to our societies. A house with an ocean view fetches a much higher price than one without and global shipping makes the ocean the global market's "circulation system," ensuring the global flow of goods. Fish and other living ocean resources make an important contribution towards meeting our nutritional needs, while the harvest of non-living materials supplies us with building materials as well as raw ingredients for myriad industries. Few, however, ever stop to consider that our very existence depends on the ocean.

We – like all other organisms – are a part of a community of interacting organisms within a physical environment. That means that we, just like all other organisms, are part of an "ecosystem." Our interactions with one another and with all other living organisms are linked across the globe. Thus, the entire Earth comprises our ecosystem. That the ocean covers almost three quarters of this ecosystem should immediately give us cause to consider what it actually means for us.

The ocean drives the Earth's water (hydrological) cycle. Evaporation causes water from the surface ocean to be transferred to the air, where it then can be transported by wind. Ultimately, it can fall as rain or snow over land. Thus, without the ocean we would have limited – if any – access to freshwater on land. Without freshwater, life could not exist on land but the ocean does more than provide us with water. It also is a decisive factor in establishing global climate conditions.

The great climate regulator

Changes in the Earth's climate conditions are caused by changes in the amount of the sun's heat that is received and stored near the surface of the Earth. Heat from the sun arrives daily on the Earth and has done so for billions of years. If there were no mechanisms for the Earth to rid itself of some of that heat, our planet would now be far too hot for living organisms to survive. The Earth does have mechanisms to rid itself of the extra heat, however, and much radiates away from the Earth's surface back into space. While passing through the atmosphere, it can come into contact with "greenhouse" gases – so called because they retain the heat radiating from the Earth's surface. For that reason, the concentration of greenhouse gases in the Earth's atmosphere is an important factor controlling temperature near the surface of the Earth. The higher the concentration of these gases in the atmosphere, the more heat is retained in our ecosystem.

It is primarily by changing the concentration of greenhouse gases in the atmosphere through the burning of fossil fuels that humans have caused the recent global warming. Information drawn from ice cores tells us that major warming or cooling events throughout the Earth's history have been associated with changes in greenhouse gas concentrations in the atmosphere. The ocean contains much more CO_2 than the atmosphere and, under some conditions, this CO_2 can readily move from ocean to atmosphere (or vice versa). Thus, many of the changes in climate the Earth has experienced in its history, i.e., entering and exiting Ice Ages, have been associated with the movement of CO_2 to and from the ocean and atmosphere.

The ocean is in contact with the atmosphere over 71 percent of the Earth's surface and the gases in both media are constantly seeking to come in equilibrium, i.e., to come in balance with one another. Today, as we increase the concentration of CO_2 in the atmosphere by burning fossil fuels, the concentration in the ocean is also increasing. Thus, the ocean is taking CO_2 out of the atmosphere and buffering climate change. Without the ocean, then, the effects of climate change would be much worse than those we experience today.

While that is good news now, many anticipate that we in the future can reduce atmospheric CO_2 concentrations by sucking CO_2 out of the atmosphere. If we ever develop the technology well enough to decrease atmospheric CO_2 concentrations to below those of the surface ocean, CO_2 will move from the ocean to the atmosphere. Thus, decreasing atmospheric CO_2 concentrations by sucking CO_2 out of the atmosphere implies that we ultimately will have to remove CO_2 from the ocean as well.

Moving CO_2 between the atmosphere and ocean also changes ocean chemistry. Most importantly, when CO_2 is dissolved in water, carbonic acid is formed. The production of carbonic acid means that the ocean becomes more acidic and, because of the increases we have made in atmospheric CO_2 concentration, the surface ocean is more acidic today than it has been at any time in human history. The ocean's level of acidity is, however, still less than in our shampoo. So, for us, this increased acidity is not an immediate problem.

However, for the myriad carbonate-(chalk) forming organisms in the ocean, including corals, oysters and the tiny ocean organisms whose fossilized shells comprise, for example, the White Cliffs of Dover, increasing acidity is a threat as chalk dissolves in acid. Therefore, the more acidic the water becomes, the harder it is for the organisms to maintain their carbonate structures. Already today, oyster aquaculture along the west coast of North America is impacted by ocean acidification caused by increasing concentrations of CO_2 in the atmosphere.

Global heat storage and distribution

Not only CO_2 but also heat is stored in the ocean. Over 90 percent of the increase in heat energy stored near the Earth that has occurred since the mid-20th century is today in the ocean. That means the ocean is warming much faster than the air. The surface ocean has been getting steadily warmer since the 1970s but, in 2023, a sudden and dramatic increase was observed. We have been monitoring surface ocean temperatures with the help of satellite mounted sensors for over four decades. The increases observed until now have been incremental, i.e., the temperature for any given year has always been similar to that of the previous year. Suddenly, in May 2023, this pattern was broken such that surface temperature of the ocean now lies well above those recorded in 2022 and in all previous years. A number of factors have been identified that may have contributed to this sudden increase, but the actual causal mechanism(s) is not yet understood. The increase has implications not only for ocean life but also for life on land as heat is released from the ocean to the air. Therefore, numerous temperature records over land were also broken in 2023.

Many storms over land get their energy from the heat stored in the ocean. Hurricanes, for example, form over the ocean but only in regions where the ocean surface temperature is at least 26°C. An ocean with a larger surface area where temperatures are > 26°C gives rise to more intensive and/or more frequent hurricanes.

The transport of heat by the ocean impacts regional climate and weather conditions. The climate, for example, in northwest Europe is much milder than that at similar latitudes in Siberia or Canada. The ocean is responsible for this difference as it transports heat from subtropical latitudes towards Europe. Paleorecords indicate that this current system does not function under all global climate conditions and one of the concerns about human-caused climate change is that this current system could be disrupted and lead to radical changes in climate/weather conditions in Europe.

Nature's rules are different in the ocean

Our planet is unique because it houses life. We do not know what life is, but we know what it does. It transforms and transports the nonliving chemical elements found on Earth. When it has been possible to extract enough energy from such a biochemical transformation to support life, an organism or organism group has evolved to do so. Life began in the ocean and has been present there much longer than it has on land, and nothing suggests that ocean nature is less worthy of or less in need of protection than nature on land. Nevertheless, ocean nature protection receives much less political and public attention than nature on land.

"Out of sight, out of mind" undoubtedly plays a role when it comes to our lack of empathy for ocean nature but that is not the only explanation. Nature in the ocean is simply harder for us to see, understand and appreciate than nature on land. On land, plants are large and can be perceived by our senses but, in the ocean, most of the plants are so small that they cannot be seen by the naked eye. That plants are so large on land seems likely to be an adaptation to life on land.

Water is essential for life. A plant, therefore, has a root system that allows it to tap into soil moisture and underground water reserves. Accessing water is not a problem for an ocean plant. Indeed, were ocean plants large and heavy like many land plants, they would run the risk of sinking out of the surface ocean, where light is accessible. The result is that most ocean plants, phytoplankton, are single-celled organisms that drift in the surface waters. They are so small that they can only be observed through a microscope. As a result, we do not appreciate the enormous diversity expressed by these plants and most textbooks simply treat them as a "black box." Because phytoplankton are very small, so are the animals that eat them. Thus, most ocean nature is invisible to us. The accidental ingestion of a mouthful of seawater means that we also swallow whole ecosystems containing hundreds of thousands of microorganisms.

On land (if we ignore the fungi), assigning organisms to either the "plant" or "animal" category is quite straight forward. This is not the case in the ocean. Most of the different groups of phytoplankton contain species that either lack the ability to do photosynthesis or combine photosynthesis with the consumption of other organisms or organic materials from the water around them. The ability to both perform photosynthesis and use

EMILIJA ŠKARNULYTĖ

Still from *Aphotic Zone* (Afotisk zone), 2022, with a digital rendering of a phytoplankton.

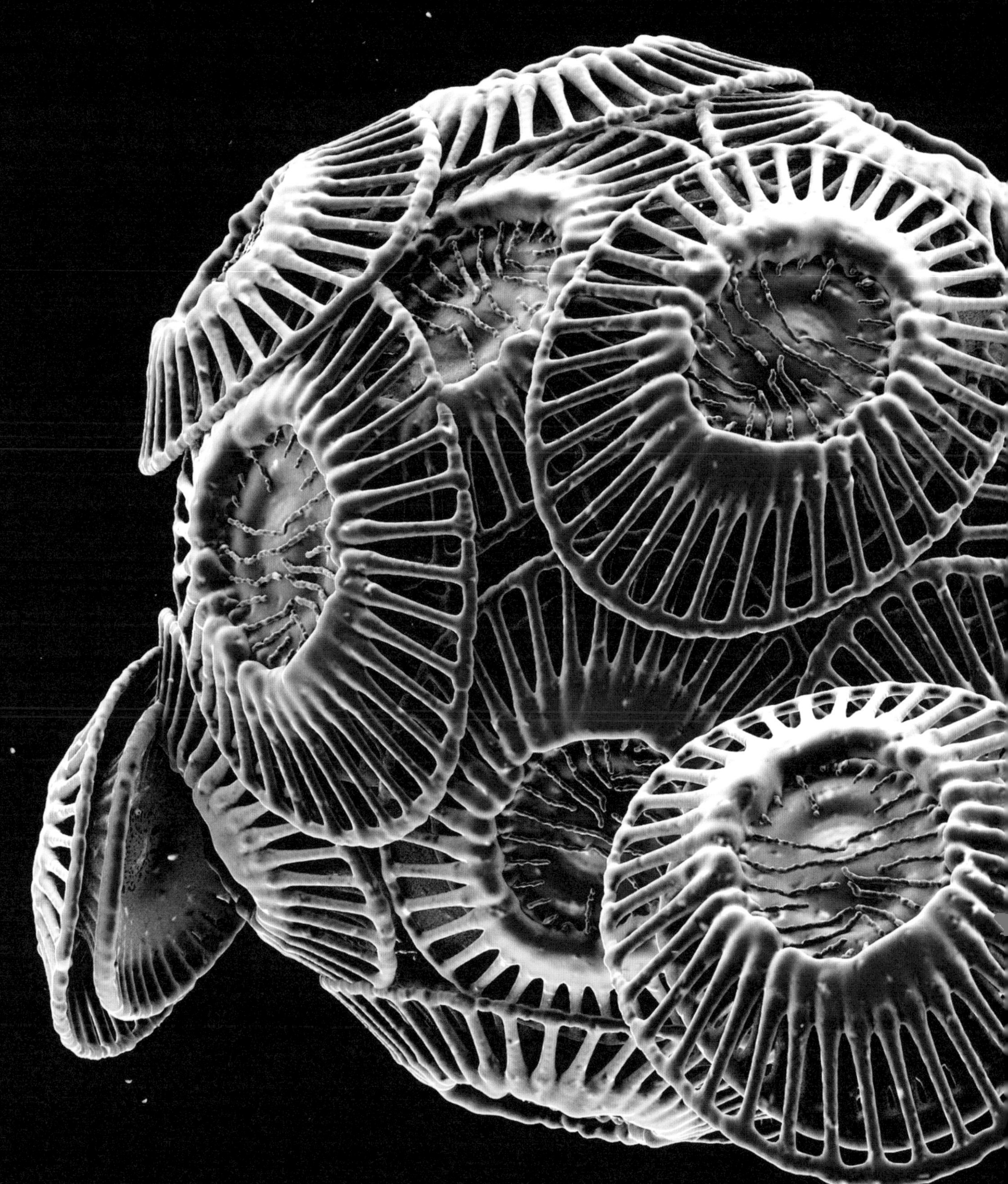

external carbon sources for nutrition is called "mixotrophy" and ocean nature has evolved myriad fantastic strategies for doing just this.

Some photosynthetic phytoplankton join forces to attack animals much larger than themselves. They inject the animal with a poison, whereby it becomes paralyzed, and the "army" of phytoplankton can then suck out and digest the animal contents. We have no idea how the attackers agree on which animal to attack. Other phytoplankton which are, themselves, unable to manufacture the basic machinery of photosynthesis, known as chloroplasts, consume organisms with chloroplasts. They then digest all the contents of the prey organism except the chloroplasts. These continue to perform photosynthesis and supply their new host with energy. Again, we have no idea how the consuming phytoplankton "knows" it would be a mistake to immediately digest the chloroplast.

There are many other forms of mixotrophy, but these examples serve to remind us that nature in the ocean operates under a different set of "rules" than nature on land. While the occurrence of mixotrophic organisms is common in the sea, it is much less so on land. Perhaps living conditions on land make it harder to have multiple nutritional strategies than in the ocean. Light is abundant in the surface layers of the ocean so, here, phytoplankton can carry out photosynthesis. However, these tiny plants are at the mercy of the water currents in which they are found and can do nothing if those currents carry them to depths where there is no or only little light. On the other hand, the same currents bring to them an abundance of potential food sources in the form of both particulate and dissolved organic materials.

Therefore, a successful nutritional strategy in the ocean might well be to invest in the infrastructure to both carry out photosynthesis and to exploit the organic material passing by. To obtain water, a plant on land needs to be stationary and sink roots. Furthermore, air does not deliver nutrition to a land plant in the same way that water delivers it to a marine plant. The result may have been that it was advantageous for organisms adapting to life on land to specialize in either photosynthesis or the consumption of organic materials.

The biodiversity of microscopic organisms is also important

That much of ocean nature is comprised of very tiny organisms does not mean that its diversity is unimportant. Genetically speaking, phytoplankton are much more diverse from one another than land plants are from each other. We intuitively recognize that food webs are very different in ecosystems where the plant life is comprised of cacti, rain forest species, or nettles. We have no such understanding of what diversity in ocean plant communities means for marine food webs.

In our eyes, all phytoplankton are very small but that is not how they appear to the animals that eat them. The relative volume difference between the largest and smallest phytoplankton is greater than the relative volume difference between a mouse and an elephant and no one would expect mice and elephants to be eaten by the same predators. The same is undoubtedly true when it comes to plankton food webs, but we do not yet understand how phytoplankton diversity influences ocean food webs or the ability of the ocean to store carbon.

Because it removes CO_2 from the atmosphere, photosynthesis is important for climate development. Therefore, the UN Intergovernmental Panel on Climate Change (IPCC) includes in its climate models estimates of the photosynthesis occurring both on land and in the ocean. There is still, however, considerable uncertainty regarding the amount of ocean photosynthesis and how it may be impacted by climate change. In fact, the IPCC models do not even agree as to whether climate change will increase or decrease the amount of photosynthesis occurring in the ocean.

On land, the CO_2 taken out of the atmosphere by photosynthesis is converted into plant biomass, where it potentially can remain for long periods (some trees live for centuries). While the CO_2 is stored in plants, it cannot reenter the atmosphere and contribute to global warming. Because phytoplankton are small and short-lived, very little of the CO_2 fixed through ocean photosynthesis gets stored in plant material. When photosynthesizing phytoplankton die and decay in the surface waters of the ocean, CO_2 is released and can again be released to the atmosphere.

However, when the photosynthesizing phytoplankton sink into the very deep ocean, any CO_2 released during their decay cannot reenter the atmosphere until that bottom water is again mixed to the surface. That can take up to 1,000 years. We call it the "biological pump" when carbon is transported from the surface layers and stored in the deepest depths of the ocean. The amount of carbon transferred to the inner ocean has varied during the history of the Earth and is believed to have played a role in the ocean-atmosphere CO_2 exchange related to the coming and going of Ice Ages. Relatively large and ballasted phytoplankton are more likely to contribute to a strong biological pump than their smaller counterparts. Therefore, phytoplankton diversity also matters in terms of the storage of carbon in the ocean and the role of ocean biology in the drawdown of CO_2 from the atmosphere.

Human-ocean interactions

Humans, like all other organisms, survive by harvesting and using natural resources. On land, the harvest of wild animals to support the nutrition of our species is very limited. Not so in the ocean. About 20 percent of the animal protein consumed by humans is in the form of fish and about half of that comes from wild stocks (the rest coming from aquaculture). Often fishing activities destroy habitats (e.g., bottom trawling) or lead to mortalities of non-target species.

Because life drives the cycling of elements on Earth, it has a critical role in establishing the overall environmental conditions on Earth. In fact, it is the interaction between the Earth's climate and life that ultimately controls living conditions on this planet. This means that the biodiversity crisis is just as important as the climate crisis and, just as for climate, the United Nations has established a panel of scientists (Intergovernmental Panel on Biodiversity and Ecosystem Services, IPBES) to advise governments on the state of biodiversity and assess how humans are impacting it. Because of the enormous impact of fisheries on ocean nature, IPBES identifies "exploitation" (fishing) as the primary cause of biodiversity loss in the ocean.

Although the impact of climate change on ocean biodiversity is not nearly as well studied or understood as the effects of fisheries, IPBES still, however, identifies it as the second most important threat to ocean biodiversity. For biodiversity on land, IPBES ranks climate change as being only the fifth most important threat (behind land use change, exploitation, introduction of alien species and pollution). That climate change impacts should be more important for ocean than for land organisms is hardly surprising given that so much of the change in heat storage on Earth is occurring in the ocean. All organisms (including humans) respond to a warmer world in the same way.

When conditions become too warm or if food becomes less available, organisms that can move away do so. Therefore, many marine organisms are currently on the move. The distribution of warm-loving species is moving poleward, while the area that can support cold-loving species is shrinking. New ecosystems are being formed. In some cases, these new ecosystems are "unbalanced," i.e., dominated by a single species that has no natural predators in the new environment. While others may function well, they may not necessarily support human activities, such as fishing, in the manner we expect.

There are, of course, also organisms in the ocean that cannot move away from adverse conditions. They have no choice but to remain and, if conditions become too detrimental, to die. Corals are a good example here and most scientists agree that even if the climate goals of the Paris Agreement are met, we will likely lose the magnificent coral reefs that adorn tropical and sub-tropical coasts. The problem here is that corals survive with the help of small organisms (zoozanthellae) living within them. When it becomes too warm, the corals, for unknown reasons, expel their zoozanthellae. This causes the corals to lose their color. This is called a "bleaching event." Often, bleaching leads to death of the corals.

Human impacts on the ocean are enormous and yet most of us know little about the ocean and seldom give it or its nature a thought. We mistakenly assume that it is only people living near or working on the ocean who are most responsible for human impacts on the ocean and marine life but, in fact, we are all sinners when it comes to managing our relationship with the sea. We impact ocean nature through our harvesting of its fruits and by using it as a waste receptacle. Climate change is a waste issue (greenhouse gases), and it is not only CO_2 waste and heat that accumulate in the sea. Chemical pollution and plastic litter also abound.

The Apollo missions of the 1960s provided us with pictures of the Earth from space. These clearly show there is no pipeline that can carry our waste away from the Earth. They also show that almost three quarters of the Earth is covered by ocean. One of the reasons we like plastic is that it is essentially non-degradable in nature. Where did we imagine the plastic, we have been throwing out since the 1950s would end its life? Where else could it be than in the ocean?

Another famous quote from Karen Blixen is that "the cure for anything is salt water: sweat, tears or the sea" but the relationship between humans and the ocean is too unequal for the sea on its own to restore and maintain robust ecosystems as well as its role in the Earth's ecosystem. Tears will not help either. Only by our building respect for the ecosystem of which we are both a part and dependent upon into all of our activities can a healthy balance between humans and the ocean be restored.

Katherine Richardson is Professor in Biological Oceanography at Globe Institute and Leader of the University of Copenhagen's Sustainability Science Centre. The focus of her research is to better understand the role of biological processes and biodiversity on the cycling of carbon in the upper ocean and how this impacts food webs and the global carbon cycle. Most of her research has been on marine plankton (primarily phytoplankton). She has published numerous articles and books on these subjects.

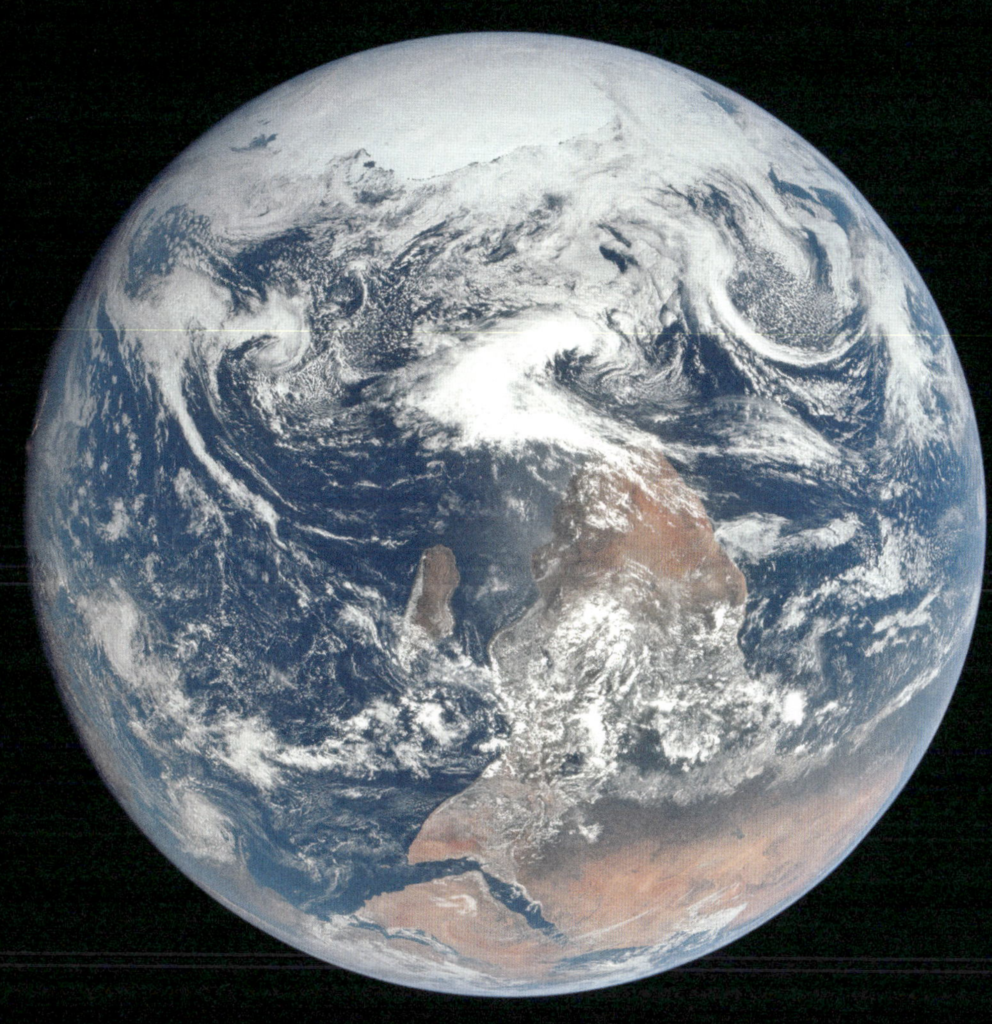

The first photograph of the planet in its entirety was taken in 1972 by an astronaut on the Apollo 17 mission. Because the crew later said the Earth looked like a marble, the sequence was named the "Blue Marble."

The third part of the exhibition explores how climate change and voracious exploitation of natural resources are putting marine ecosystems under pressure. In the age of globalisation, the ocean is becoming increasingly trafficked – crossed by container ships and cruise liners the size of small cities, while undersea internet cables tie our digital world together. For centuries, the ocean floor was thought to be barren and lifeless. Now it too is increasingly in the sights of mining companies, as it holds many of the rare metals to be used in the green transition. A debate is currently raging over who owns the deep sea, and whether fragile ecosystems should be disrupted because we need batteries for electric cars.

3.

Tales from the Human Sea

LENA MARIA THÜRING
Hanjin Palermo, 2015

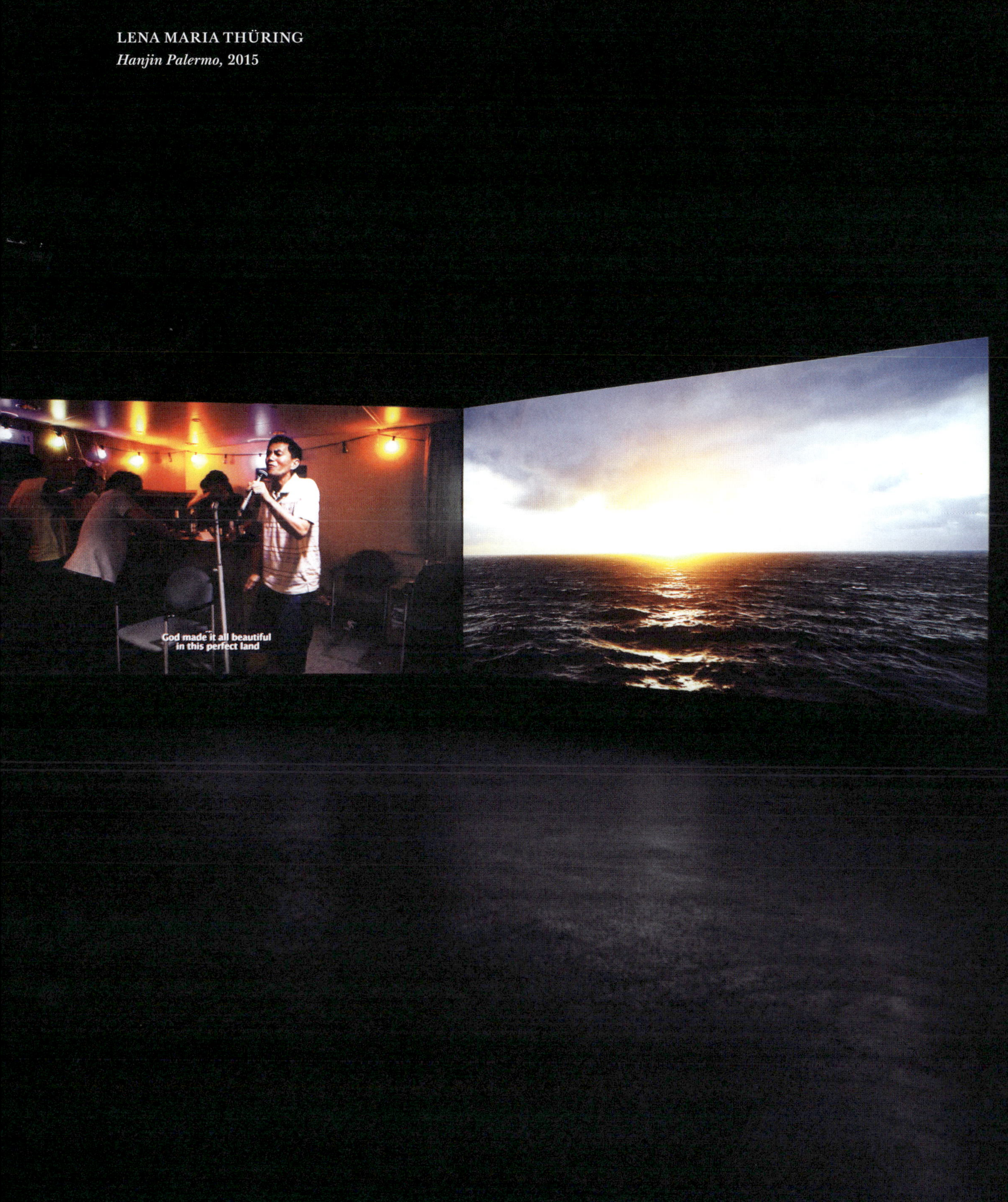

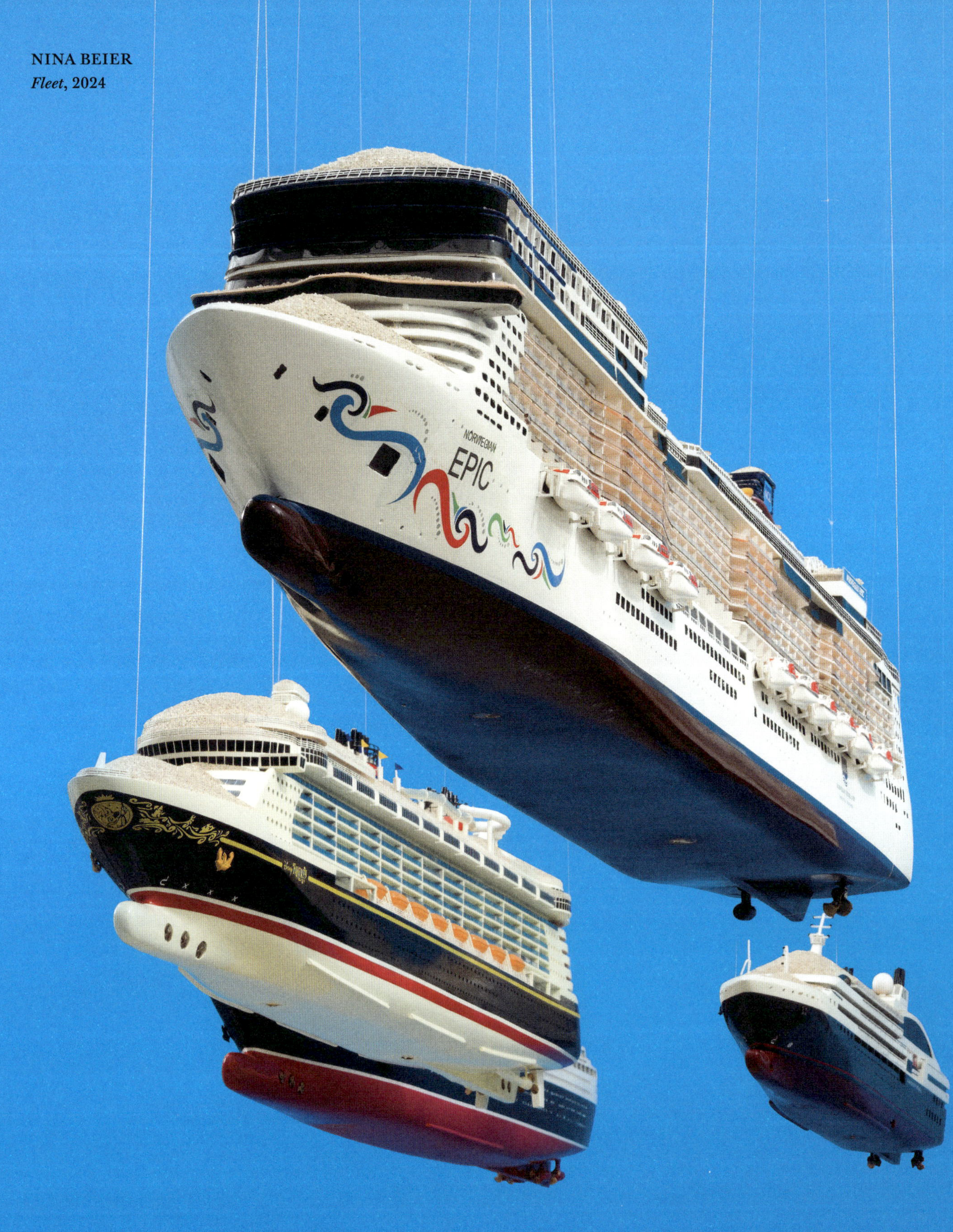

NINA BEIER
Fleet, 2024

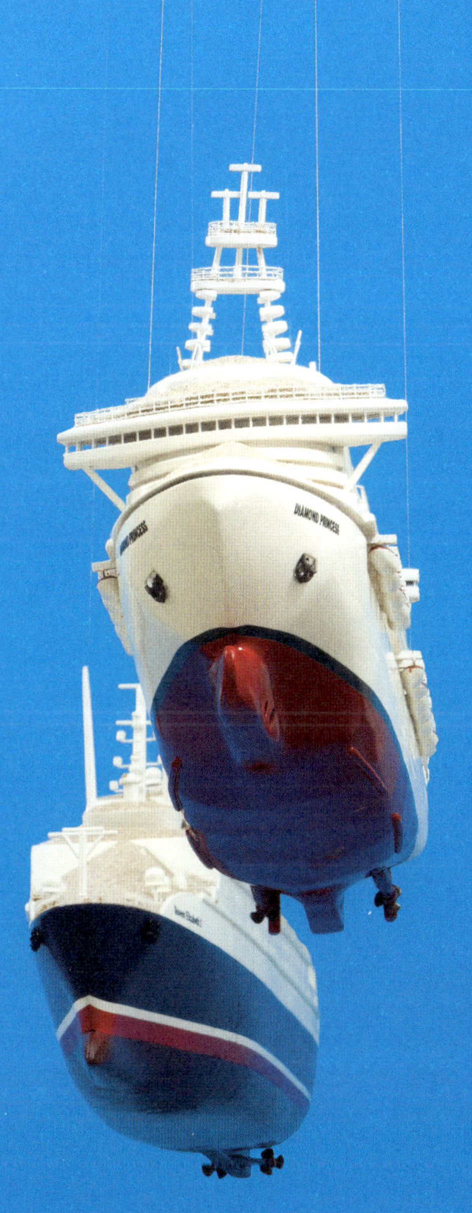
DIAMOND PRINCESS

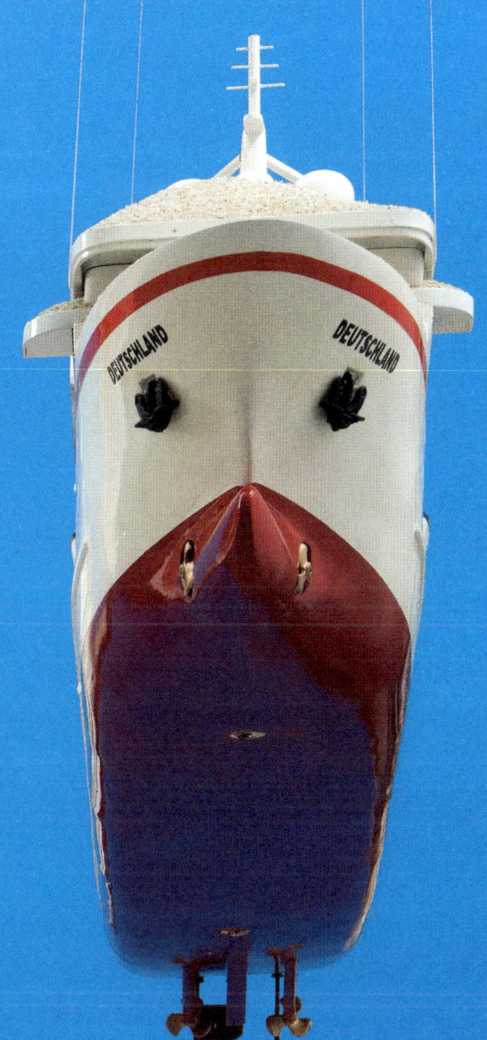
DEUTSCHLAND
DEUTSCHLAND

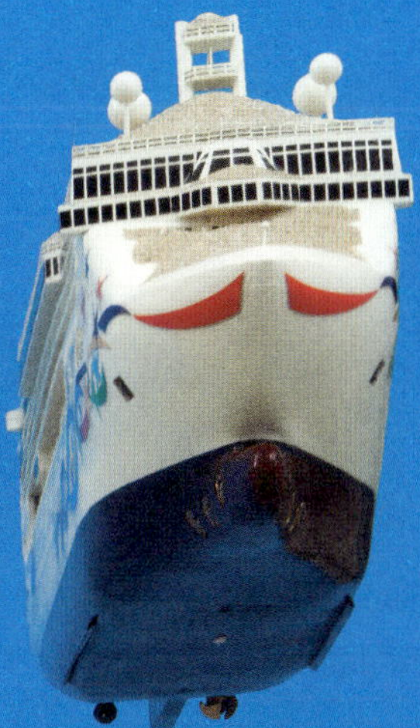

ALLAN SEKULA
Detail of *"Middle Passage", Chapter 3, Fish Story*, 1994

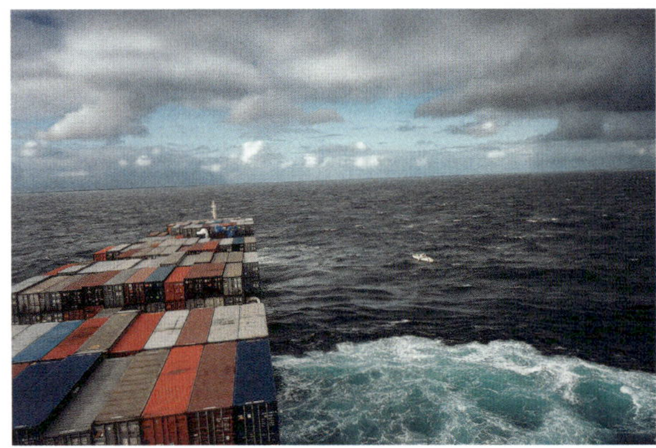

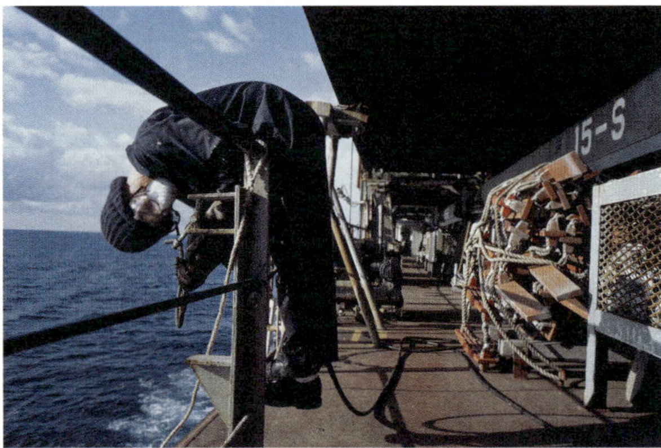

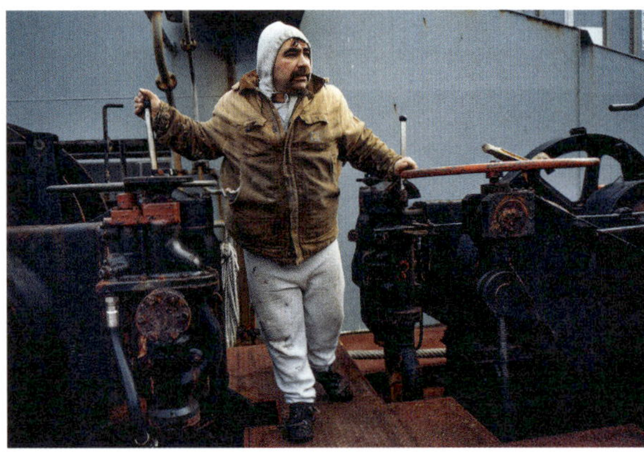

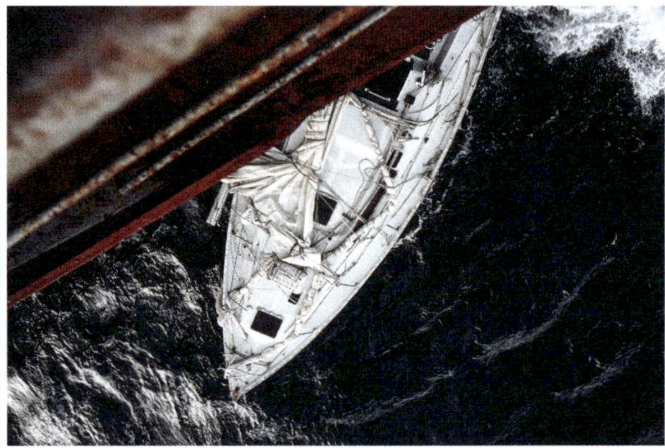

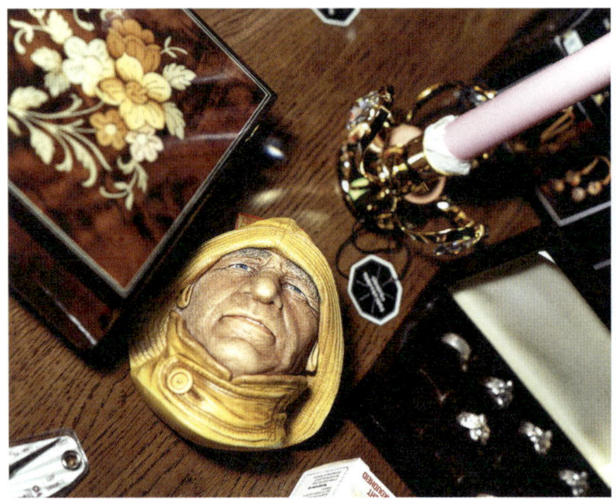

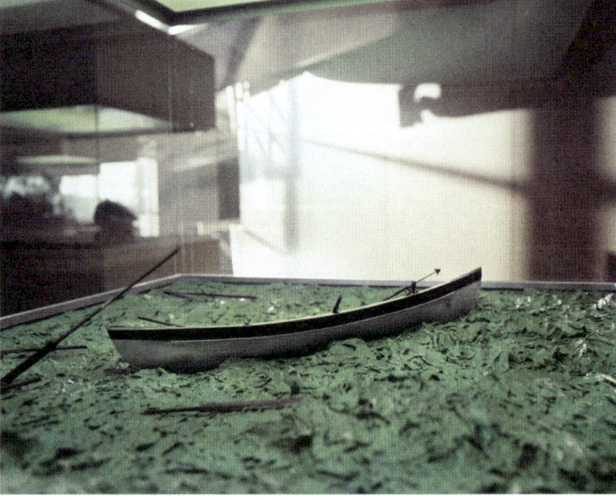

November 30, 1999

Dear Bill Gates,

I swam past your dream house the other day, but didn't stop to knock. Frankly, your underwater sensors had me worried. I would have liked to take a look at Winslow Homer's Lost on the Grand Banks. It's a great painting, but, speaking as a friend and fellow citizen, at $30 million you paid too much.

HIGHEST PRICE EVER PAID FOR AN AMERICAN PAINTING!!!

So why are you so interested in a picture of two poor lost dory fishermen, momentarily high on a swell, peering into a wall of fog? They're about as high as they're ever going to be, unless the sea gets uglier. They are going to die you know, and it won't be a pretty death.

And as for you Bill, when you're on the net, are you lost? Or found?

And the rest of us--lost or found--are we on it, or in it?

Your friend

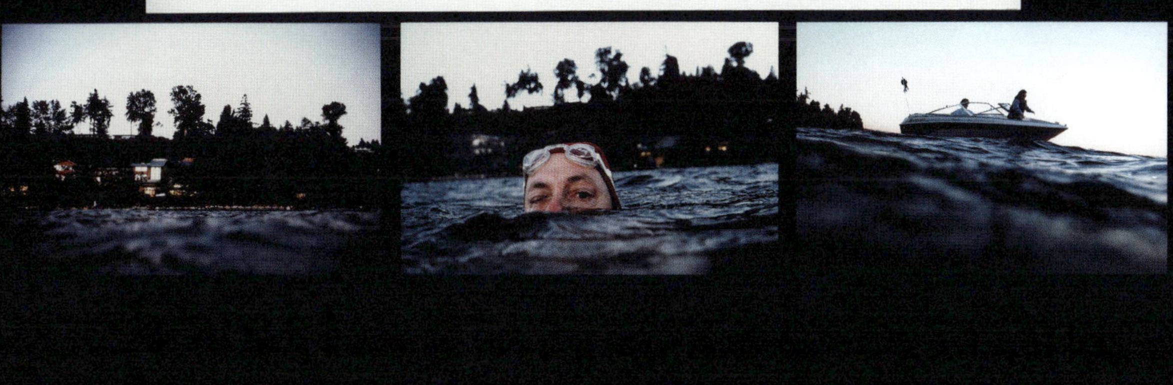

ALLAN SEKULA
Dear Bill Gates, 1999
The photographer, writer and cultural theorist Allan Sekula (1951-2013) looked at social and economic structures in the late-capitalist world. Fusing performance, photography and text, *Dear Bill Gates* questions the Microsoft founder's acquisition of the Winslow Homer painting *Lost on the Grand Banks.*

KIRSTEN JUSTESEN
Mer Maid / Hav Frue, 1990

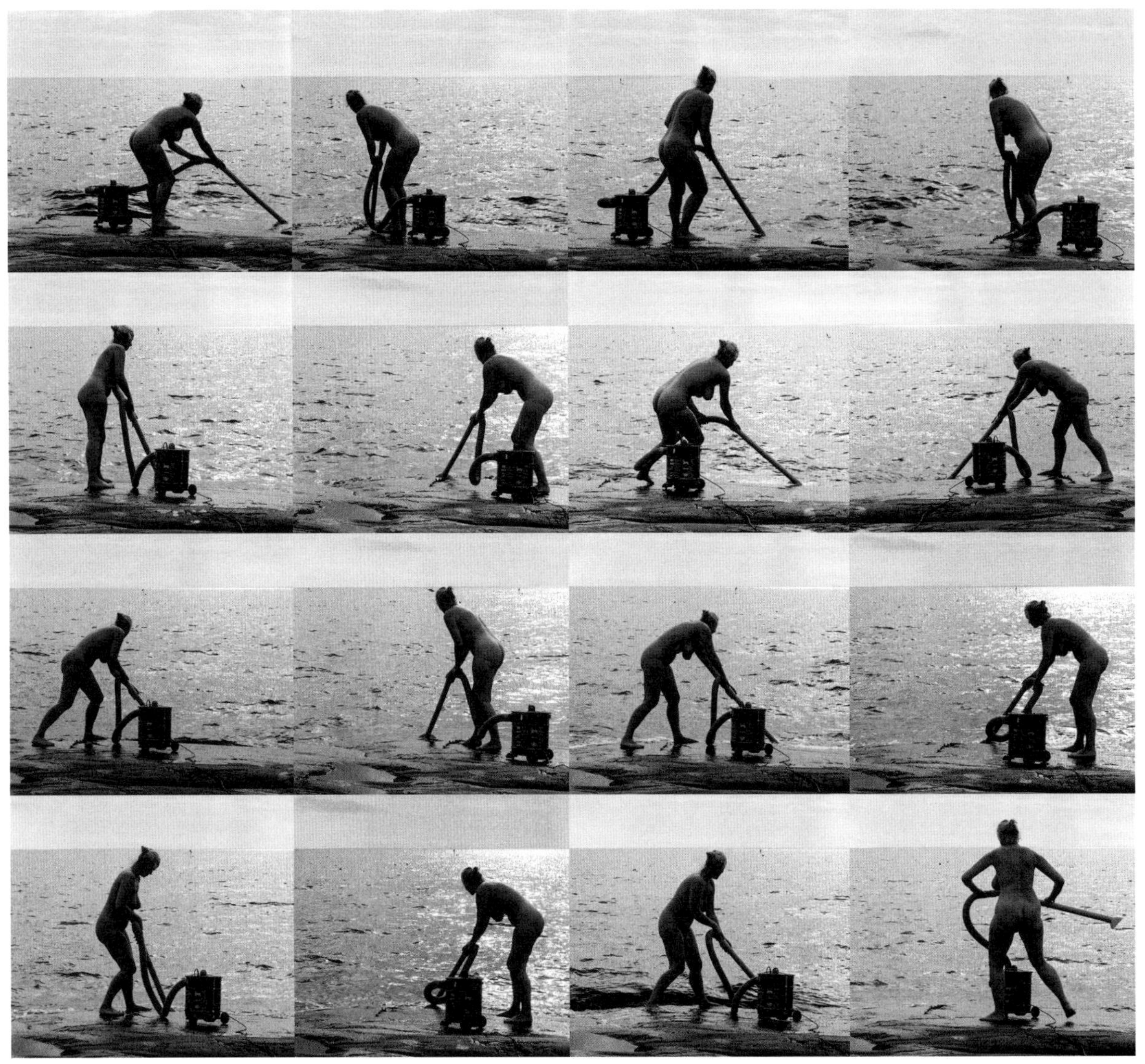

Opposite page:
NICEAUNTIES
Stills from *Auntlantis*, 2024

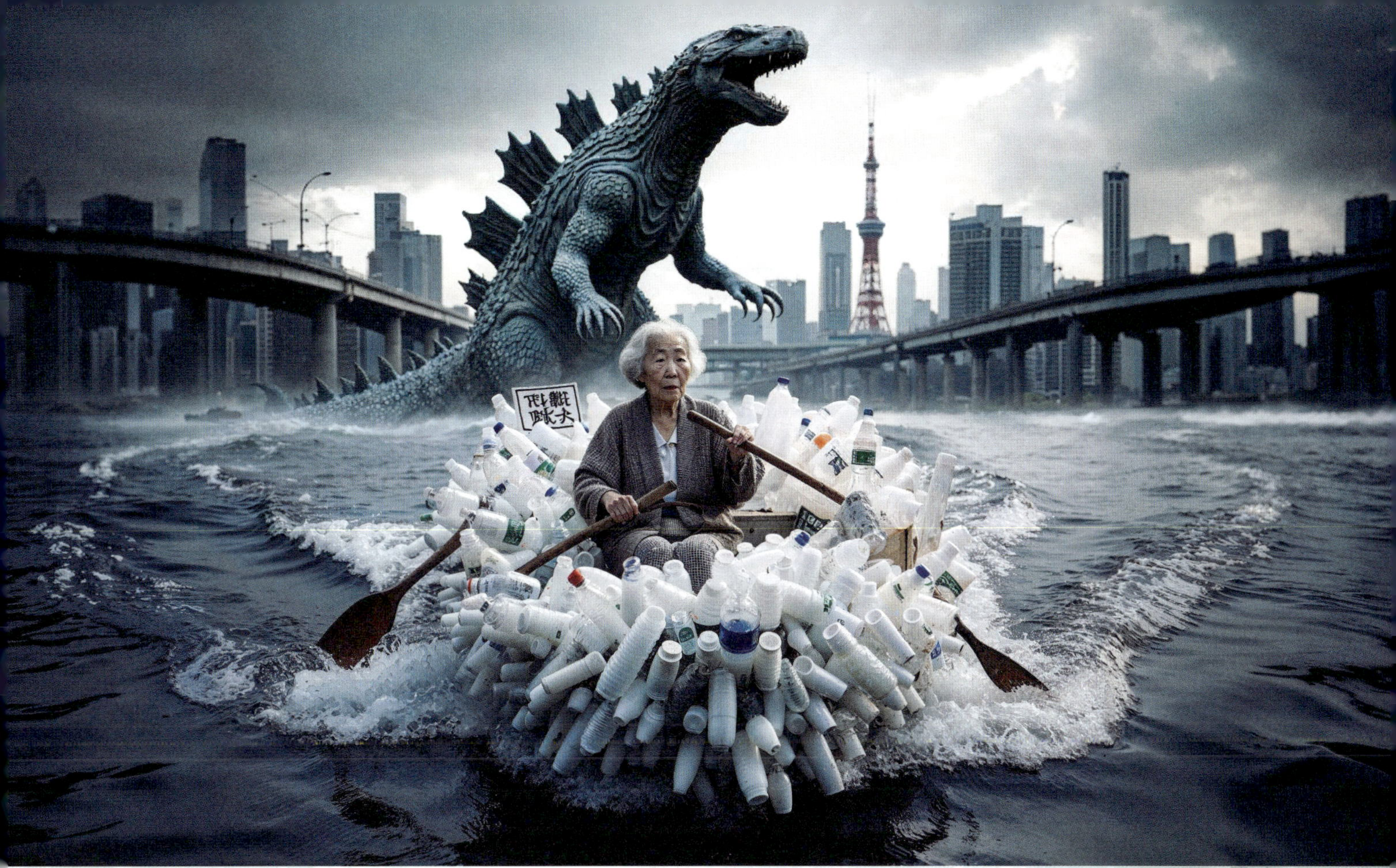

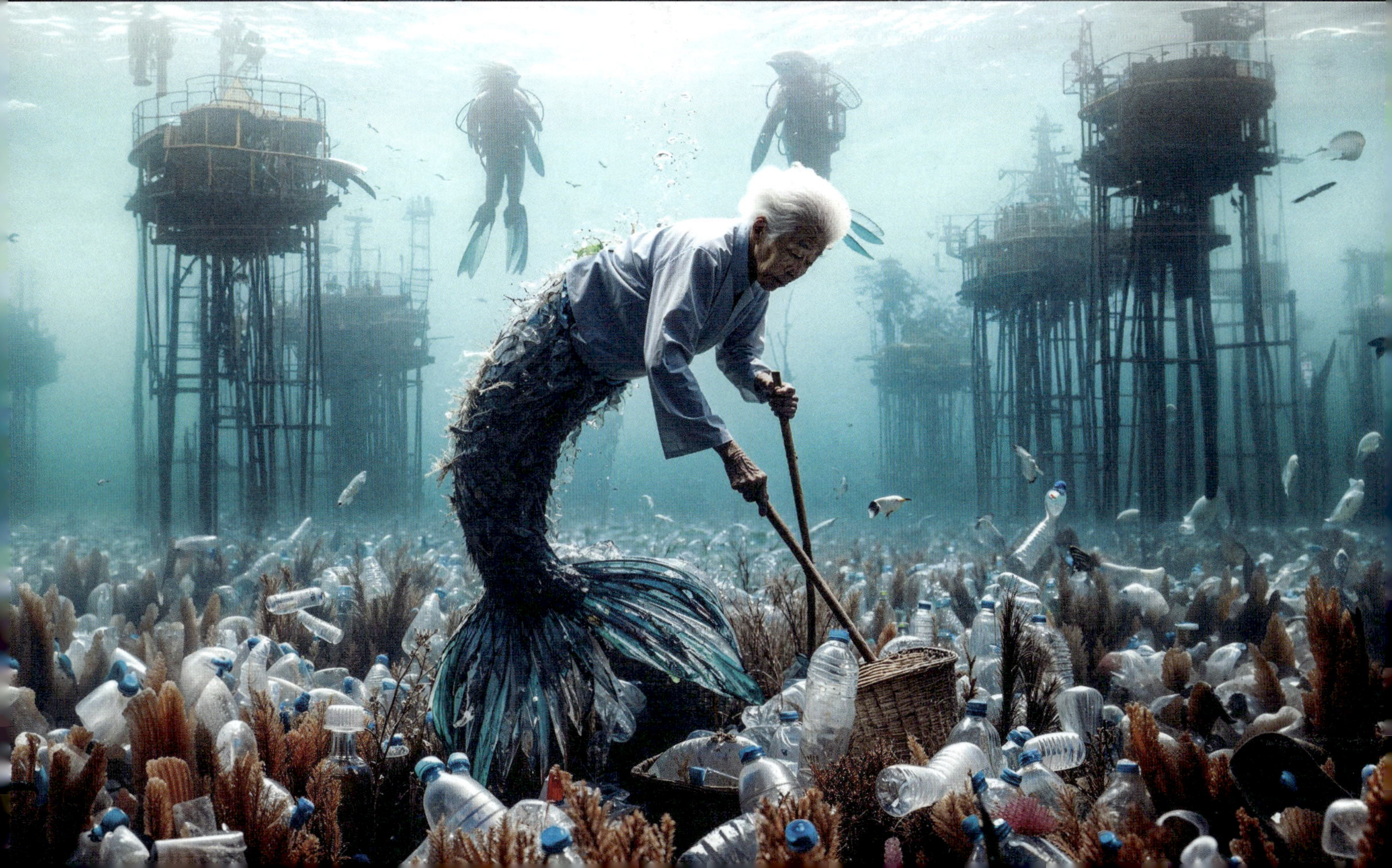

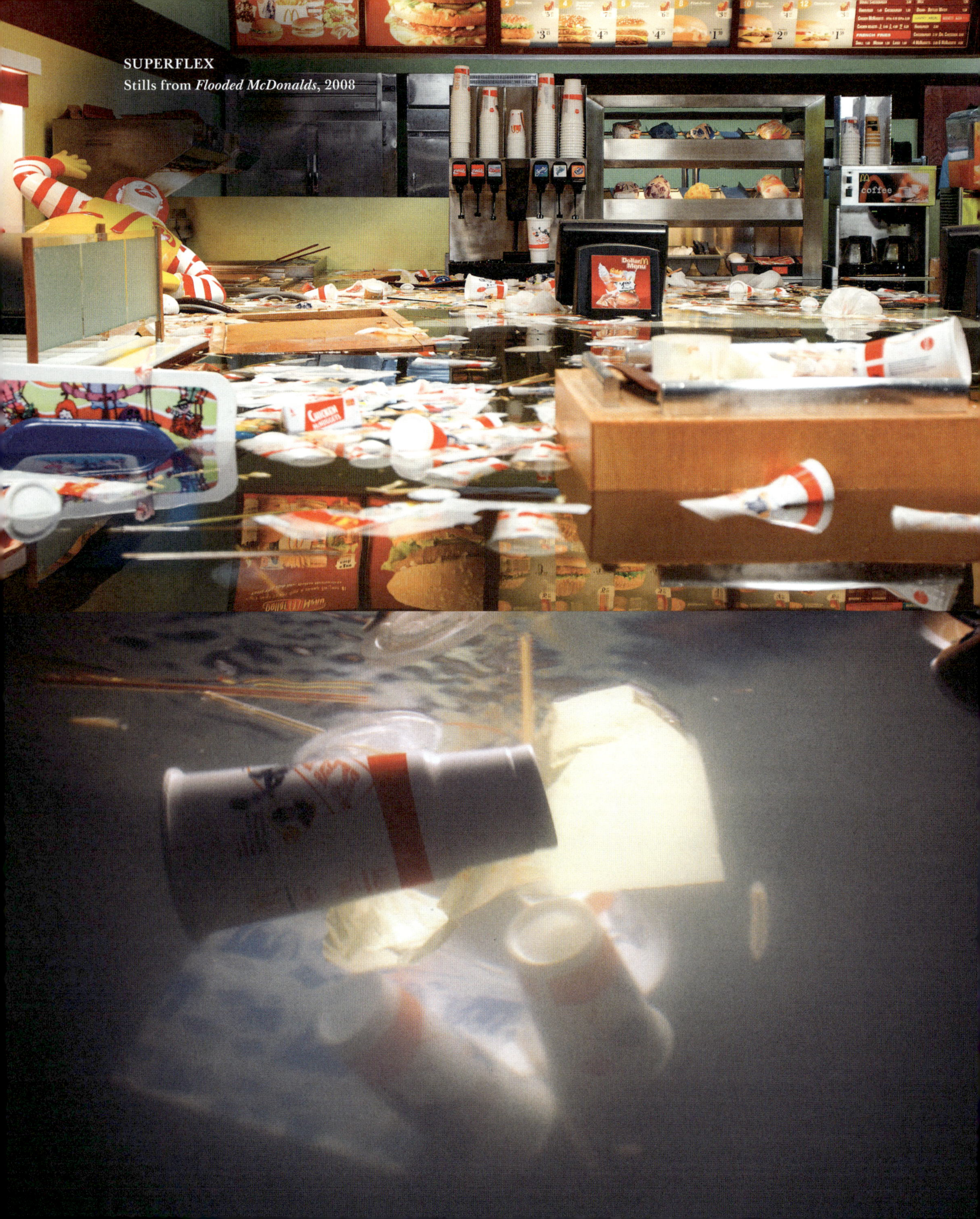

SUPERFLEX
Stills from *Flooded McDonalds*, 2008

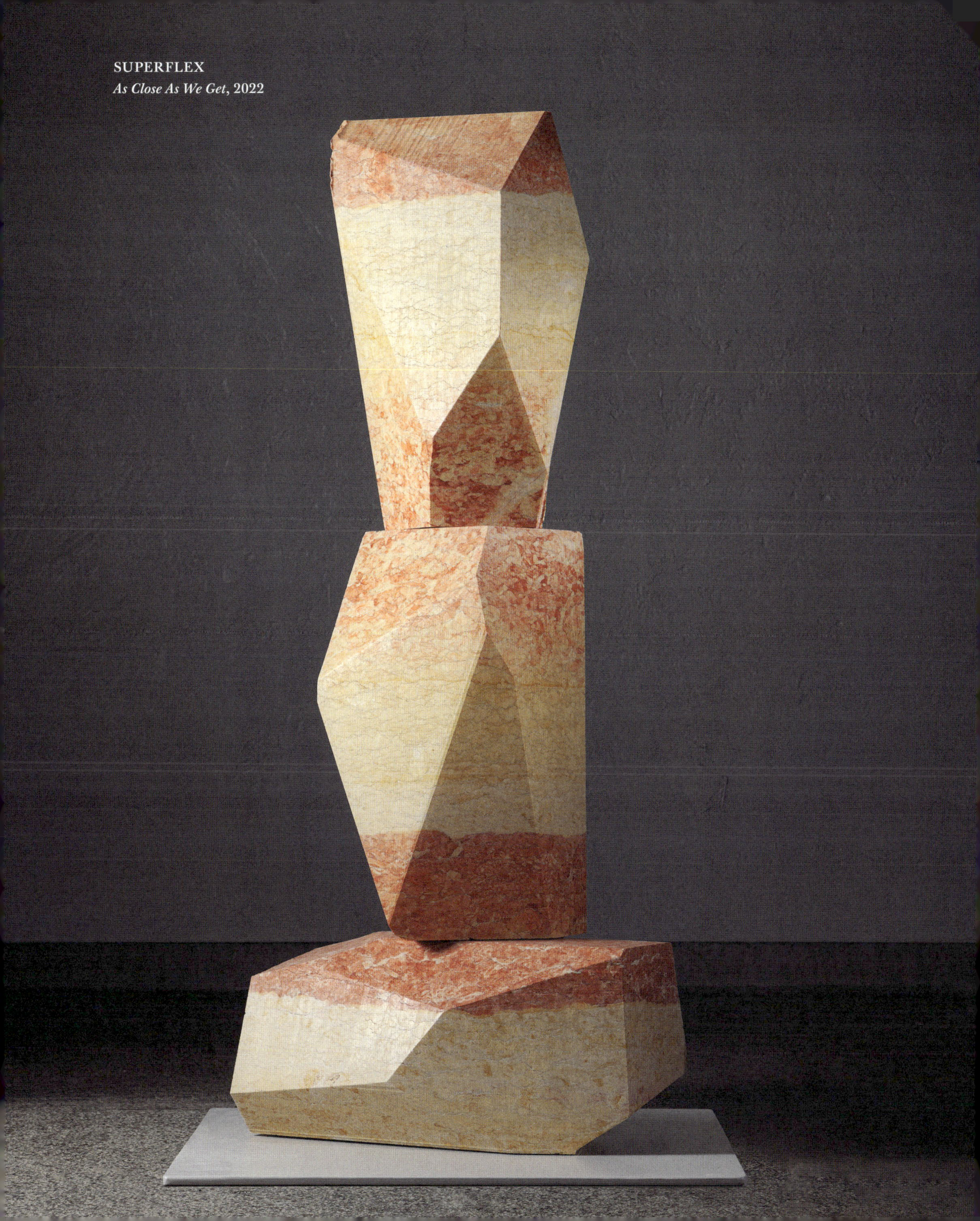

SUPERFLEX
As Close As We Get, 2022

PIERRE HUYGHE
Zoodram 2, 2010/2021

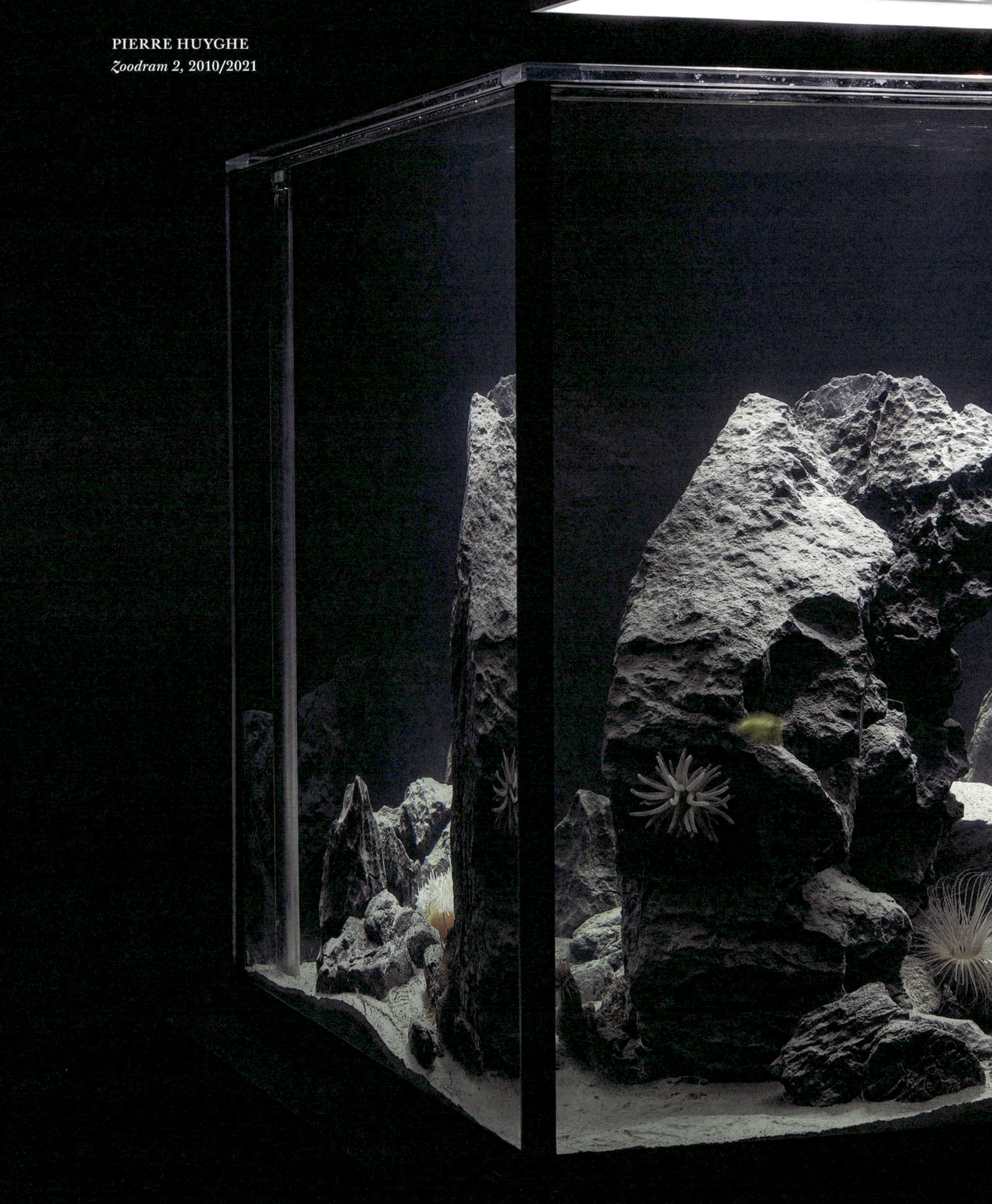

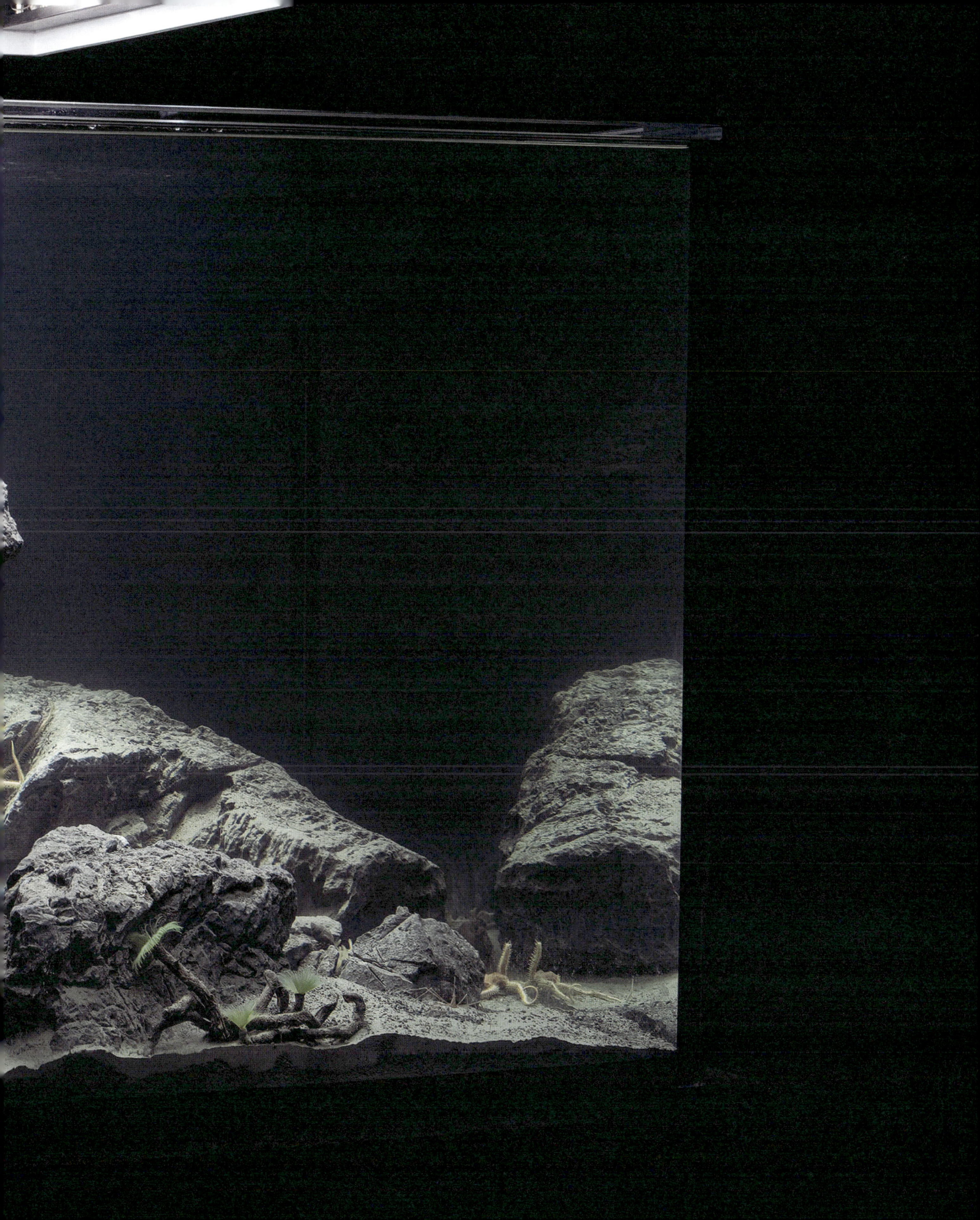

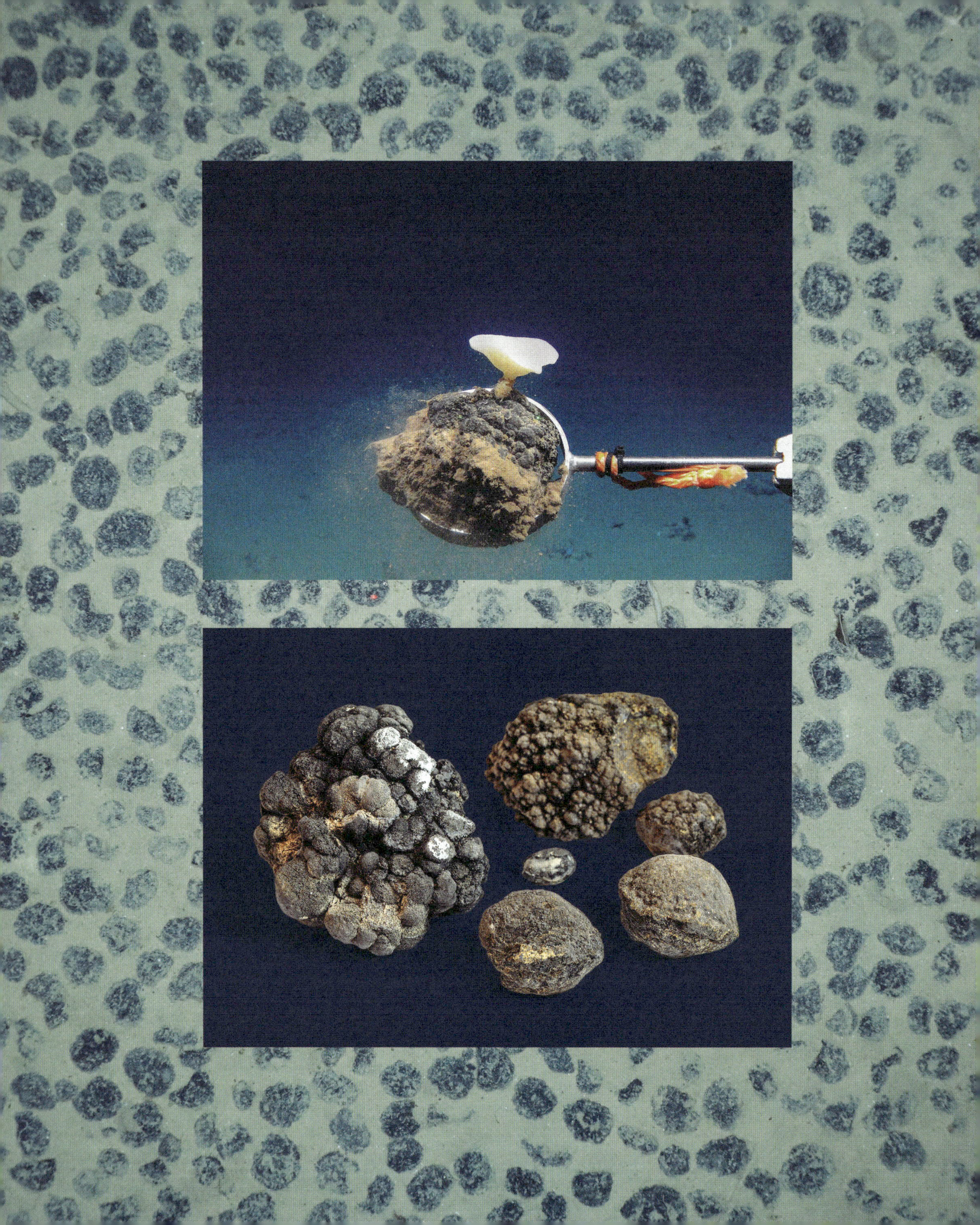

HOWARDENA PINDELL

Deep Sea #2, 2024

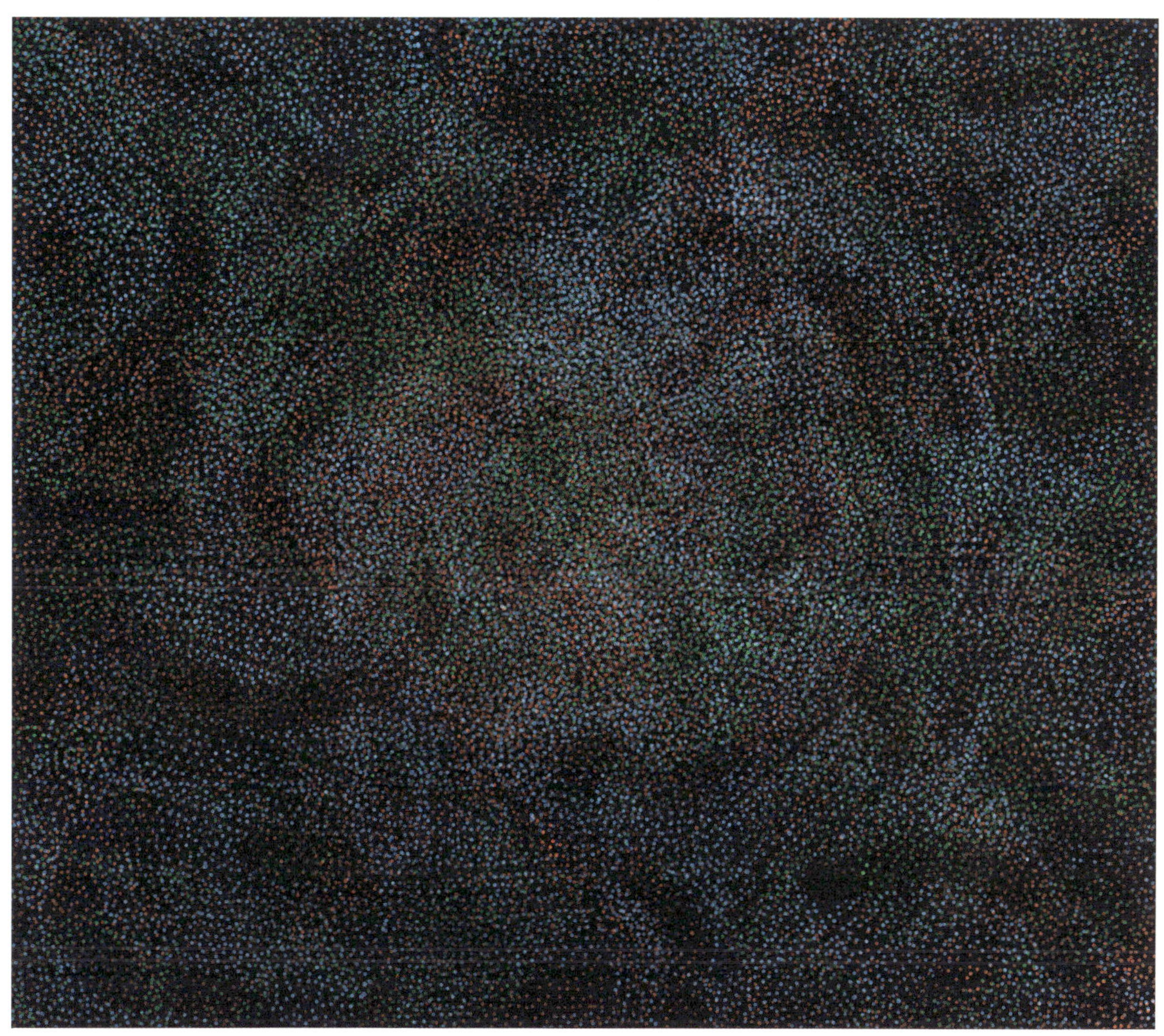

Opposite page:
Manganese nodules contain metals like nickel, copper and cobalt that are used in the green transition (solar panels, windmills, electric car batteries). Allowing mining companies to remove them from the seabed risks the collapse of a rich variety of deep-sea life and vital biogeochemical cycles.
Top and background: Manganese nodules from the so-called Clarion-Clipperton Zone, a 4.5 million sq. km area in the Pacific ocean between Hawaii and Mexico.
Bottom: Manganese nodules from the Pacific and Atlantic Oceans.

TREVOR PAGLEN

Colombia-Florida Subsea Fiber (CFX-1) NSA/GCHQ-Tapped Undersea Cable Caribbean Sea, 2015

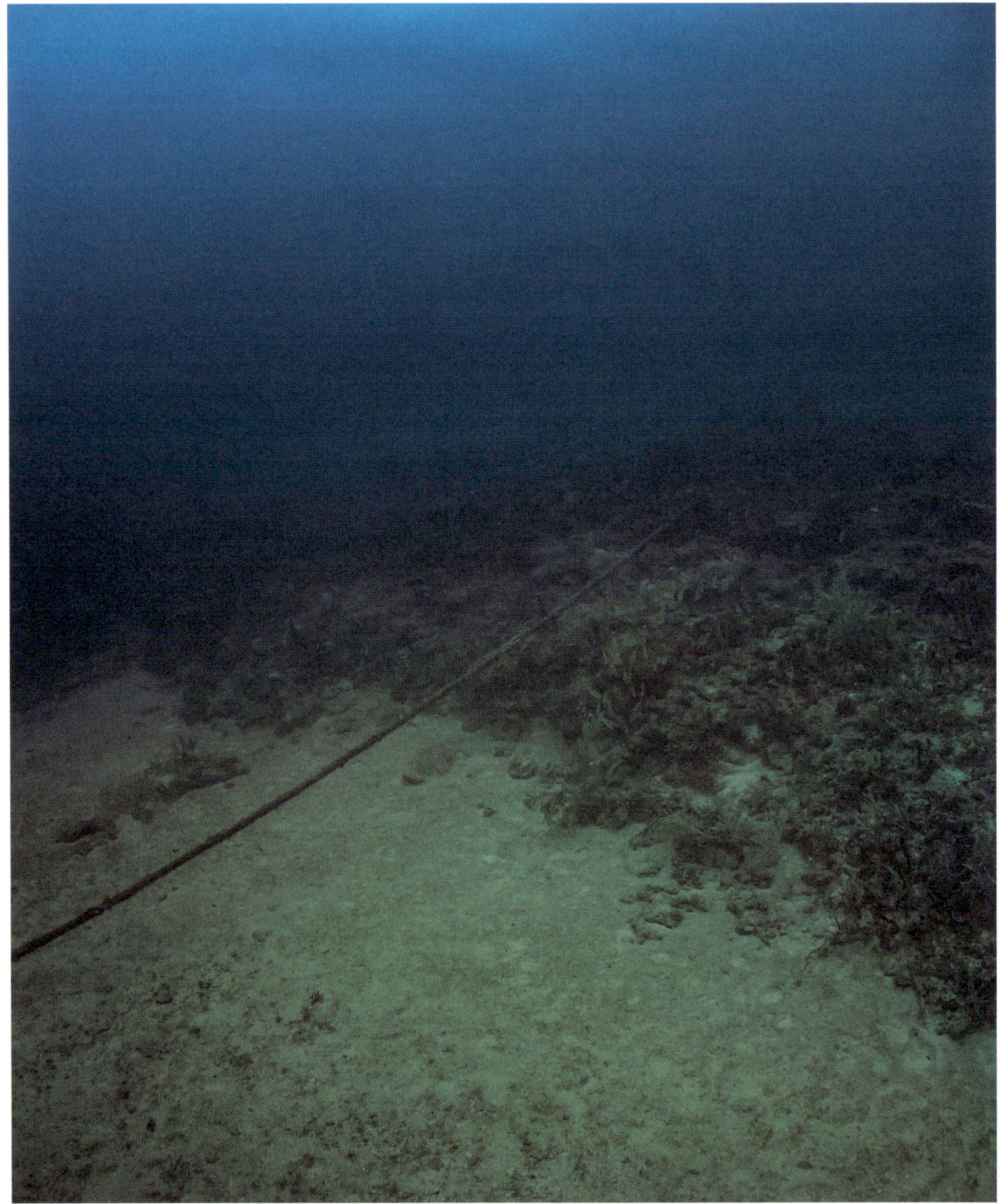

TARYN SIMON

Transantlantic Sub-Marine Cables Reaching Land, VSNL International, Avon, New Jersey, 2007

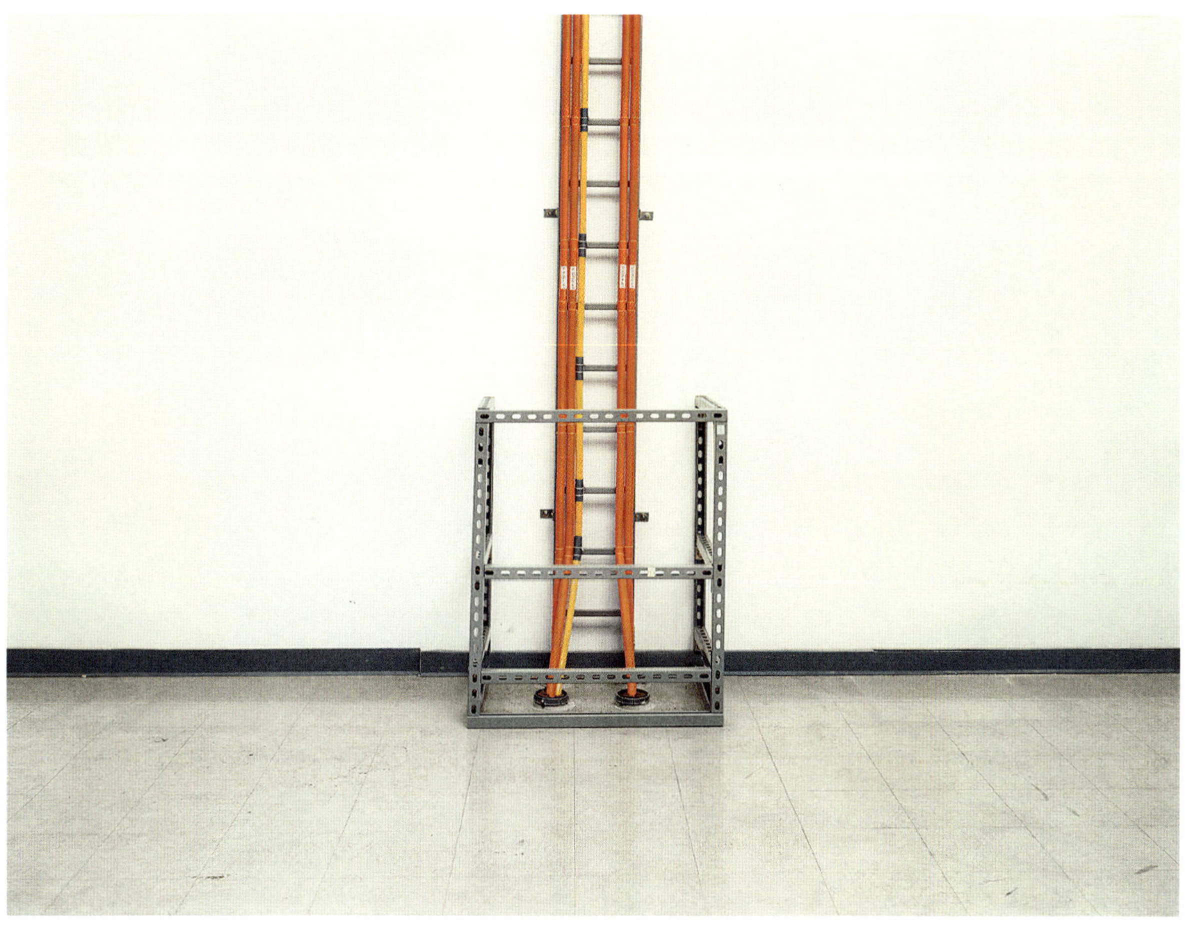

Transatlantic Sub-Marine Cables Reaching Land
VSNL International
Avon, New Jersey

These VSNL sub-marine telecommunications cables extend 8,037.4 miles across the Atlantic Ocean. Capable of transmitting over 60 million simultaneous voice conversations, these underwater fiber-optic cables stretch from Saunton Sands in the United Kingdom to the coast of New Jersey. The cables run below ground and emerge directly into the VSNL International headquarters, where signals are amplified and split into distinctive wavelengths enabling transatlantic phone calls and internet transmissions.

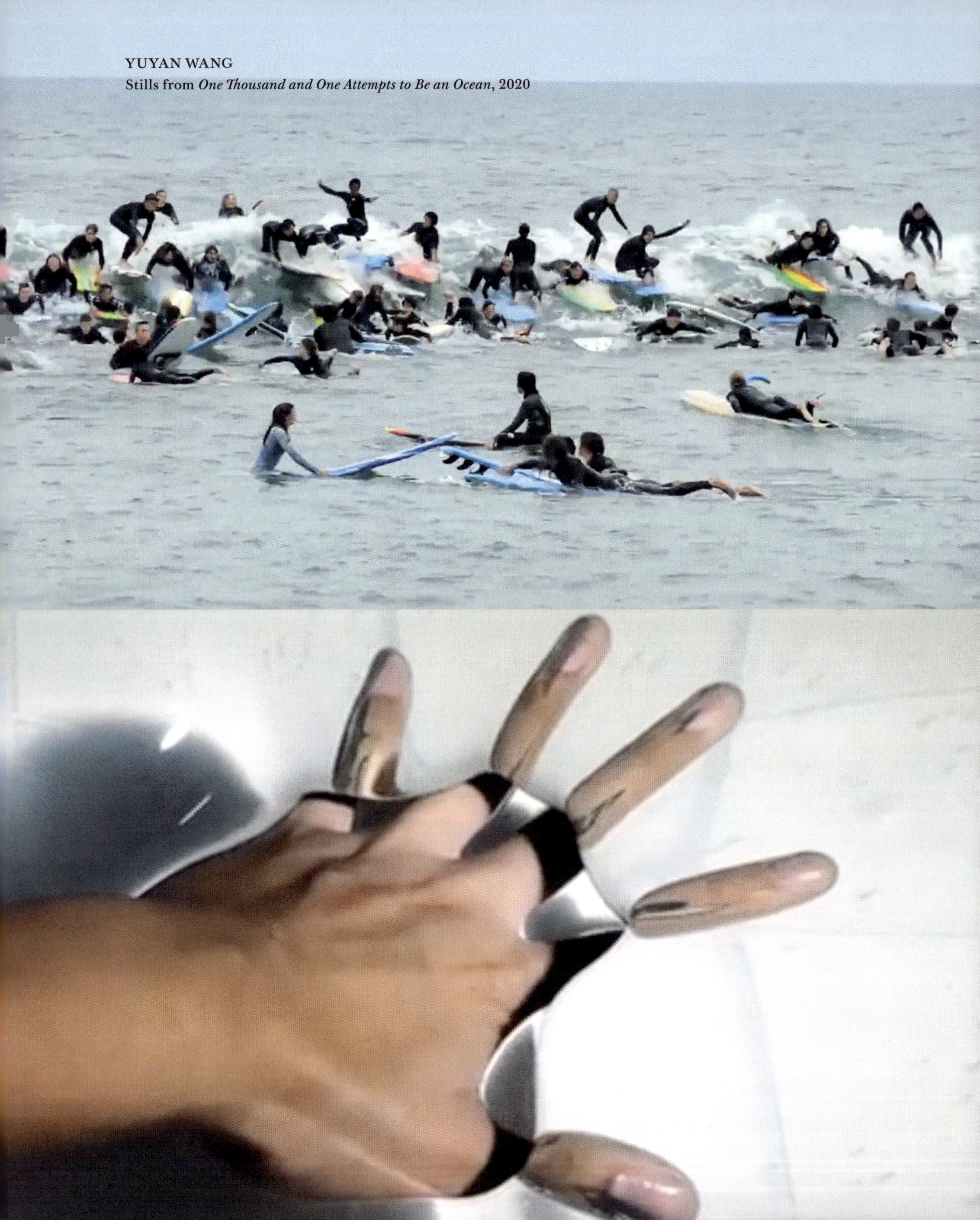

YUYAN WANG
Stills from *One Thousand and One Attempts to Be an Ocean*, 2020

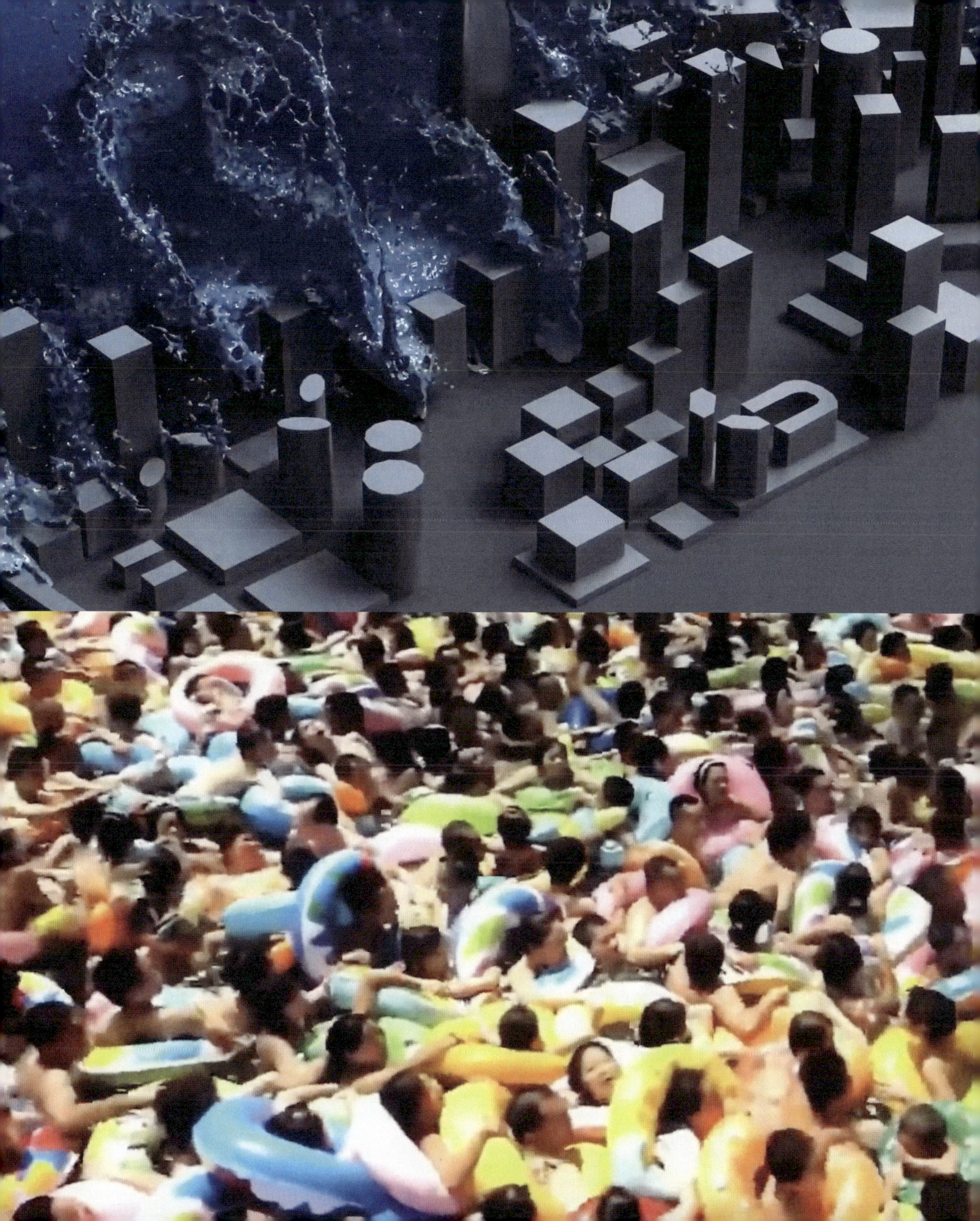

The Sea, the Human and Nature

Dorthe Jørgensen

In *Havbrevene* (The Sea Letters, 2018), the Danish writer Siri Ranva Hjelm Jacobsen offers a poetic portrayal of what oceanographers and environmental scientists have long said: that the sea, which is essential to all life on Earth, is threatened by human behaviour. The book takes the form of letters between the Atlantic Ocean and the Mediterranean Sea. The Atlantic recounts the birth of "the creepers" and the far younger Mediterranean their demise. Jacobsen's message is critical: we creepers are mistreating the seas, our maternal origins, which are suffering from our behaviour. This message can also be put in academic terms to no great effect. For decades, reports have been written on the critical state of the oceans, but we haven't changed our behaviour. Poetry, however, can do something science cannot: it can make things come alive. In *Havbrevene*, the Atlantic and the Mediterranean appear as living beings with feelings, thoughts and desires. This poetic representation brings the sea closer to us. It lets us empathize with it and better understand how it is doing.

Poetry doesn't only make existing things come alive; it can also give birth to new things. From poetry grows empathy and understanding – or spiritual life – just as organic life grows from the sea. Originally, poetry, philosophy, theology and science were connected, but over time they've become separate discourses. In the 1600s, philosophy began to liberate itself from theology, which created new conditions for science, which no longer had to legitimize itself in the eyes of theology. Meanwhile, science, which could now focus on empirical discoveries and rational explanations, was emptied of poetry and philosophy. Moreover, poetry was seen as only capable of containing feeling, as opposed to knowledge, and at most, as a source of entertainment for those with a taste for it. Finally, philosophy, which was still guided by ideas and thinking in wholes, wanted to become a science in the new sense of the word. From a poetical-philosophical-theological-scientific approach to the world, we therefore moved toward a one-sided scientific approach, driven by the intellect.

This modern scientific approach, as far as the sea is concerned, has excelled at describing its biology and explaining the dangers it faces, but it doesn't make us understand the sea's intrinsic value or the existential significance it has historically had for humans. At the same time, modern science dismisses older ways of thinking and formulations as dated. But is it wise to ignore ideas and symbols that have been essential to others before us? The alternative to this insistence on progress, however, is not to seek to recover what has been lost in its original form. History is neither linear nor circular, but rather a multilayered tapestry composed of endless threads. It contains different histories that represent both actualized and not-yet-actualized possibilities. Maybe we could learn something from the thoughts of the past – and from the sea? Why does the sea draw us? What does it mean to us, and what do we mean to it? How does our thinking affect the sea, and what does the sea do to our well-being? These questions invite reflections on philosophy and the history of ideas, with which I will argue for an expanded view of nature and a poetic approach to the sea.

The modern view of nature

In recent years, many books have been written about nature that, for a change, are not absent of poetry or philosophy. Examples include the American philosopher John Sallis' *The Return of Nature* (2016), the Italian philosopher Emanuele Coccia's *The Life of Plants* (2016) and the British religious thinker Karen Armstrong's *Sacred Nature* (2022). There are also several recent books that focus on the sea, including the German philosopher Gunter Scholtz's *Philosophie des Meeres* (Philosophy of the Ocean, 2016), the American philosopher David Farell Krell's *The Sea* (2018) and the French philosopher Laurence Devillairs' *Petite philosophie de la Mer* (A Little Philosophy of the Sea, 2022). These books contain critiques of the modern view of nature and propose a deeper understanding of nature as well as its significance for us. Coccia, for example, suggests a new philosophy of nature based on plant life to heal the broken bond between humans and nature, and Devillairs draws lessons from the sea and all that is proper to it.

This is a welcome development. For a long time, we have lived with a view of nature characterized by the grave omission of the fact that everything small is a part of something greater, and that greatness can be experienced in small things. In this view of nature, the human is the subject (of its cognitive exercises), and nature is the object (of these). Humans have souls and consciousness; nature is soulless matter, disenchanted. Humans investigate nature, analyse and categorize its individual parts, while nature exists at our disposal. This *dualistic* view of nature has inverted the proportions of the universe by making nature into a small thing in the large hands of humans. The result, as far as the sea is concerned, is that the sea and humans are not seen as parts of a greater common whole. They are separated, transformed into consumer and natural resources, and we can consume as we wish. Or so we thought.

However, there have been many other philosophical formulations of nature over time. Around the year 1800, Romantic and Idealist thinkers such as the German poet Novalis and the German philosopher F.W.J. von Schelling saw nature as a manifestation of spirit. For these thinkers, humans and nature were parallel parts of a greater whole. Later, the Austrian philosopher Martin Buber similarly reflected in *I and Thou* (1923) on the possibility of humans relating to nature (and everything else) as a "you" rather than an "it." When we relate to something or someone as an "it," we objectify them; we don't speak *with* them but only *about* them. If instead, we relate to them as a "you," they appear as living beings we are in *dialogue* with, whom we feel for and take consideration of. In an I-it relationship to the sea, the sea serves only to satisfy our own needs. The modern view of nature is an expression of this I-it relationship, and the consequence is the current state of the sea. In an I-you relationship, however, the sea has intrinsic value and is treated with respect. We find traces of this I-you relationship in recent books, including *Havbrevene*, in which the seas don't only speak with each other, but also bring the reader into dialogue with them.

Philosophy of nature

The reader's experience of the sea as a "you" is enabled by the text's poetic vitalization of the sea and the receptiveness of the reader. Together these enable the empathy that is the condition of conversation and thereby also of comprehension. In §40 of the *Critique of Judgment* (1790), the

German philosopher Immanuel Kant writes that genuine connection requires transcendence. Kant differentiates between the ways of thinking appertained to understanding, reason and judgment, respectively. He describes judgment's way of thinking as *expanded* because it is both empathetic and transcendent – and precisely therefore, it can link understanding and reason's different ways of thinking. In judgment's way of thinking, the power of imagination flourishes, which enables us to empathize with others; and because judgment's way of thinking also involves transcendence to something greater, that doesn't mean one needs to sacrifice oneself. Without losing sight of anyone, neither oneself nor anyone else, we encounter, in judgment's expanded way of thinking, the idea of the good, which is the condition for acting in our *shared* interest.

Kant recognized the necessity of an expanded way of thinking at a time when the consequences of modern thought were beginning to be felt. The more science was emptied of poetry and philosophy, the more it came to represent rational understanding without reason or judgment. The same could also be said of philosophy, which has itself striven to become a science in the modern sense of the word. The result is the dualistic view of nature, in which humanity exists at a remove from nature instead of being part of it; nature is thus seen as something "out there." As the Danish theologian K.E. Løgstrup describes in *Ophav og omgivelse* (Origin and Environment, 1984), modern humans understand nature not as their origin, but only as something surrounding them. Among other things, this view of nature prompts us to think and talk about the sea as a means to an end without intrinsic value, as even happens in contemporary critical discourses on the state of the sea. Arguments for restoration are rarely made for the sake of the sea, but rather to ensure our own survival.

Modern thought, which is driven by rational understanding, privileges concepts and is only interested in the particular: it is one-dimensional. A more reason-driven way of thinking, which privileges ideas, thinks in wholes and is therefore multidimensional, can be found in texts from the Renaissance and Romantic period, including the Italian philosopher Giordano Bruno's *Cause, Principle and Unity* (1584), Schelling's *Ideas for a Philosophy of Nature* (1797), Novalis' *The Novices of Sais* (1802) and the Danish scientist H.C. Ørsted's *The Soul in Nature* (1850). Such works of natural philosophy could provide inspiration now, as researchers in many fields are attempting to change our view of nature through ecophilosophy, deep ecology and biocentricism. However, few people nowadays – among them the French philosopher Jean-Louis Chrétien – are willing to really study tradition and actualize its hidden potential. But in the aforementioned books, a brave reader will meet thinkers who fostered the notion of a creative force in nature, which they called the soul, the spirit or the light of nature. Nature isn't just matter. We are part of nature not only insofar as we come from the sea, but also because there is spirit common to it and to us. As Schelling would say, nature is visible spirit, and spirit is invisible nature.

The holy sea

Spirit is omnipresent; it transcends all. Spirit challenges thought, which must reach as far as the imagination takes it without fanaticism. If anything, this *expands* the mind. At the same time, the idea of spirit in nature helps us to comprehend the sea's historical symbolic function. Old Levantine mythologies recount a primordial darkness, from which the firmament, or first land, emerged and the first gods were born. In the Bible's creation narrative, we also find a primordial darkness in the forms of the water God's spirit floats above, before He gathers the waters and calls them "Seas." It may therefore not come as a surprise that in the Swedish author Pär Lagerkvist's novel *Pilgrim at Sea* (1962), the priest Giovanni believes that the sea knows all secrets because it is the oldest thing in the world. Perhaps more surprisingly, however, he claims that the sea can teach a human to live, and that the sea is the only thing he experiences as holy. Both because the sea is a clear symbol of "that which is greater than us," and because the idea of the sea's wisdom recalls something that Krell, Devillairs and others would sign off on.

First, the *symbolism*: the sea is both eternal and infinite. In evolutionary history, the origins of life exist in the World Ocean, where they are invisible to the naked eye. Additionally, large parts of the ocean's depths remain unturned and contain forms of life we can only imagine. At the same time, we see forces in the sea that are so powerful that Kant, in the *Critique of Judgment*, cites the turbulent sea as an example of the *sublime*. In fact, according to Kant, it is not the sea that is sublime but human reason. Historically, however, God has been described this way, described as both *beautiful* and *sublime*, as the sea is too. The sea reflects the sky in more than one sense. As Krell recounts in *The Sea*, the sea can rock us like we were still in our mothers' bellies, and therefore be *beautiful*, but as Kant claims, it can also both threaten and lure us in and thus seem *sublime*; and if we attempt to deny its power, it can crush us.

Next, the *wisdom*: Lagerkvist's priest suggests that the way to discover the soothing and threatening wisdom of the sea is by *surrender* – to become indifferent to the conflicts and efforts of daily life and rather let oneself be "carried, aimless, out into the unknown," to submit to "uncertainty as the only certainty, the only really dependable thing when all's said and done."[1] Krell and Devillairs too argue for a submission to the sea, which they describe as both difficult and delightful. According to the priest, the act of surrender can offer peace, and only the sea, which itself never finds rest, can provide this rest. The sea can't give us security, but however ruthless it might be, it can give us peace. It can rage like the Old Testament God and demand humility and awe, but it is also gracious. In Krell's account of the longing to become one with the sea, however, surrender is a kind of utopia; our survival instincts are always getting in our own way. In addition, Devillairs focusses more on opening the mind to the freedom symbolized by the sea than surrender, but she too acknowledges the healing power of the sea – the peace – though she never calls the sea "holy."

Intrinsic value

What is great, divine or absolute has, by definition, *intrinsic value*, which, according to the ancient Greeks, means *beauty*. In antiquity, the beautiful, or *to kalon* in Greek, was not just what was pleasing but what had intrinsic value. For the Greeks, philosophy and philosophical truth had intrinsic value; later, the medieval Church Fathers saw God and Christianity the same way, and today some would talk about love, others their own freedom. But where do we end up if we choose to see the sea through a lens that ascribes intrinsic value to it? Does this imply, in the vein of the priest's use of the word "holy," a pseudo-religious deification of the sea? Are we, as the subjects behind this lens, merely reproducing the anthropocentricism (centring humans) that the sea is enduring today? Or could it instead reveal a fertile mode of co-existence, in which we protect the diversity of the sea while the sea continues to support us?

When the priest calls the sea "holy," this might sound like a deification of the natural phenomenon of the sea. In line with the German American theologian Paul Tillich's "The Lost Dimension in Religion" (1958), we might, however, say that the priest has rediscovered a depth that modern humans have forgotten. From antiquity until the present day, humans have lived in two dimensions: a vertical dimension (of faith, the "ultimate concern" of the past) and a horizontal dimension (of daily life and the level of practical tasks). The vertical dimension gave the horizontal dimension structure and meaning but was lost with modernization. Humans, however, seek meaning. We may no longer look up to find it – we rarely call on God – but instead look down, at the opposite end of the vertical axis, which, like the sea, reflects the skies. According to Tillich, if the dimension of depth opens itself to us, it is there we will seek an ultimate concern. We seek something we won't sacrifice, which isn't a means to something else, but has intrinsic value, absolute and ultimate value. In this vein, ascribing intrinsic value to the sea may be the most meaningful thing we can do today. Not only because the sea is "gasping for air," but also because the conditions for experiencing meaning have changed.

The idea of the sea's intrinsic value, however, doesn't arise from the sea but from us, which brings its legitimacy into question. To this, the German philosophers Martin Heidegger and Hans-Georg Gadamer might say that humans cannot experience or know anything independent of their own presence. All that appears to us is, in the act of its appearance, marked by us, and this is not a problem but a fundamental condition. The fact that we are present in the encounter with whatever we encounter in the world is not itself anthropocentric (human-focussed). Therefore, we need not remove ourselves from the equation, nor would we ever be able to do so. We only become a threat to nature when we act without considering the aforementioned condition, believing that we have knowledge about things we will never know. To say that the sea has intrinsic value is not the same as saying what the sea *is*. This is not a statement of the sea's essence, but rather of *what we ought to do*; namely see it as a fellow being. This is a matter of ethics, and if someone says the sea doesn't care, the response must be: how do you know?

An expanded view of nature

We need an *expanded view of nature*, which is less driven by rationality, I-it, resources, and characterized rather by empathy and transcendence, I-thou, intrinsic value. In her essay collection *The Condition of Secrecy* (2000), the Danish poet Inger Christensen takes a related stance. The essays are inspired by Novalis' thinking about nature's "magic writing" and about language as a reflection of "the strange interplay of things."[2] With this as her starting point, she makes a poetic break with the dualistic view of nature. Nature doesn't exist on the other side of an imaginary line separating humans and nature. "We're bound to the forms of nature, in that we ourselves are one of its manifold forms." "Human beings' use of language [is] part of the world," and "whenever we express ourselves through language, the world too is expressing itself."[3] The state of the planet is therefore not only interpretable by how the rainforest lives and breathes, but also by how we live and breathe. Measurements of melted ice are not the only way to understand what is happening to the sea. Our language and thinking also bear witness to its state, for we are a part of the natural world of which the sea is part.

Oh, to speak with the sea and its fish; with plants, animals and things, maybe even with God. But this is precisely what poets do – and natural philosophers, children, worshippers and mourners. In "On the Mimetic Faculty" (1933), the German philosopher Walter Benjamin recounts how in antiquity, humans could interpret nature's signs, and suggests that we find traces of this ability to speak with nature in poetic language. In *Berlin Childhood around 1900* (1930s), moreover, he writes that for the child, things are animate in ways that adults only vaguely remember. Further back, the Italian philosopher Giambattista Vico was well aware of the importance of magical thinking. In *The New Science* (1725), he argues that the rationality of modern science has historical roots in a magical, poetic way of thinking that scientists ought to retain more of. He argues for an understanding of science that challenges what, in his time, was already becoming the established definition of science. He wants science to have an ear for the poetry of the universe.

In *The Year of Magical Thinking* (2005), the American author Joan Didion similarly portrays the world of the bereaved as enchanted. Many would agree with her account of how grief opens up dimensions of reality usually closed to us. For Didion this is a form of magic that, to her relief, eventually passes, but for Jean-Louis Chrétien this magic is a gift of faith. In *The Call and the Response* (1992), he describes, in poetical and philosophical language, how the universe constantly echoes the call we hear when our senses aren't dulled, which we unconditionally answer. This call, according to Chrétien, is the beauty of all things we call beautiful, their intrinsic value, and we respond to this call by bringing beautiful things into the world ourselves – for instance, poetry and philosophy. When we perceive the sea as beautiful – not just pretty, but sublimely beautiful and beautifully sublime – we hear its call and, in this call, something greater too. This experience expands our view of nature. It invites us to describe nature in new ways, to adjust our understanding of the relationship between it and us, and to rediscover a shared origin.

Dorthe Jørgensen, PhD, Dr. phil. habil. and Dr. theol. habil., is a philosopher, theologian and historian of ideas. Author of numerous books on faith, nature, ethics, religion, aesthetics, modernity and pedagogy. Dorthe Jørgensen is a boardmember at the think tank HAV (Ocean) and is currently writing a book about the sea.

1 Pär Lagerkvist, *Pilgrim at Sea*, Vintage Books, 1982, p. 14.
2 Inger Christensen, *The Condition of Secrecy*, A New Directions Paperbook Original, 2018, pp. 73 and 64.
3 Ibid., pp. 43 and 42.

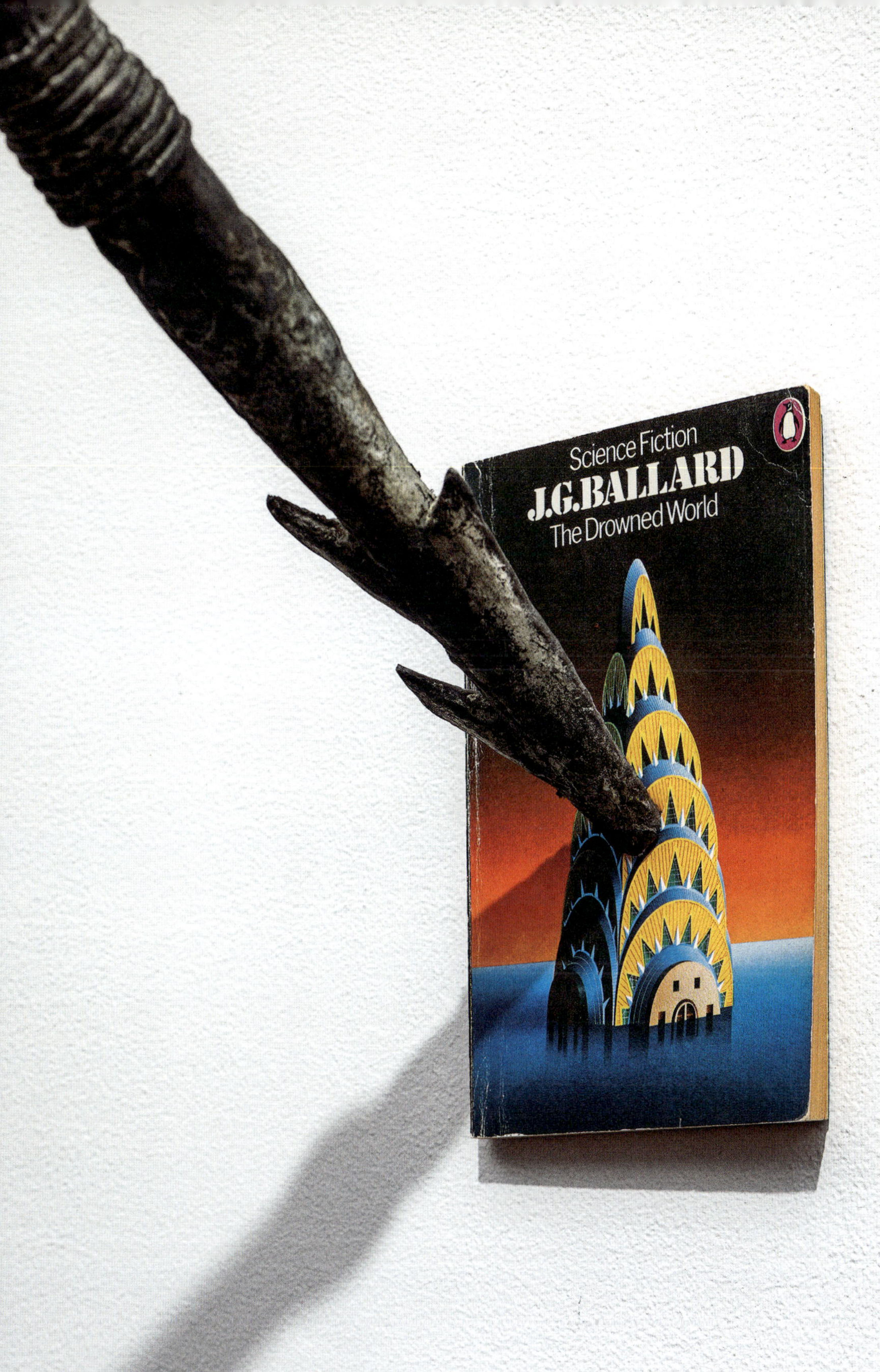

ELISABETTA BENASSI
The Drowned World, 2023

LIST OF WORKS

BAS JAN ADER
The Netherlands 1942-
disappeared 1975
Bulletin 89: In Search of the Miraculous (Songs for the North Atlantic), 1975
Offset-printed, black and white
Louisiana Museum of Modern Art, Humlebæk

JOHN AKOMFRAH
Great Britain 1957
Vertigo Sea, 2015
Three channel HD colour video installation, 7.1 sound
Duration: 48:30 min.
© Smoking Dogs Films; Courtesy of Smoking Dogs Films and Lisson Gallery

EL ANATSUI
Ghana 1944
Akua's Surviving Children, 1996
Found wood and iron
Variable dimensions
Courtesy the Artist and October Gallery, London

BALTHASAR VAN DER AST
The Netherlands 1593/4-1657
Still life with Shells, c. 1640
Oil on panel
47 × 30 cm
Collection Museum Boijmans Van Beuningen, Rotterdam. From the estate of Mr and Mrs Dr Ir. G.L.P. Philips-van der Willigen

ANNA ATKINS
Great Britain 1799-1871
Photographs of British Algae: Cyanoptype Impressions, 1843
Reproduction
Halstead Place, Sevenoaks, England, 1843-1853

PEDER BALKE
Norway 1804-1887
Nordkapp, 1860s-1870s
North Cape
Oil on paper mounted on panel
8.2 × 11 cm
The Gundersen Collection

Seileskute i opprørt sjø, 1860s-1870s
Ship in Rough Seas
Oil on panel
8.5 × 11 cm
The Gundersen Collection

Svart hav med Skytteren, 1860s-1870s
Black Sea with Skytteren Cliff
Oil on panel
8 × 11 cm
The Gundersen Collection

Hav og tåke, mid 1860s
Sea and Fog
Oil on paper mounted on panel
34.5 × 26
The Gundersen Collection

Marine, 1870s
Seascape
Oil on panel
9 × 11.5 cm
The Gundersen Collection

Marine med klipper, 1870s
Seascape with Cliffs
Oil on panel
11.8 × 16.2 cm
The Gundersen Collection

Nordkapp, 1870s
North Cape
Oil on panel
8.5 × 11 cm
The Gundersen Collection

Opprørt hav, 1870s
Rough Sea
Oil on panel
8.5 × 11.5 cm
The Gundersen Collection

Opprørt sjø, 1870s
Rough Sea
Oil on panel
8.2 × 11.6 cm
The Gundersen Collection

Opprørt hav med dampbåt og seilskute, 1870s
Rough Sea with Steamboat and Sailing Ship
Oil on panel
8.5 × 11 cm
The Gundersen Collection

Skip i opprørt hav, 1870s
Vessel in Rough Sea
Oil on panel
9 × 11.5 cm
The Gundersen Collection

Skipbrudd, Nordkapp, 1870s
Shipwreck, North Cape
Oil on panel
9.7 × 12 cm
The Gundersen Collection

ELISABETH JERICHAU BAUMANN
Poland, Germany, Denmark
1818-1881
Havfrue, 1863
Mermaid
Oil on canvas
135 × 95 cm
Kunstmuseum Brandts

NINA BEIER
Denmark 1975
Fleet, 2024
Model cruise ships, sand and sugar
Variable dimensions
Louisiana Museum of Modern Art, Humlebæk

ELISABETTA BENASSI
Italy 1966
The Drowned World, 2023
Book, bronze
83.8 × 11.1 × 116.2 cm
Courtesy of the artist and Peter Freeman, Inc. New York

LEOPOLD & RUDOLF BLASCHKA
Germany 1822-1895 / 1857-1939
26 models (cephalopods, jellyfish, sea slugs, flat and bristle worms, sea cucumbers, protists, sea anemones, starfish, radiolarians, coral)
Glass
Variable dimensions
Ar fenthyg gan / Lent by Amgueddfa Cymru - Museum Wales

3 models (cephalopods, jellyfish)
Glass
Variable dimensions
Zoological Collection of the University of Rostock

LOUIS BOUTAN
France 1859-1934
Pied lourd, 1898
Heavy shoe
Vintage print
37.3 × 29.2 cm
Archives Jean Painlevé / Les Documents Cinématographiques

Plongeur avec bâton, 1898
Diver with stick
Vintage print
37.3 × 29.2 cm
Archives Jean Painlevé / Les Documents Cinématographiques

MARK BRADFORD
USA 1961
Playing with the Ocean's Ceiling, 2014
Paper and laquer on canvas
259.1 × 365.8 × 5.5 cm
Louisiana Museum of Modern Art, Humlebæk
Donation: Mr. & Mrs. Diamond og Mr. & Mrs. Braman

CARL CHUN
Germany 1852-1917
Die Cephalopoden, 1915
Reproduction
Gustav Fischer, Jena, 1910-1915

ADRIAEN COORTE
The Netherlands c. 1665-after 1707
Shells on a Stone Plinth, 1698
Oil on paper on panel
29 × 22.5 cm
Rijksmuseum. On loan from a private collector

JACQUES-YVES COUSTEAU
France 1910-1997
Le monde du silence, 1956
The Silent World
Directed by Jacques-Yves Cousteau & Louis Malle
Duration: 86 min.
© Cousteau Society

JOHAN CHRISTIAN DAHL
Norway 1788-1857
Seascape with Wreck, 1831
Oil on canvas
22 × 40.3 cm
SMK, National Gallery of Denmark

DREXCIYA
Wave Jumper
from the CD *The Quest*, 1997
Duration: 6:40 min.
Submerge

ALBRECHT DÜRER
Germany 1471-1528
The Sea Monster, c. 1498
Etching
25 × 18.8 cm
SMK, National Gallery of Denmark

JEANNETTE EHLERS
Denmark / Trinidad and Tobago
1973
Atlantic (Endless Row), 2009
Photography
3 parts, each 60 × 120 cm
Jeannette Ehlers Studio

CASPAR DAVID FRIEDRICH
Germany 1774-1840
After the Storm, 1817
Oil on canvas
22.2 × 30.8 cm
SMK, National Gallery of Denmark

ELLEN GALLAGHER
USA 1965
Fast-Fish and Loose-Fish, 2023
Oil, pigment, palladium and paper on canvas
295.9 × 201.9 cm
THE GEORGE ECONOMOU COLLECTION

Fast-Fish and Loose-Fish, 2023
Oil, pigment, palladium and paper on canvas
295.9 × 201.9 cm
Private collection

HENDRICK GOLTZIUS
The Netherlands 1558-1617
Portrait of the Haarlem Shell Collector Jan Govertsen van der Aer, 1603
Oil on canvas
82.7 × 107.5 cm
Collection Museum Boijmans Van Beuningen, Rotterdam.
Loan P. & N. de Boer Foundation

NICCOLÒ GUALTIERI
Italy 1688-1744
Index testarum conchyliorum quae adservantur in museo Niccolo Gualtieri, 1742
Reproduction
Florence, Albizzini, 1742

SIGURDUR GUDMUNDSSON
Iceland 1942
Horizontal Thoughts (study), 1970-1971
Gelatine silver print
32 × 38 cm
Louisiana Museum of Modern Art, Humlebæk
Acquired with funding from The Augustinus Foundation

ERNST HAECKEL
Germany 1834-1919
Kunstformen der Natur, 1904
Reproduction
Leipzig & Wien, Verlag des Bibliographischen Instituts, 1904

CORNELIS VAN HAARLEM
The Netherlands, 1562-1638
Neptune and Amphidrite, c. 1616/1617
Oil on panel
72 × 92.5 cm
P.& N.de Boer Foundation, Amsterdam

MARSDEN HARTLEY
USA 1877-1943
Still Life No. 4, c. 1929
Oil on linen
24.5 × 33.5 cm
Louisiana Museum of Modern Art, Humlebæk
Acquired with funding from The Augustinus Foundation

SUSAN HILLER
USA, Great Britain 1940-2019
On the Edge, 2015
Rough Sea postcards. Monochrome and duotone, with map
15 panels, each 77.5 x 107.3 cm
© Estate of Susan Hiller; Courtesy of Lisson Gallery

UTAGAWA HIROKAGE
Japan, active c. 1797-1858
Great battle between vegetable and fish army, 1859
Colour woodcut, triptych
94.5 × 59.5 cm
MAK – Museum of Applied Arts, Vienna

UTAGAWA HIROSHIGE
Japan 1797-1858
Awa Province, Naruto Rapids, 1855
Woodblock print
35.7 × 24.5 cm
Victoria and Albert Museum, London

PIERRE HUYGHE
France 1962
Zoodram 2, 2010/2021
Aquarium, live marine ecosystem, seiryu rock, sand
146 × 110 × 118.8 cm
Kunsten Museum of Modern Art
Acquired with funding from Ny Carlsbergfondet

PIETER DE JODE II
Belgium 1606-1674
The Birth of Venus (after Peter Paul Rubens), 1606-1674
Etching
37.4 × 52.3 cm
SMK, National Gallery of Denmark

KIRSTEN JUSTESEN
Denmark 1943
Mer Maid / Hav Frue, 1990
Archival Pigment Print on Somerset Satin Enhanced
135 × 147 cm
Kirsten Justesen, courtesy Galleri Tom Christoffersen

WILLEM KALF
The Netherlands 1619-1693
Pronk Still Life with Holbein Bowl, Nautilus Cup, Glass Goblet and Fruit Dish, 1678
Oil on canvas
68 × 56 cm
SMK, National Gallery of Denmark

ANSELM KIEFER
Germany 1945
Inflammation, 1983-1986
Oil and lead on canvas
330 × 280.5 × 13 cm
Louisiana Museum of Modern Art, Humlebæk

YVES KLEIN
France 1928-1962
Untitled, Blue Sponge Sculpture (SE 100), 1960
Dry pigment and synthetic resin, natural sponge on a metal rods mounted on marble
18.2 × 25.5 × 21cm
Louisiana Museum of Modern Art, Humlebæk
Donation: Rotraut Klein

UTAGAWA KUNISADA I
Japan 1786-1865
Collecting Shells on the Beach at Akashi, 1855
Colour woodcut, triptych
35.6 × 25 cm, 35.5 × 24.8 cm, 35.5 × 24.9 cm
Rijksmuseum. Purchased with the support of the F.G. Waller-Fonds

The scrap dealer Jiemon and the carpenter Rokusaburo, 1854-1859
Colour woodcut, diptych
36 × 24.8 cm, 36 × 25 cm
MAK – Museum of Applied Arts, Vienna

UTAGAWA KUNIYOSHI
Japan 1798-1861
Benkei on the Boat, c. 1842
Woodblock print
22.5 × 29 cm
Victoria and Albert Museum, London

Calming the Waves at Kakuta on the Way to Exile at Sado Island, 1835-1836
Woodblock print
23.4 × 36.5 cm
Victoria and Albert Museum, London

Diver Recovers Jewel from the Palace of the Dragon King, 1847-1848
Woodblock print
36 × 75 cm
Victoria and Albert Museum, London

Tamakazura, the Diver Brings Back the Pearls. From the series *Comparison of Scenes from the Tale of Genji and the Floating World*, 1843-1847
Woodcut
37.7 × 25.5 cm
MAK – Museum of Applied Arts, Vienna

Kintaro struggling with carp, 1834
Colour woodcut
37.6 × 24.8 cm
Rijksmuseum. Gift of F. Bobeldijk, Zwolle

Yoshitsune attacked by Taira ghosts, 1853
Colour woodcut
36.4 × 25.5 cm
Rijksmuseum. Gave: E. Both

ÉTIENNE DE LA VILLE-SUR-ILLON, COMTE DE LACÉPÈDE
France 1756-1825
Histoire naturelle des quadrupèdes ovipares, des serpents, des poissons et des cétacés, 1836
Reproduction
Paris, P. Duménil, 1836

OLAUS MAGNUS
Sweden 1490-1557
Carta marina, 1572
Map of the Sea
Reproduktion
Rome: Antoine Lafréry, 1572
Library of Congress, Washington, D.C.

ANDREA MANTEGNA
Italy c. 1431-1506
Battle of the Sea Gods, left half, c. 1470-1500
Etching
27.8 × 39.4 cm
SMK, National Gallery of Denmark

Battle of the Sea Gods, right half, c. 1470-1500
Etching
28.2 × 40.6 cm
SMK, National Gallery of Denmark

JACOB MATHAM
The Netherlands 1571-1631
Neptune and Thetis, 1611-1614
Etching
27 × 40 cm
SMK, National Gallery of Denmark

NICEAUNTIES
Singapore
Auntlantis, 2024
-Sweeping the Floor
-Trashy Friends
-Day in the Life Of
Duration: 2:48 min.
AI film
Niceaunties

GEORGIA O'KEEFFE
USA 1887-1986
Open Clam Shell, 1926
Oil on canvas
51.1 × 23.2 cm
Dallas Museum of Art, The Eugene and Margaret McDermott Art Fund, Inc., bequest of Mrs. Eugene McDermott

Closed Clam Shell, 1926
Oil on canvas
51.1 × 23.2
Dallas Museum of Art, The Eugene and Margaret McDermott Art Fund, Inc., bequest of Mrs. Eugene McDermott

TREVOR PAGLEN
USA 1974
Bahamas Internet Cable System (BICS-1), 2015
C-print
152.4 × 121.9 cm
Courtesy of the Artist and Pace Gallery

Colombia-Florida Subsea Fiber (CFX-1) NSA/GCHQ-Tapped Undersea Cable Caribbean Sea, 2015
C-print
152.4 × 121.9 cm
Courtesy of the Artist and Pace Gallery

Globenet NSA/GCHQ-Tapped Undersea Cable Atlantic Ocean, 2015
C-print
121.9 × 152.4 cm
Courtesy of the Artist and Pace Gallery

JEAN PAINLEVÉ
France 1902-1989
Le Pieuvre, 1928
The Octopus
Film, silent
Duration: 12 min.
Archives Jean Painlevé / Les Documents Cinématographiques

Oursin de roche, piquants, 1928
Rock Sea Urchin, Quills
Vintage print
33.5 × 27 cm
Archives Jean Painlevé / Les Documents Cinématographiques

Pieuvre, 1928
Octopus
Vintage print
67.5 × 81 cm
Archives Jean Painlevé / Les Documents Cinématographiques

Pieuvre tentacules, 1928
Octopus Tentacles
Vintage print
74 × 101 cm
Archives Jean Painlevé / Les Documents Cinématographiques

Anémone de mer, 1930
Sea Anemone
Vintage print
42.3 × 52.4 cm
Archives Jean Painlevé / Les Documents Cinématographiques

Pince de crabe, 1930
Crab Claw
Vintage print
65 × 77 cm
Archives Jean Painlevé / Les Documents Cinématographiques

Tête d'hippocampe d'Arcachon, 1931
Head of Arcachon Seahorse
Vintage print
74.6 × 62.6 cm
Archives Jean Painlevé / Les Documents Cinématographiques

Pince de homard ou "de Gaulle", c. 1931
Lobster Claw or "de Gaulle"
Vintage print
87 × 70 × 4 cm
Archives Jean Painlevé / Les Documents Cinématographiques

Buste d'hippocampe, 1933
Seahorse Bust
Vintage print
141 × 98 cm
Archives Jean Painlevé / Les Documents Cinématographiques

Deux hippocampes mâles, 1933
Two Male Seahorses
Digital print
41 × 32.8 cm
Archives Jean Painlevé / Les Documents Cinématographiques

Hippocampe femelle, 1933
Female Seahorse
Vintage print
40.6 × 33.9 cm
Archives Jean Painlevé / Les Documents Cinématographiques

L'Hippocampe, 1933
The Sea Horse
Film, silent
Duration: 15 min.
Archives Jean Painlevé / Les Documents Cinématographiques

Ouverture de poche chez l'hippocampe mâle, 1933
Opening of Male Seahorse Belly Pouch
Vintage print
33.5 × 27 cm
Archives Jean Painlevé / Les Documents Cinématographiques

HOWARDENA PINDELL
USA 1943
Video Drawings: Abstract (Eel and Coral), 1976
C-print
20.3 × 25.4 cm
Courtesy of the artist and Garth Greenan Gallery, New York

Video Drawings (Cephalopod), 1976
C-print
20.3 × 25.4 cm
Courtesy of the artist and Garth Greenan Gallery, New York

Video Drawings (Fish), 1976
C-print
20.3 × 25.4 cm
Courtesy of the artist and Garth Greenan Gallery, New York

Video Drawings (Sand Worm), 1976
C-print
20.3 × 25.4 cm
Courtesy of the artist and Garth Greenan Gallery, New York

Video Drawings (Sea Slug), 1976
C-print
20.3 × 25.4 cm
Courtesy of the artist and Garth Greenan Gallery, New York

Video Drawings (Sea Slug), 1976
C-print
20.3 × 25.4 cm
Courtesy of the artist and Garth Greenan Gallery, New York

Video Drawings (Sea Slug and Coral), 1976
C-print
20.3 × 25.4 cm
Courtesy of the artist and Garth Greenan Gallery, New York

Deep Sea #2, 2024
Acrylic on canvas
198.1 × 223.5 cm
Courtesy of the artist and Garth Greenan Gallery, New York

Deep Sea #5, 2024
Acrylic on canvas
198.1 × 223.5 cm
Courtesy of the artist and Garth Greenan Gallery, New York

LOUIS RENARD
The Netherlands 1678-1746
Poissons, ecrevisses et crabes, de diverses couleurs et figures extraordinaires, que l'on trouve autour des isles Moluques et sur les côtes des terres Australes, 1754
Reproduction
A. Amsterdam, Chez Reinier & Josué Ottens, 1754
Harvard University, Museum of Comparative Zoology, Ernst Mayr Library

PIPILOTTI RIST
Switzerland 1962
Sip My Ocean, 1996
Single-channel video installation with two projections, colour and audio
Duration: 8 min.
Louisiana Museum of Modern Art, Humlebæk

JAN SAENREDAM
The Netherlands 1565-1607
Stranded whale near Beverwijk witnessed by Prince Ernest of Nassau, 1602
Etching
40.7 × 59.5 cm
SMK, National Gallery of Denmark

ALLAN SEKULA
USA 1951-2013
"Middle Passage", Chapter 3, Fish Story, 1994
22 cibachrome prints and 4 text panels
Various dimensions
TBA21 Thyssen-Bornemisza Art Contemporary Collection

Dear Bill Gates, 1999
Cibrachrome print and typewritten letter
With frame:
37.5 × 31.1 × 4.4 cm
Louisiana Museum of Modern Art, Humlebæk

TARYN SIMON
USA 1975
Transatlantic Sub-Marine Cables Reaching Land, 2007
VSNL International, Avon, New Jersey
Archival inkjet print on paper
94.8 × 114 × 4.2 cm
Louisiana Museum of Modern Art, Humlebæk
Acquired with funding from The Augustinus Foundation

EMILIJA ŠKARNULYTĖ
Lithuania 1987
Aphotic Zone, 2022
Single channel installation, 4K, 5.1 sound, 16'
Duration: 15 min.
Courtesy of the artist, Erik Cordes and the Schmidt Ocean Institute, and Fondazione In Between Art Film

AUGUST STRINDBERG
Sweden 1849-1912
Storm in the Skerries. "The Flying Dutchman", Dalarö, 1892
Vax colour on cardboard
62 × 98 cm
SMK, National Gallery of Denmark

The Wave V, 1901
Oil on canvas
101 × 69.9 cm
Lillehammer Art Museum, deposited by The Savings Bank Foundation DNB

HIROSHI SUGIMOTO
Japan 1948
Marmara Sea, Silivli, 1991
Gelatine silver print
55 × 42.5 cm
Louisiana Museum of Modern Art, Humlebæk

English Channel, Weston Cliff, 1994
Gelatine silver print
55 × 42.5 cm
Louisiana Museum of Modern Art, Humlebæk

Tyrrhenian Sea, Conda, 1994
Gelatine silver print
55 × 42.7 cm
Louisiana Museum of Modern Art, Humlebæk

SUPERFLEX
Denmark
Flooded McDonalds, 2008
One-channel video installation with sound
Duration: 20:59 min.
Louisiana Museum of Modern Art, Humlebæk
Acquired with support from private donor and Museumsfonden af 7. december 1966

As Close As We Get, 2022
Pink and gold lioz coral, steel plate
155 × 60 × 35 cm
By SUPERFLEX, courtesy of L. Gomard

As Close As We Get, 2022
Pink and gold lioz coral, steel plate
120 × 60 × 35 cm
By SUPERFLEX, Courtesy of Nils Stærk

As Close As We Get, 2022
Pink and gold lioz coral, steel plate
95 × 60 × 60 cm
By SUPERFLEX, Courtesy of Nils Stærk

WILLEM VAN SWANENBURGH
The Netherlands 1580-1612
Neptune Riding on two Dolphins, 1603-1607
Etching
34.3 × 21.3 cm
SMK, National Gallery of Denmark

MARIE THARP, BRUCE C. HEEZEN, HEINRICH C. BERANN
USA 1920-2006 / USA 1924-1977 / Austria 1915-1999
World Ocean Floor Map, 1977
Reproduction
Library of Congress, Geography and Map Division, Washington D.C.

LENA MARIA THÜRING
Switzerland 1981
Hanjin Palermo, 2015
HD video installation, colour, sound
Duration: 15:03 min.
Lena Maria Thüring

WOLFGANG TILLMANS
Germany 1968
Louisiana, 1996
Chromogenic print mounted on Dibond aluminum in artits's frame
198 × 145 cm
Louisiana Museum of Modern Art, Humlebæk
Acquired with funding from The Augustinus Foundation

WERNER VAN DEN VALCKERT
The Netherlands 1575-1635
Neptune, 1609
Oil on wood
108 × 80 cm
SMK, National Gallery of Denmark

Galathea, 1619
Oil on wood
108 × 80 cm
SMK, National Gallery of Denmark

KARA WALKER
USA 1969
Rift of the Medusa, 2017
Gouache, Sumi ink and collage on paper with gessoed ground
351.5 × 449.5 cm
Louisiana Museum of Modern Art, Humlebæk
Long-term loan:
Schroeder Collection

YUYAN WANG
China 1989
One Thousand and One Attempts to Be an Ocean, 2020
Film
Duration: 11:30 min.
Director: Wang Yuyan
Sound Design: Raphaël Hénard
Producer: Le Fresnoy

FRANCESCA WOODMAN
USA 1958-1981
Untitled, c. 1975-78
Gelatin silver print
12.7 × 12.7 cm
Courtesy Woodman Family Foundation © Woodman Family Foundation / Artist Rights Society (ARS)

Untitled, c. 1975-78
Gelatin silver print
24.1 × 31.1 cm
Courtesy Woodman Family Foundation © Woodman Family Foundation / Artist Rights Society (ARS)

Anguilla #2 (from *Eel series*), 1978
Gelatin silver print
15.1 × 15.1 cm
Courtesy Woodman Family Foundation © Woodman Family Foundation / Artist Rights Society (ARS)

Untitled (from *Eel series*), 1978
Gelatin silver print
14.9 × 14.8 cm
Courtesy Woodman Family Foundation © Woodman Family Foundation / Artist Rights Society (ARS)

Untitled (from *Eel series*), 1978
Gelatin silver print
14.9 × 15.1 cm
Courtesy Woodman Family Foundation © Woodman Family Foundation / Artist Rights Society (ARS)

FRANTZ ZÉPHIRIN
Haiti 1968
Indian Spirits Facing Colonization, 2000
Oil on canvas
60 × 105.4 cm
Collection of Marcus Rediker

The Slave Ship Brooks, 2007
Oil on canvas
83.8 × 109.2 × 7.6 cm
Collection of Marcus Rediker

Ceremonie Por Dambalah, 2007
Ceremony for Dambalah
Acrylic on canvas
76.2 × 101.6 cm
Courtesy Zephirin/Giannetta Gallery

Queen of the Deep, 2023
Acrylic on canvas
50.8 × 40.6 cm
Courtesy Zephirin/Giannetta Gallery

STATUE OF A WRESTLER, EARLY 1ST CENTURY BC.
Parian marble
100.1 cm
Hellenic Ministry of Culture,
National Archaeological Museum

THE RIGHT LEG OF A MARBLE MALE STATUE, EARLY 1ST CENTURY BC.
Parian marble
46 cm
Hellenic Ministry of Culture,
National Archaeological Museum

RIGHT HAND OF A MARBLE MALE STATUE, EARLY 1ST CENTURY BC.
Parian marble
31 cm
Hellenic Ministry of Culture,
National Archaeological Museum

PART OF THE TORSO OF A MARBLE MALE STATUE, EARLY 1ST CENTURY BC.
Parian marble
81 cm
Hellenic Ministry of Culture,
National Archaeological Museum

PART OF THE TORSO OF A MARBLE MALE STATUE, EARLY 1ST CENTURY BC.
Parian marble
80 cm
The Hellenic Ministry of Culture,
National Archaeological Museum

SHELL CABINET, 1762
Wood, paint, sea shells
250 × 198 × 49 cm
Private collection

10 MANGANESE NODULES
(GEOMAR expedition SO268, 2019)
Multible dimensions
Julia M. Otte, MPI/AWI, Germany

6 MANGANESE NODULES
Multible dimensions
Natural History Museum Denmark

2 MANGANESE CRUSTS
75 × 26 × 10 cm
40 × 19 × 12 cm
GEUS (Geological Survey of Denmark and Greenland)

ANNA ATKINS

Pages of the book *Photographs of British Algae: Cyanoptype Impressions*, 1843-1853

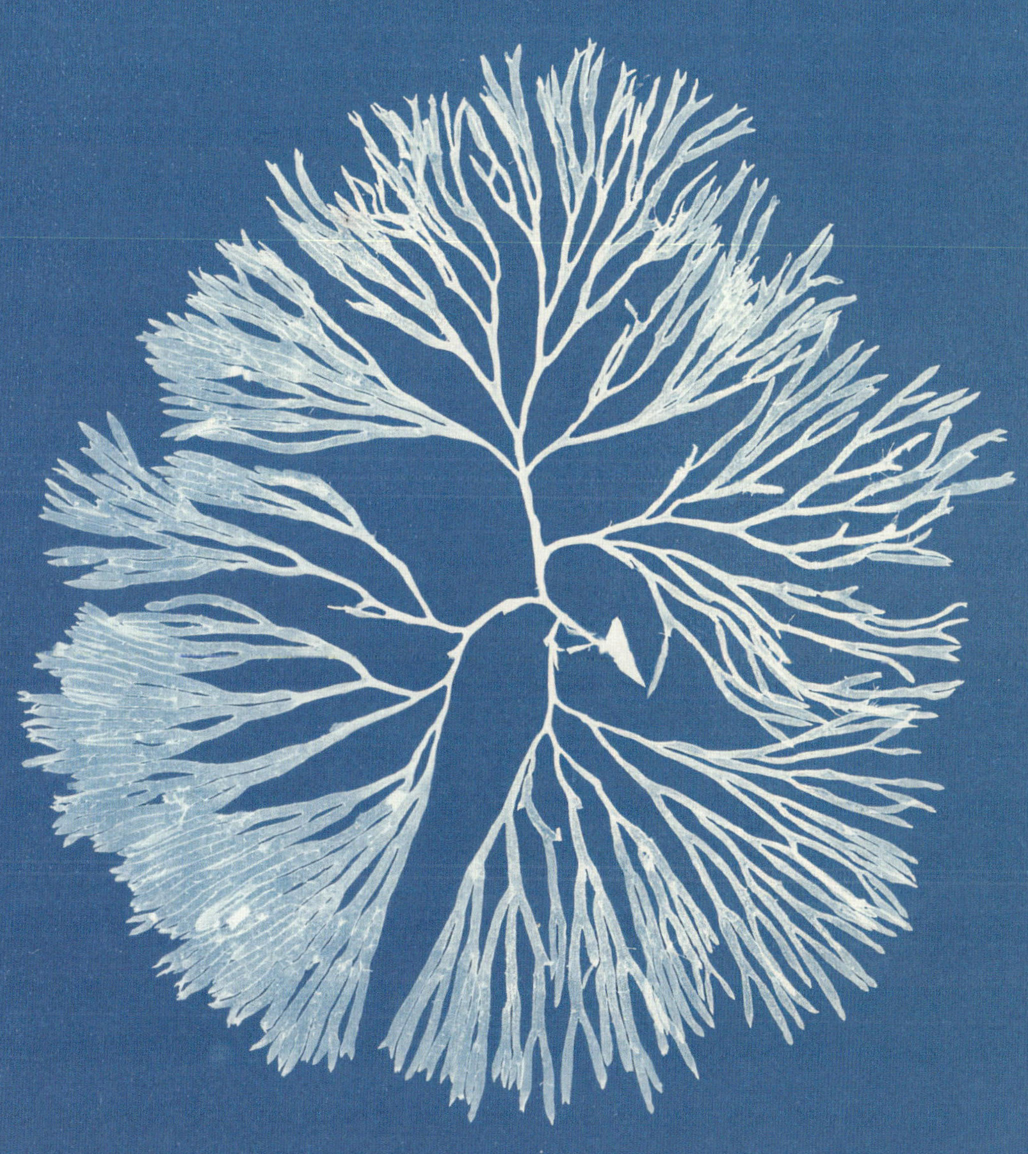

Halymenia furcellata.

OCEAN

Edited by Lærke Rydal Jørgensen, Tine Colstrup and Kaspar Thormod
Graphic Design: Marie Lübecker
Photo Editors: Grethe Røndal Christensen, Kim Hanssen
Translations: Adam King (Poul Erik Tøjner), Glen Garner (Tine Colstrup and Kaspar Thormod), Sherilyn Hellberg (Dorthe Jørgensen)
Proofreading: Henry Broome
Kaspar Thormod's and Dorthe Jørgensen's articles have been peer-reviewed
Cover, front: Utagawa Hiroshige: detail of
Awa Province, Naruto Rapids, 1855
Woodblock print, 35.7 × 24.5 cm
Victoria and Albert Museum, London
Photo: © Victoria and Albert Museum, London
Cover, back: Leopold & Rudolf Blaschka: detail of cephalopod
Glass, 10 × 10 × 20 cm
Ar fenthyg gan / Lent by Amgueddfa Cymru – Museum Wales
Photo: James Turner
Frontpapers: Emilija Škarnulytė: still from *Aphotic Zone*, 2022
Single channel installation, 4K, 5.1 sound, 16'
Duration: 15 min.
Courtesy of the artist, Erik Cordes and the Schmidt Ocean Institute, and Fondazione In Between Art Film
Endpapers: Howardina Pindell: detail of *Deep Sea #5*, 2024
Acrylic on canvas, 198.1 × 223.5 cm
Courtesy of the artist and Garth Greenan Gallery, New York

Litho/Print: Narayana Press
ISBN: 978-87-93659-82-7
Printed in Denmark 2024
www.louisiana.dk

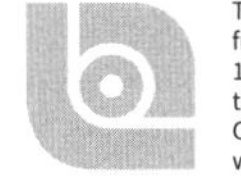

The emission of greenhouse gases from production of this book is 1,0 kg CO2eq evaluated according to www.climatecalc.eu.
Cert.nr. CC-000159/DK
www.narayana.dk

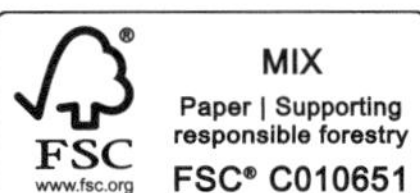

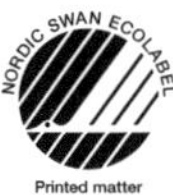

The catalogue is published on the occasion of the exhibition
OCEAN
Louisiana Museum of Modern Art, Humlebæk
11 October 2024 – 27 April 2025

Curators: Tine Colstrup, Poul Erik Tøjner and Kaspar Thormod
Curatorial Coordinator/Registrar: Arne Schmidt Petersen
Exhibition Architects: Lovisa My Lorén and Brian Lottenburger
Conservator / Exhibition Producer: Camilla Thorsen Vilslev
Graphic Design: Maria Hviid Bengtson, Marie Lübecker and Thomas J. Winther

Photo: p. 15, 17, 64-65, 69, 89, 103, 106, 113: Louisiana Museum of Modern Art; p. 18-19, 93: Fondazione In Between Art Film; p. 21: Louis Boutan. Archives Jean Painlevé/Les Documents Cinématographiques; p. 25: Videostill, Louisiana Museum of Modern Art; p. 26-27: Smoking Dogs Films; p. 29 top: K. Xenikakis/Hellenic National Archaeological Museum, Athens, NAM Γ 15550; bottom: V. Pettas/Hellenic National Archaeological Museum, Athens, NAM Γ 15541); p. 31: Ronald Grant Archive/Ritzau Scanpix; p. 33: © Frankie Fultz; p. 36-37: Andy Keate; p. 41-43: Archives Jean Painlevé/Les Documents Cinématographiques; p. 44-45: Alle fotos: James Turner undtagen bottom left: Robin Maggs; p. 52, p. 54 top: P. & N. de Boer Foundation, Amsterdam; p. 53: Louisiana Museum of Modern Art/Kim Hansen; p. 54 bottom: Studio Tromp; p. 55, 74 bottom: Rijksmuseum, Amsterdam; p. 56: © Woodman Family Foundation; p. 57: Image courtesy Dallas Museum of Art; p. 66, 72, 73, 78 top, 78 bottom left, 79, 80, 82: Statens Museum for Kunst/SMK; p. 67: Lillehammer Kunstmuseum/Camilla Damgård; p. 68: The Gundersen Collection/Morten Henden Aamot; p. 70-71: Lisson Gallery; p. 74 top, p. 75, p. 76 top: © Victoria and Albert Museum, London; p. 76 bottom: MAK – Museum of Applied Arts, Vienna; p. 77: © MAK/Georg Mayer; p. 78 bottom right: Statens Museum for Kunst/SMK/Jacob Schou-Hansen; p. 81: Kunstmuseum Brandts; p. 83, 84: K. Xenikakis/Hellenic National Archaeological Museum, Athens, NAM Γ 2773; p. 85: Nikolaj Recke; 86, 87: Jon Etter; p. 88: Sikkema Jenkins & Co., New York; p. 97: Shutterstock/Evertt Collection; p. 99: ©Lena Maria Thüring; p. 100-101: David Stjernholm, Art Direction: Lorenz Klingebiel (Frieze Magazine); p. 102: Allan Sekula Studio; p. 104: Kirsten Justesen, courtesy Galleri Tom Christoffersen; p. 105: Niceaunties; p. 107: Robert Damisch; p. 108-109: © Pierre Huyghe. Marian Goodman Gallery; p. 110 top: ROV KIEL 6000/ GEOMAR; p. 110 bottom: Kim Hansen; p. 111: Courtesy of the artist and Garth Greenan Gallery, New York; p. 112: © Trevor Paglen; p. 114-155: Videostills ©Wang Yuyan; p. 121: Nicholas Knight

The exhibition is supported by

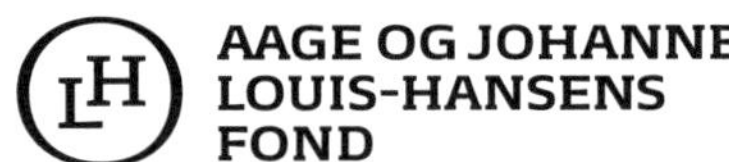

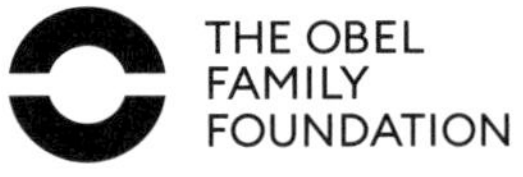

Main Corporate Partner
FRITZ HANSEN

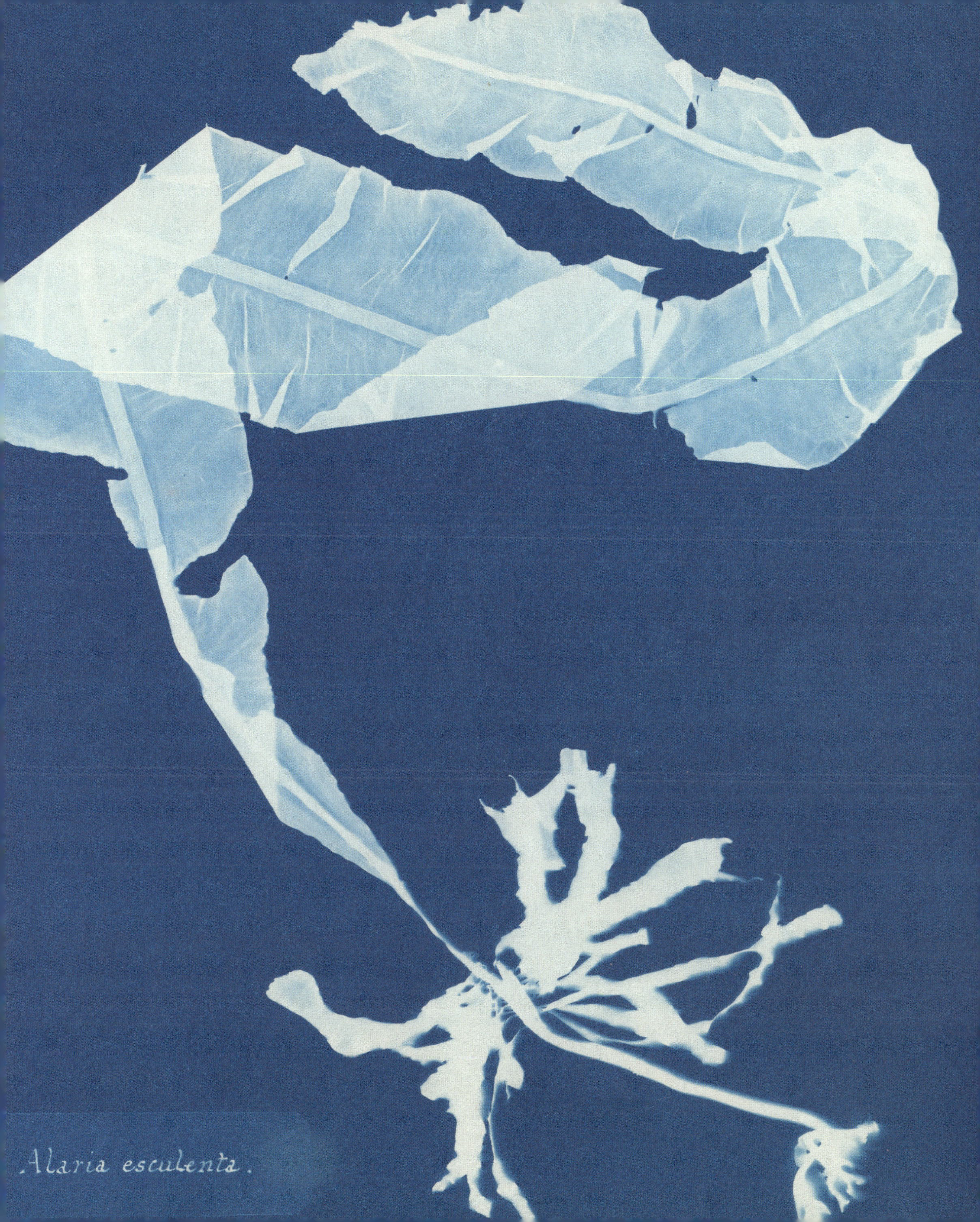
Alaria esculenta.

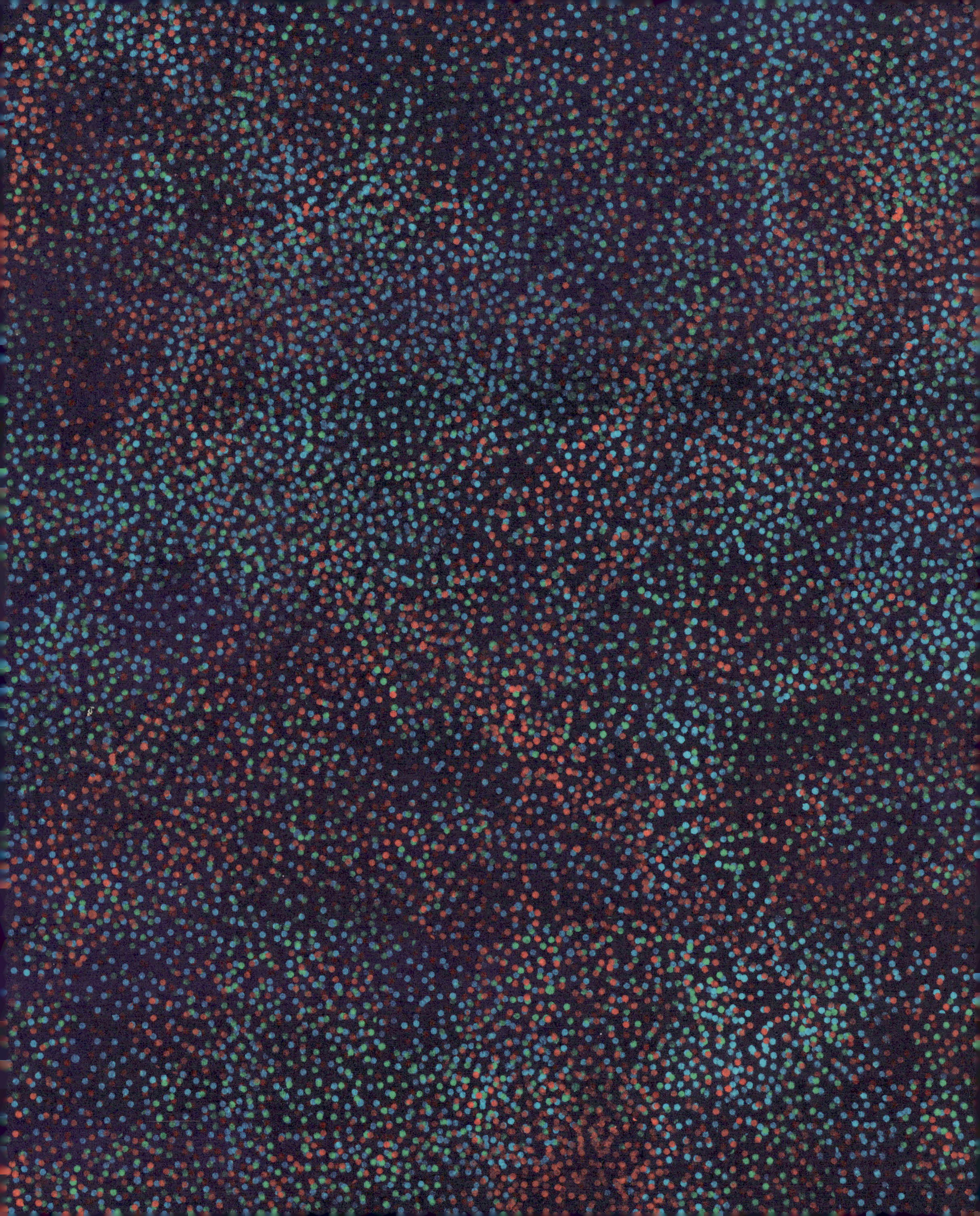